A NEW STUDY

OF

ASTROLOGY

together with

Astrology Reborn

and

The Discrimination of Birth Types

by

John M. Addey, M. A.

The Urania Trust

The Urania Trust

396 Caledonian Road
London N1 1DN, UK.

A registered educational charity,
number 31780.

A New Study of Astrology.

Published 1996.

ISBN 1 871989 06 X

British Library Cataloguing-in-Publication Data.
A catalogue record for this book is
available from the British Library.

Printed in England by Antony Rowe,
Chippenham, Wiltshire, SN14 6QA.

Dustjacket designed by Phillip Bentley
Tel/fax 0181 314 5068

CONTENTS

LIST OF ILLUSTRATIONS

Acknowledgements

The production of this book has been long delayed and no precise details have been found of the many people who helped in the several years of its original preparation and the research which made it possible. Certainly first and foremost John Addey would have wished to thank the late Neil F. Michelsen and his wife Maria Kay Simms owners of Astro-Computing Services, (now Astro-Communications Services) for their generous hospitality in their home and the use of their computing facilities at ACS in San Diego. Without their support and the expertise, imagination and unstinting labours of Tom Shanks, ACS's brilliant head of programming and research, the crucial harmonic analysis of the vast quantities of character trait data which made John's work possible would not have been available. John often mentioned how important his dialogue with Tom Shanks had been in working out ways of presenting and statistically evaluating the data in a way which would minimise the risk of the creation of artifacts in the data. Many members of the Astrological Association research group were involved in preparing and checking data, and graphs, most notably Alison Wells and Peggy Lance, who was also responsible for a great deal of the typing and preparation of much of the first and subsequent drafts of the MS. As with *Harmonics in Astrology* the ever modest Colin Bishop offered John important insights about the use of harmonics. An especial debt of gratitude is due to David Holmes who drew most of the diagrams, but also retained invaluable correspondence and material without which this book would be much less complete. No doubt John's final accolade would have gone to Michel and Francoise Gauquelin, without whose Herculean and heroic work, in collecting their original data, few of his ideas could have been adequately tested and elaborated. Finally a great debt is owed to John's son Tim Addey who has laboured long in preparing the final text of this MS and piecing together the final form of this book from the partially prepared material that John was working on at the time of his death. The trustees of the UT would also like to express their thanks to Peter Roberts, long term colleague and co-worker of John Addey for writing the Foreword to this book.

v

PREFACE

The 400th anniversary of the publication of Johannes Kepler's first book, *Mysterium Cosmographicum* in 1596 would seem to be a highly appropriate occasion on which to publish this major posthumous work, *A New Study of Astrology* together with a re-issue John Addey's seminal *Harmonics in Astrology*.

Kepler with his Pythagorean background viewed the universe as being governed by geometric relationships that conform to the inscribed and circumscribed circles of the five regular polygons. This idea may now seem rather quaint to some but it was the genesis of his later insights about the solar system's underlying order. Equally John Addey, another Pythagorean, was led by his researches, outlined in this book and in *Harmonics in Astrology*, to propose that it is the dynamic geometry of Cycle and Number, the harmonics of cosmic periods, that are the fundamental basis by which the Ideas that shape the cosmos are unfolded in space and time. Once again we are alerted to the potential importance of Form and Number in understanding the deeper scheme of things. And there is every indication that Addey's insights will equally have the power to transform our conception of the inner relationship between cosmos and psyche.

This major, if incomplete, *New Study*, which contains so many startling and provocative insights about the underlying nature of astrology, has been waiting publication for some fourteen years. Some of this delay has been practical: the lack of time for editing and the lack of resources with which to publish it. But another significant delay in recent years has been the on-going debate about the validity of the Gauquelins' Character Trait Hypothesis (CTH), the idea, which seems self-evident to anyone working in astrology, that the planets do not determine profession so much as character, and that it is the possession of a certain kind of temperament and character that inclines one to excel in certain professions rather than others.

The CTH was supported by a series of massive experiments, described in this book, in which the Gauquelins extracted the character traits of several thousand leading professionals and then related them to the planetary positions at birth. It was found by the Gauquelins that people born with, for example, Mars angular tended to be described by martial traits such as "energetic", "courageous" and so on. However Ertel's attempts to replicate this finding have so far proved unsuccessful.

Since the core of *The New Study of Astrology* centres upon the use of the Gauquelins character trait data, and the CTH, it was judged appropriate to delay publication pending the results of some seemingly definitive experiments on the CTH being conducted by Michel Gauquelin, Suitbert Ertel and others in the late 1980s. It was, perhaps naively, assumed that the new experiments being undertaken would quickly demonstrate the essential validity of the character trait approach and move the focus of research into the territory which John Addey pioneers in this book.

In the event, it has turned out, while the Gauquelins continued to get positive results only negative results greeted the new experiments by Suitbert Ertel, the Professor of Psychology at Göttingen University. As a result, Ertel, who has done so much to vindicate the Gauquelins findings on planets and professions, currently believes that the CTH approach is not the way forward in understanding the Gauquelins results. His position is that a link between planets and profession has been unequivocally established but that, surprising as it may seem, he can find no replicable experimental evidence for there being a link between planets and character traits.

In the circumstances Ertel has had to suggest that the apparent results obtained by the Gauquelins, if not the result of deliberate bias or deception in the selection of traits, is essentially the result of unconscious bias in favour of character traits associated with planets known to be prominent at the time of birth of the individual

His position has not gone unchallenged. Michel Gauquelin was embroiled in debate with Ertel on this matter up until the time of Michel's tragic death in May 1991. This debate has continued between Ertel and Francoise Gauquelin who persists in her conviction that their original character trait work is essentially sound. She cites her own analysis of ten major astrology texts, including Ptolemy's Tetrabiblos which shows beyond any doubt that the character traits that she and Michel had found associated with each planet, agreed very closely with both ancient tradition and modern textbooks.

At present the position is a stand-off, as summarised by Francoise Gauquelin in a recent article on the subject in her Schneider-Gauquelin research journal[2]

Clearly in these circumstances it is of the utmost importance that all those involved in this crucial CTH research should closely study John Addey's findings as outlined here in *A New Study*. For quite independently of the Gauquelins analysis, Addey's findings suggest very strongly indeed that the CTH is not only vindicated but that, when applied in this much wider harmonic way, it opens the door to far more subtle analysis than the Gauquelins or Ertel have as yet contemplated. Equally it throws up a wealth of significant findings for testing and replication.

Ertel has objected[3] that from his perspective John Addey's analysis is based upon what he considers to be a highly distorted selection of character traits and this, if true, would contaminate all studies based on those selections.

Here it should be said that, though it has been alleged that the Gauquelins character trait selections are biased, this has not in fact been quantitively demonstrated. It has not been shown, for example, that the Gauquelins, or their helpers, ever included character traits in biographical listings that were not possessed by that individual. Nor has it been shown that character traits were omitted from biographies which should have been included. Thus any distortions would be more likely to be of degree, *e.g.* of additional weight being given to particular traits by repetition which was not fully justified.

If this is the case, then Addey's approach, which entails the analysis of individual character trait words across all professional groups, and which uses the highly conservative method of counting any one case only once, regardless of the number of times a character trait is mentioned for that case, would seem, by and large, to by-passes any distortions or fact fudging or unconscious bias on the part of those extracting the character traits.

In studying the analyses and findings in this book it should be remembered that when Addey was analyzing the distribution of each planet (by computer) in relation to each character trait, he had no preconceptions as to where each character trait should be strong or weak, nor had he any means for predetermining which other character traits might show similar distributions. The fact is that when such an analyses is done it is found that certain character traits and groups of character traits show similar distributions for the same planet across independent samples, regardless of profession.

That these harmonic distribution patterns found by Addey replicate so well between samples, for example see Chapter VIII, Figs 41a-47d, is compelling enough. Perhaps even more persuasive is the fact that some of the highly significant and replicated distributions are for clusters of character traits in harmonic patterns entirely unknown or unsuspected by the Gauquelins, as for example Saturn's 5th harmonic distribution among those with the characteristic traits of the scientist and their opposite type: see Fig. 35, p. 106 - or Mars in the 3rd harmonic for typical writers' characteristics and their opposites, see Fig. 36a, p. 107.

For some years now these facts have been repeatedly drawn to the attention of Suitbert Ertel and Geoffrey Dean,[4] who has been advising Ertel on the evaluation of Addey's work. Since neither Ertel nor Dean, who are normally swift to demolish poor research design, have responded to repeated requests for a critique of Addey's methods, as herein demonstrated, it can be assumed that there are no obvious errors in this approach.

Even allowing for some distortions, that may be present due to inconsistencies in character trait extraction, Addey's work as here presented shows that his approach opens up a wealth of new insights about the way in which planets express themselves in terms of the diurnal cycle. These findings have dramatic implications not only for research but also for the way in which practising astrologers go about interpreting their charts and most of all for the overall philosophical implications they have for the nature of reality and the way it is unfolded.

We strongly urge all students of astrology to given this book their fullest attention, and for those with an interest in astrological research to follow up and adopt the methods and approaches advocated in these studies. Further replication of these findings will help to transform our understanding of astrology and help to reinstate her as a Queen of Sciences.

Charles Harvey June 1996

Notes

1. Gauquelin, Francoise, *Psychology of the Planets*, ACS Publications, San Diego, California 1982.

2. CTH Yes? or CTH No? by Francoise Gauquelin, *The Schneider-Gauquelin Research Journal*, Vol 11, No 1, March 1995, pp 8-17. This gives a balanced presentation of the current standing of the character trait hypothesis.and the evidence for and against.

3. Personal communication from Suitbert Ertel 26th September 1992

4. A 7pp detailed letter explaining John Addey'methods which was faxed and mailed to Suitbert Ertel 30th Sept 1992, with copies sent to Geoff Dean and Michael O'Neill on the same day. Copies have been sent on various occasions since and the matter raised in person and by phone without as yet any response.

Notes on the original plan for *A New Study*

and the present form of this book

This book is not the polished work that John Addey would have written had he lived longer. It amounts to about 75% of the volume he envisaged. For this reason the reader will need to make allowances when reading it and "piece out our imperfections with your thoughts."

John Addey had intended *The New Study of Astrology* to be the first of three companion volumes which would open up astrology to the wider thinking public and to those interested in exploring its fundamentals. The first volume, the one you hold, was about 75% complete at the time of John's death in the Royal Homoeopathic Hospital in London on 27th March 1982. At that time neither Chapter One or Two had been written though notes survive indicating what he intended to cover. Likewise there was to have been a Chapter 10 in which the threads were to have been drawn together.

In order to give the book a context and make it more approachable. I have pieced together a brief, ersatz Chapter One from John's notes and earlier writings, interpolating additional material where appropriate.

The missing Chapter Two presented a more difficult problem. It was to be called, as here, *Some Philosophical Considerations*. Exactly what John was going to write we cannot know, but we do know that he intended it to focus in part on the different kinds of causality, elaborated by Aristotle. He was concerned to emphasise that astrology is essentially concerned with formal causes rather than the material causes beloved of current contemporary science. To this end we have printed the detailed notes for his lecture to the Astrological Association on the subject of Causality on 1st October 1981. This was almost the last lecture John gave before his fatal cancer incapacitated him, and so represents some of his final thoughts on this matter. In any case we can be fairly certain that this would have formed an important part of this chapter. However we can also be certain that he intended to elaborate on the ideas he originally formulated in his 1971 Carter Memorial Lecture, *Astrology Reborn*. As this is no longer readily available, and is a beautiful statement of his understanding of astrology's philosophical position this has been included as Appendix I. For those unfamiliar with John's thinking this should be read alongside the present Chapter Two.

No attempt has been made to provide a Chapter Ten.

The series of important Appendices John had planned for this book are noted on p. 196 before the present Appendices. The most important of these, the provision of the basic data and harmonic analyses of Gauquelins' character trait distributions, on which John's conclusions are based, will be issued by the UT in image format on CD in the near future. If there is the demand we hope that a text format of this same information can also be made available later on disc.

Volume Two and Three of *A New Study* never got beyond loose notes and at the time of his death John Addey had done no substantial work on them. Volume II was intended to be a comprehensive study of Number symbolism directed primarily at astrologers to help them better understand this fundamental aspect of astrological science and art. Volume III was to have been a systematic delineation of each harmonic in terms of horoscopic interpretation with illustrative examples. It was also to include the interpretative synthesis of different phases of different harmonics yielding interpretation of degree areas in different circles. John described this to Neil F. Michelsen as "a practical harmonic interpretation cook-book type of job" which, like Volume II, he thought "would no doubt sell well". Alas these were not to be, and it remains for future students to elaborate such texts.

Charles Harvey, June 1996

FOREWORD

It is both an honour and a pleasure for me to write a foreword for this posthumous publication of John Addey's writings. John occupied a unique position among 20th century astrologers in being prepared to marry his own awareness of astrological concepts with contemporary empirical science, in order to develop a philosophy with its roots in the earth but soaring way beyond the constraints of empiricism.

I knew John Addey from back in the '50s when he taught classes for the Faculty of Astrological Studies and I was one of his pupils. We became close research collaborators for some periods of time during subsequent decades. Thus, the subject matter of this text is very familiar to me. I shared in the excitement when we discovered the twelves family of harmonics present in each separate set of polio data.

Apart from sharing the empirical research on data sets, I was also a witness to John's intellectual struggle with the contrasts between our findings and the traditional teachings of astrology. He was profoundly convinced of the ultimate unity to be found in the cosmos and sought for the patterns which would accommodate our research findings within the overall grand design. He found what he sought in the underlying significance of numbers. The diurnal planetary patterns found by Michel and Francoise Gauquelin show very clearly a 3rd and also a 4th harmonic. Among the different professions which the Gauquelins investigated, sometimes the 4th harmonic was quite dominant and for others the 3rd was equally important. John set himself the task of discovering why there should be this difference between the measured amplitudes of the two harmonics in different collections of data. His conclusion, explained with a wealth of detail in the text, is that there are separate sets of personality attributes associated with each of these two harmonics - indeed essential attributes of the numbers 3 and 4. From this important discovery he was led to develop a comprehensive synthesis of the significance of harmonics in all parts of the horoscope (not just the diurnal positions of the planets.) He was concerned to show that harmonics were present in distributions of solar longitude for many diverse collections; and also to find meaning in the phase angle of each harmonic, in addition to the harmonic numbers themselves.

John's vision of astrology was that of a sublime scheme whose various facets had been glimpsed to only a partial extent by past astrologers. His own findings now carried our appreciation of the beauty and universality of that scheme to new heights. He saw his work, not as any contradiction with tradition, but rather as an expansion and an enhancement.

The second important message which John brings is the idea of expanding the vision of contemporary empirical science beyond what he defines as 'efficient' and 'material' causes, out to (in Aristotelian terms) 'formal' and 'final' causes. Thus, he points out that although being born with Mars close to an angle in the birth chart might appear at first sight to be the cause of the observed martial qualities in the subject, the true state of affairs is that this soul-body combination has found an appropriate time to appear as an individual in the world. Mars has not 'caused' the martial qualities (they are latent) - it is the timing of the birth which has made it seem so. The world of science - and particularly the study of genetics - is not in conflict with that of astrology. The two are complimentary, referring to different causes, with science always concentrating on the efficient and material.

John had strong hopes that the scope of contemporary science would be expanded to embrace the wider vision which astrology offers. Indeed, he wrote that signs of this awakening would be apparent in the next 20 years (i.e. before the end of the century). I think that there are some signs of this coming to pass. Writers with impeccable scientific credentials have emerged to declare that there is a 'hidden' side to our world lying beyond that weighed and measured by science. The most direct involvement of science appears in Seymour's *Astrology, the Evidence of Science*[1], but one should also note Sheldrake's conjuring up of noumenous worlds lying beyond the observable. Similarly, Bohm's *Wholeness and the Implicate Order*[2] contemplates a wider vision of the universe. My own *Message of Astrology*[3] comes very much from a scientific viewpoint but puts forward a similar picture to the one offered in John Addey's writings.

These few signs are hardly more than a 'leavening of the lump' and I am sure that John was contemplating a much more radical change in the world of science. However, it would be a bold spirit who prophesied such a revolution in the world of orthodox science during the next century, let alone the next decade. We have to work for the change and this collection of John Addey's writings is another valuable contribution among all the efforts necessary for that change.

PETER ROBERTS, May 1994
Professor of Systems Science
City University, London.

1. Seymour, Percy, *Astrology the Evidence of Science*, published Lennard Publishing 1988, ISBN 1-85291-025-9

2. Bohm, David, *Wholeness and the Implicate Order*

3. Roberts, Peter, *The Message of Astrology*, Aquarian Press 1990, ISBN 0-85030-823-2

A NEW STUDY

OF

ASTROLOGY

CHAPTER I

THE PROBLEM OF ASTROLOGY

John Addey only left an outline of what he intended to include in this chapter. The brief account which follows is based as closely as possible on his specific notes and my understanding of his intentions as expressed elsewhere in our numerous discussions over 20 years and his many lectures, summer school seminars and his earlier writings. References to the sources for each of the main points are given at the end of the chapter. C. H. May 1996

To make astrology credible in the modern world two things are needed:

A) To show that it **is** true in the light of empirical, scientific criteria.

B) To show that, in terms of the soundest philosophical traditions, *i.e.* in terms of the higher reason, astrology **is** a thoroughly rational and intelligible subject.

Both of these approaches are needed. No scientific demonstration of the truth of astrology will be accepted without a coherent account of **how** and **why** it is true. Strictly speaking the "how and why" should come first but in these days science is not open to explanations in truly rational terms but must first be convinced in terms of empirical evidence that astrology appears to be valid.[2]

The problem of demonstrating empirically that astrology is true in essence, if not in every particular detail of its tradition, is complicated by the fact that the "building materials" of which traditional astrology is made up consists of a wealth of seemingly disparate constituent parts. Let us consider[3] some of our astrological building materials.

First and foremost we have signs and houses, planets and aspects; these are supported by such things as rulerships, mid-points, degree areas, etc.etc. and of course various sorts of directions and other predictive techniques.

I said "we have" these things - but have we? Before one can say that one "has" something one must be able to say what it is, describe it, define its limits and if it is made up of parts, say what the parts are.

What then are the **divisions of the ecliptic** - signs for example - are we happy about these? Do we know where we stand? Obviously not, for the Tropical-Sidereal controversy cuts deep; and if you feel no doubts on that score there are plenty of other problems. Our Indian friends, for example, whose testimony we cannot ignore. have numerous other ecliptic divisions, such as navamshas, Lunar Mansions, and so on. If these are valid we are missing something.

The **houses;** no need to labour the uncertainties here. There are plenty of problems about the Quadrant systems; plenty, too, about Equal Houses. What for example is the true difference between Equal Houses from the Ascendant and from the M. C.? And then why not Equal Houses from the Prime Vertical or the East-West Meridian? All must have their symbolism.

But this is only a start. What about cusps as boundaries or centres of houses? And again, Cyril Fagan and others assure us that there are really eight and not twelve houses, and so on.

Aspects seem at first to be definite enough, but they are not really so. Even putting aside the important question of "minor" aspects and glossing over the problem of "orbs" (for which we can do no better than propound quite arbitrary rules which seem "about right") we are still left with the whole problem of *interpreting* aspects. Our rough and ready divisions into "good or bad", or "hard or soft" or "harmonious or inharmonious", is really only serviceable for as long as one does not look too closely at it. In reality, just as each sign is not simply "good" or "bad" but embodies a definite *principle,* so too does each aspect embody a definite principle which can operate to our advantage (even a square) or disadvantage (even the trine). These principles are in need of clear delineation.

So one could go on. One could take each and every factor in use in present-day astrology and show it to be surrounded by a host of uncertainties.

Of course, those who practice astrology must make up their minds how they are going to deal with these uncertainties. They must, and do, adopt whatever plan of practical procedure seems best and most sensible to them and one admires them for this and is grateful that there are those who, despite the difficulties, manage to produce something really worthwhile and of value to their fellows out of this rather patchwork science.

Still, there is a time for taking stock of our deficiencies and for asking ourselves if there is to be found a means of *co-ordinating, simplifying* and *unifying* some of our present heterogenous conceptions. This is surely the great need of astrology today. For before any science can be truly unfolded so as to realise its full potentialities, it **must be reduced to its fundamental concepts,** to the simple units of which it is really composed. A man who tries to build up a science without first finding the real units with which it is to be built is like a man who must try to build a house out of the rubble from other buildings. Every time he picks up a brick h finds part of another brick sticking to it and probably part of the original brick missing, too, The pieces are the wrong shape and mixed up with other, non-essential elements. They are not flexible enough; they help him but they hinder him at the same time.

As I have suggested in *Harmonics in Astrology*[4], there is reason to think that we are at last in sight of a solution. The evidence would suggest that, apart from the planets themselves. **all astrological effects, such as signs, houses, aspects, midpoints, degree areas, can be understood in terms of the harmonics of cosmic periods,** *i.e.* in terms of Circle, or cycle, and Number, and that these are the fundamental building blocks, with which, when understood, we can construct a systematic and intelligible science of astrology.

The following pages show, using the copious data supplied by the Gauquelins, how this harmonic approach offers a key to astrology as a whole and to unravelling the deeper significance of some of the details of the Gauquelins results in particular.

Prior to that, in the next chapter and again in Chapter Nine and in the text of *Astrology Reborn* (Appendix I) a ground work is set out for helping the reader understand that astrology is in fact a thoroughly rational and intelligible subject in terms of the soundest philosophical traditions, i.e.in terms of the higher reason.

CHAPTER I - NOTES

1. The following three paragraphs are based closely on Notes about the book sent to Neil F. Michelsen of Astro-Computing Services (now Astro-Communication Services) who, with his principle researcher Tom Shanks, had done so much to support John Addey's researches through computer and statistical expertise, and by helping John get to San Diego and housing him whilst he was there. John at that stage was hoping that Neil and his company might be interested in publishing the book.

2. *Astrology: Science or Superstition* by Hans Eysenck and David Nias, published Maurice Temple Smith 1982, appeared shortly almost simultaneously with John Addey's death and was reviewed by Nicholas Kollerstrom in the same Summer 1982 issue, Vol XXIV, No 3, pp 202-3 of the Astrological Association Journal which contained John Addey's obituary notices. Written by Britain's most eminent psychologist the Professor of Psychology at London University and a colleague, it concluded that the work of the Gauquelins had to be taken seriously. Perhaps because it was too recent and difficult to assess in a simple way, the book fails to give serious attention to Addey's work and harmonic theory of astrology, which was a pity. Its courageous, if guarded, stand put down a marker in the orthodox academic world, indicating that astrology should be taken seriously as a field for future study.

3. Most of what follows is adapted from John Addey and Peter Roberts paper, *The Basis of Astrology*, Part 1, Astrological Journal Vol VI, No 3, pp 8-17, Summer 1964, and reprinted in *An Astrological Anthology*, Vol One 195-1970, Edited by Zach Matthews, published by the Astrological Association, London 1995, ISBN 0 9502658 7 X.

4. *Harmonics in Astrology*, by John Addey, published in a new edition by the Urania Trust 1996.

CHAPTER II

Some Philosophical Considerations

A summary of a lecture delivered to the Astrological Association in London, 1 October '81

Only some brief notes survive for this chapter, but we do know that John Addey had intended to devote this section to some philosophical consideration regarding the nature of astrology. Central to this was to have been a presentation of the importance of an understanding of Aristotle's four causes. The following is a transcript with minor additions or John's notes for what was to be one of his last lectures to the Astrological Association in London on 1st October 1981. A fuller working out of these ideas and the philosophical basis of astrology is also given in Chapter IX and in *Astrology Reborn*, which is reproduced as Appendix II.

What is the cause of an astrological effect?

Causality

Aristotle defined four causes:-

1 **Final Cause** - The reason for a thing's existence; the purpose for which it exists, eg in the case of a book, the demand for it or to gratify one's own desire to see oneself in print.

2 **Formal Cause** - The idea behind or substanding a thing; that which makes it what it is. In the case of a book, this would be the subject matter which gives it its shape and content. To produce a "good" book, ie a book which fulfils the purpose for which it exists, the author would have to be thoroughly familiar with the Formal Cause. A sculptor who is commissioned to make a likeness of the god Venus would have to be imbued with the idea of Venus.

3 **Efficient Cause** - That which produces a thing. In the case of a book, the author, typesetter, printer etc.

4 **Material Cause** - In the case of a book, the material out of which it is made.

Each Cause may embody a series of subordinate causes; to take an example:-

Efficient Cause of a book - Author writes the book
                The book is typed
                The book is typeset
                Printer prints it
                Publisher markets it

Given that the steps which go to make up an Efficient Cause are in order, the highest step, upon which all the others necessarily depend, will require the most intelligence, and the lowest step will require the least.

It is the job of the Efficient Cause to look at the Formal Cause or unitive idea and split it up into parts so that it may be manifested.

Does a hierarchy of causes apply to the Macrocosm as well?

According to the great sages and philosophers, the same process is indeed evident in the production of the universe. There are always four Causes. The Final Cause can be seen as a Unity or One which expresses Itself through the Trinity of the Formal, Efficient and Material Causes. The One and the Three are evident in all things.

What is the Efficient Cause of the Macrocosm?

Most religions would say the "Divine Creative Intellect" or "Creator Lord". In Greek mythology, Jupiter represents the idea of Divine Creative Intellect. Hindus believe Brahma to be Divine Creative Intellect.

The One and the Three dominate the whole scheme of things; unities continually yield trinities.

From the point of view of Formal Causes, the whole of manifestation is a body of Ideas.

From the point of view of Efficient Causes, the universe is a body of lives and activities; a body of beings engaged in activities who are expressing ideas.

Astrology has retained an understanding of **Formal Causes** as well as Efficient Causes; thus astrologers can think about life in a more satisfactory way than can scientists. Currently, science concerns itself, almost exclusively, with Efficient and Material Causes, and consequently it sees only the tail end of things. For instance, scientists say that the origin of the universe was a "big bang" without bothering to ask themselves the Cause of the "big bang"! Astrology, however, uses a language of symbols designed to cover all aspects of life. It is concerned with expressing **Formal Causes**, which are always, in some sense, ideas.

The hierarchy of Formal Causes begins with the most all-embracing archetypal Ideas and works down to universal Ideas, thence to particular ideas and finally to matter. In a sense, the seeds in nature are the tail end of ideas which are "designed" to **inform** the different species. Every species grows into one of its own members simply because it has a Formal Cause which is absolutely consistent. If we understand Formal Causes, we are able to understand synchronicity.

In the Trinity, the Formal element should be feminine. An all-male Trinity is really disastrous. Such primary Ideas dominate whole civilizations, percolating down through every level of life. Conflict is caused because of the omission of the female element in the Trinity. (The Catholic faith, however, does place emphasis on the female element, ie Virgin Mary.)

The particular events in our lives, no matter how small, continually show us the outworkings of archetypal ideas as symbolized in our charts. Events and our reactions to them do, of course, differ because we are all individuals with particular characteristics and needs, but beyond individual circumstance can be seen the unity of archetypal ideas which the whole of humanity has in common.

In order to consider the action of Efficient Causes, we have to look at the doctrine of substance - the first principle of nature and very illuminating. That which has real being is independent and can act of itself and by itself. There are three substances:-

1 Divine.
2 Human.
3 Natural.

Each of these substances has its own characteristic mode of action.

What kind of substances are the planets?

Plato says in the *Laws* that we are not looking at "lumps of dirt" but spiritual existences of some sort. In order to make up our own minds, we have to ask ourselves with what kind of activity we think we are dealing.

Every kind of substance in the hierarchy of being has its own characteristic action. The natural substances are at the bottom of this hierarchy, ie atoms - compounds - vegetables and animals. As we ascend this scale of being, the ratio of activity to passivity becomes greater; for instance, a snail is passive compared to, say, a cat, but a snail is more active than a cabbage, and so on. The higher we ascend along the scale of being, the higher do we ascend on the scale of substance. The further we go in this chain, the more we see "being done" and the less "being done *to*" a thing.

Human substance

Again, the "higher" type of man has a much higher ratio of activity to passivity. He is a more integrated and diverse being. The "higher" man also has a greater unity of activity; his life is dominated by fewer and simpler ideas. This imparts a coherence to his life which will be notably missing from the life of the "less developed" individual who, on the contrary, has too many aims and objects, many of which are inconsistent with one another.

One of the great paradoxes of action seems to be that the more self contained and interior the activity, the more far reaching are its effects. An activity beginning and ending in the same substance without going outside of itself has a considerably more far reaching effect than one that goes outside of itself. For instance, if we point a gun at someone, we naturally influence them for as long as we continue to hold the gun, but afterwards when we drop the gun, we influence that person negatively, ie they don't like us! The formal activity we have used to influence them is very extrinsic - we have to go outside of ourselves. If we wish to truly influence that person, we are using the wrong method. This applies to the whole scale of human activity, eg a comedian's private interior sense of fun naturally communicates itself to his audience; he isn't forcibly trying to impress.

Taoist text

Shun cultivated the ground. When men had settled on the land at the end of the year, he gave them good land and fishing places. Shun didn't appear to direct the people, but held the principle of virtue firmly in his mind. The reformation of the people was spiritually achieved through his own unswerving state of mind. Certainly, as this goes to show, the power of example is very potent. The more a person acts within themselves, the more are they cultivating their own integrity of being and the more widespread their influence. Action, therefore, is not necessarily a physical thing. The contemplative life, for instance, is a life of action.

The more that substances act within themselves, the more do they become spiritualized. God is the highest substance of all; continually enacting; active in relation to everything; passive in relation to nothing. "He" never goes outside of "Himself" to act and yet sustains the whole universe. Necessarily, "He" has no unused powers. "His" acting begins and ends in "Himself" and is absolutely coincident with "His" very Being. Indeed, the higher the spiritual substance, the more do being and activity become one and the same thing.

The Planets - what kind of activity?

1   They stay within themselves and their influence is very widespread.

2   Are they active or passive in relation to things? Do they "influence" us or do we "influence" them? They "influence" us regardless of whether we are conscious of them or not.

3   Are they continuously enacting or do they run to a timetable? They are continuously enacting - Mars never looks at his watch and says "at 10.15 I'm squaring Jupiter"! They are in a continuous relationship with one another.

It seems correct to conclude from what we have already said that the planets cannot be mere "lumps of dirt". Indeed, if they were, their activity would be less than that of a cabbage, and we would obviously be mistaken in affirming this. The planets, then, are spiritual existences or substances and their influence is universal.

CHAPTER III

The Work of Michel and Francoise Gauquelin

Part One - The Background

In our approach to the new study of astrology, it is desirable, first, to examine at some length the work of Michel and Francoise Gauquelin. The work of the Gauquelins is so extraordinary and of such importance that it is hoped that those who are eager to get to the meat of the evidence will be patient if we take a few pages in which to describe the background and personal history of this partnership. Although such material may seem peripheral to the main theme of the book, yet it does contain some instructive elements which are worth recording. Furthermore, although we shall have some serious criticisms to make of this work at a later stage, it is important that these criticisms should be seen in the context of the larger achievement.

Michel Gauquelin was born in Paris on 13 November 1928 at 10.15 pm. according to his birth certificate, or at 10.20 pm. he tells us according to his mother. His father, who was a dentist, had become interested in astrology through an artist friend. Gauquelin pere did not address himself to this subject in any profound or philosophical spirit, but regarded it rather as a kind of party piece with which to entertain his friends.

As a result of this interest, however, the youthful Michel received an early introduction to the subject and he records that when he was only ten years old, he was already pressing his father to show him how to calculate and read a horoscope.

It is, or certainly was, unusual to find an enthusiasm for this hoary subject among the very young, but the idea of astrology must have touched some chord in the mind of Michel Gauquelin, for during his boyhood years, he avidly read all the books on the subject he could find. Perhaps his interest was partly sustained by a certain kudos he enjoyed among the young ladies in his class at school by virtue of this unusual accomplishment, yet he pursued the topic with an earnestness which suggested that there was more to it than that, and he was still only seventeen when his first treatise on astrology, to which he was putting the finishing touches, was confiscated during a Latin lesson, to be returned later, however, by a somewhat puzzled master.[1]

After he left school, he worked for a year at a preparatory course for the Ecole des Arts Decoratifs, intending to take up a career in interior design, and during this time he intensified his studies and began writing to registrars of births for the birth certificates of notabilities in order that he might have the correct time for calculating their horoscopes.[2] However, these copies cost one franc each and as he was usually too poor to afford both this fee *and* a stamped, addressed envelope he enjoyed only a modest success in obtaining the data he sought.[3]

At about this time, he began making a detailed study of the researches of the two writers on astrology whose work seemed to him best to satisfy the standards of evidence and objectivity needed for a modern reassessment of astrological ideas. These were the Frenchman, Colonel Paul Choisnard (1867-1930)[4] and the Swiss, Karl E Krafft (1900-1945).[5] Each of these men had tried to tackle astrology in a scientific spirit, seeking through the accumulation and analysis of factual data to throw light on the workings of astrology and to establish a demonstrable case for its validity.

It is not necessary here to discuss the work of these two men; Gauquelin considered Choisnard to be both sounder and clearer but the point is debatable and in any case the researches of each had been wide-ranging and each had shown ingenuity and persistence in his investigations. Gauquelin admits that, because of the complexity of their work and the limitations of his statistical knowledge at this time, he experienced much difficulty in coming to grips with it. Krafft's *Traite d'Astro-biologie* (1939), in particular, is a monumental work which posed many problems, but Gauquelin struggled with this, section by section, until he felt that he had acquired a good grasp of its contents.

By the time he had finished, he was very conscious, as anyone must be who enters this field, of the extreme difficulties and uncertainties occasioned by the demographic and astronomical factors which bear upon the statistical assessment of probabilities in such work. Nevertheless, despite some misgivings he was impressed and set out to try to repeat such of the experimental studies done by these men as seemed to him the most convincing.

Alas, he found that he was unable to reproduce or confirm their results. This was a disappointment to him for although sometimes irritated by the uncritical credulity and frivolous attitude to the subject displayed by some of his acquaintances, he remained convinced that there was an underlying truth in astrology.

Another book which Gauquelin examined was one by Leon Lassons. Lassons' first venture into the field of astrology was inauspicious, to say the least; it took the form of a book on Mundane Astrology,[6] published in 1938 and subtitled "Fifteen years of peace"! But in a later work[7] he studied, albeit on a very limited scale, the positions of the planets in their diurnal circles (that is, in their daily rising, culminating and setting) in the nativities of men belonging to different professional groups and maintained, as a result of these studies, that the members of such professional groups showed a significant tendency to be born with that planet which was, in a broad way at least, traditionally associated with that profession (such as Mars for soldiers) near to its point of rising. However, Lassons insisted on one departure from astrological tradition.

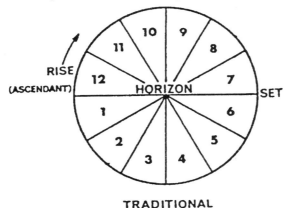

TRADITIONAL

Fig. 1a

Virtually all modern astrological teachings give a certain priority to the ascendant and planets in the first house, that is to say, the sector of the diurnal circle which lies immediately *below* the eastern horizon. (The "houses" are then numbered anticlockwise round the chart as in Figure 1a.) Lassons said that planets immediately *above* the horizon were stronger than those below and he therefore proposed that the sector above the horizon should be the first house and that the houses should then be re-numbered as in Figure 1b.

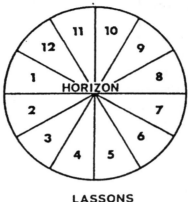

LASSONS

Fig. 1b

Lassons' writings have only a very minor place in astrological literature, in no way comparable to those of Choisnard or Krafft, and the chief effect of this book on Gauquelin was to raise further doubts in his mind about the methodology of such researches and to make him even more convinced of the need for a much deeper study of the demographic and astronomical factors involved. (Nevertheless, in the light of subsequent events, Lassons' insistence upon the strength of planets above the horizon is interesting, as also his attempt to examine professional groups.)

With these considerations in mind and feeling by now the need for more specialised knowledge in following up his researches, Gauquelin decided to avail himself of an opportunity which presented itself to enter the Sorbonne University, there to study psychology and statistics. His period at the Sorbonne was interrupted by a year's military service and there, as luck would have it, Gauquelin found that a free issue of stamps was available to conscripts for the purpose of writing home. Soldiers are not famous for their diligence in letter-writing and in this situation Gauquelin found he was able to collect enough stamps to step up his applications for copies of birth certificates.

It was also during this time at the Sorbonne (actually in 1952) that Gauquelin decided that he needed to improve his indifferent command of English, and to this end he sought the services of one Marie Schneider, a multi-lingual young lady who had recently arrived in Paris from her native Switzerland and was giving lessons in an assortment of languages conveniently nearby. Marie Schneider found Michel Gauquelin a rather tiresome student who seemed to come for lessons far too often and with but little progress to show for it, but one day he confided in her his interest in astrology and told her something of his researches in that field. From that moment (although she was deeply sceptical about the subject) she began to look upon this "tiresome student" with new eyes and even to feel, as she puts it, that "something might yet be made of this boy".

Notwithstanding this improved rapport Gauquelin, ever a cautious man, was evidently not prepared to take chances. Although he would often meet Marie after her classes were over for the day, she noticed that for a whole year he was always "otherwise engaged" on a Thursday and began to wonder what other acquaintances he might be cultivating at this time, especially as he volunteered no explanations. It later transpired that Gauquelin had obtained permission through a friend in the judiciary to go through the police files on the pretext of studying 'morpho-psychology' - (what used to be called physiognomy, I believe). This job could only be done on a Thursday afternoon but by these means Gauquelin was able to acquire the birth data of 600 outstanding murderers! It struck him, however, that this preoccupation with criminal nativities might seem to the young lady to constitute a somewhat unhealthy, even sordid, streak in his make-up and it was not until much later that he ventured to account for his missing Thursdays.

From this time on, two heads being better than one, the partnership prospered. Marie Schneider began reading for a degree in psychology and two or three years later she followed this up with a degree in statistics at the Institut de Statistique of the University of Paris. As often happens in these cases, providence took a hand in allotting to her a professor from the Institut National d'Etudes Demographiques (INED) and in selecting a subject for her thesis she chose to make a study of the whole question of times and seasons in the incidence of births. Asked by the learned professor why she chose this unusual topic she said she would tell him when she had got her degree. When she did and he found that it was to examine astrological concepts, he never spoke to her again. (Such are the hazards for those who depart from the straight and narrow path of orthodox scientific investigation.) Her paper on "L'heure de la naissance" (dealing with the nychthemeral curve or daily rhythm of births) was published in *Population*, the journal of the INED.

By these means, their native determination being reinforced by the fruits of their university courses, our two researchers successfully came to grips with the complex demographic and statistical problems inherent in their subject-matter and, after a number of pilot studies to test the ground and to bring Gauquelin's earlier studies into focus, they found that the most promising line of enquiry - indeed the only one which yielded convincing results - involved the study of planetary positions in their diurnal circles.

The problem, of course, was to show that specific groups of people who had some common characteristic (intrinsic or extrinsic) exhibited a statistically significant tendency to share also some common planetary position in their nativities which was not otherwise a significant feature of the generality of births.

In looking for such a group, the astrological investigator must take his data where he can find it from what is available to him (a fact which is not always remembered by those who cavil at a choice of data). One of the few sources from which the birth data of those with a common characteristic is generally available on a large scale is in published works of the "Who's Who" variety covering different professions. (In Britain we have *Who's Who in the Theatre, The Writers and Authors Who's Who*, and so on.)

By making use of such works of reference (full details being given in their scientific publications) and by obtaining the *time* of birth of each subject from the registrar of births (of which more later), Gauquelin was able to show to his own satisfaction that different professional and such-like groups did in fact show a statistically significant tendency to have certain planetary positions in common and this, for some years, was to form the principal basis of the Gauquelins' enquiries.

There can be little doubt that the driving force and unifying intellect behind the researches of this partnership has been Michel Gauquelin and he has always insisted that all results and research material should pass through his hands. Yet it takes more than one kind of virtue to achieve success in matters of this kind. It is clear that at this stage Gauquelin's natural impulse was, after the manner of the true-born researcher, to press on with the work, trying to perfect and refine the results in pursuit of some ever-receding ideal goal of scientific finality. It was Marie Schneider who said bluntly and after the manner of womankind that if he had not published his first book by the time he was 25 he would never be a success.

But the question was how to secure publication of a book full of dry statistics which would never be a best-seller, which would not please the scientists (though the author may have supposed it would) since it struck at the heart of their cherished beliefs, and would not please most astrologers either, since it threatened to kill off a number of their sacred cows.

Fortunately, Marie Schneider, who had evidently given the matter some thought, had the answer. She told Gauquelin that she had saved up 1000 francs and that he could use this to publish his book on condition he married her!

This brilliant solution looked, on close inspection, like a good bargain to all concerned and so Gauquelin began putting together *L'Influence des Astres*[8] (published in 1955), our research team was united in wedlock and Marie Schneider become Francoise Gauquelin.

To balance the books, it was Michel who saved up to publish his second book *Les Hommes et les Astres*[9] in 1960, but in 1969 they started the Laboratoire d'Etude des Relations entre Rythmes Cosmiques et Psycho-physiologiques and from them on virtually all the scientific works of the Gauquelins (which now number over 20 volumes, all with French and English texts on facing pages) were published under this impress, although a number of semi-popular works have been produced through other publishing houses over the years and many other articles and papers[10] have been published by the Gauquelins, separately or jointly in scientific and other periodicals.

We can now proceed to a full description of the whole range of the Gauquelins' researches, reserving a detailed assessment of these and the role they have played in the modern restoration of astrology until the facts have been fully set out.

CHAPTER III - NOTES

1 Michel Gauquelin still has this early treatise!

2 On the Continent (and in Scotland) the time of birth is recorded on the birth certificate; only the rest of the British Isles neglects to record this important information, except in the case of twins.

3 The first birth certificate Gauquelin succeeded in obtaining was that of Louis Braille, inventor of the embossed type for the blind.

4 Choisnard's main work is perhaps *Preuves et Bases de l'Astrologie Scientifiques* (1921) but an earlier and better known work was *Langage Astral*.

5 Krafft has often been referred to in later times, falsely and foolishly, as "Hitler's Astrologer", a story which Gauquelin himself does nothing to dispel in his *Astrologie devant la Science* (Astrology and Science), first published in 1966 and in English in 1970 by Peter Davies. For a more accurate account, see *Urania's Children* by Ellic Howe.

6 Leon Lassons: *Astrologie Mondiale*, Editions Demain, Brussels, 1938.

7 Lassons: *Ceux qui nous guident*, 1946.

8 Gauquelin M: *L'Influence des Astres*, Editions du Dauphin, Paris 1955.

9 Gauquelin M: *Les Hommes et les Astres*, Edition Denoel, Paris 1960.

10 A full list of such publications relating to their astrological work is given in *Birth and Planetary Data*, Series C, Vol 1 (Profession-Heredity) Michel and Francoise Gauquelin; Pub: Laboratoire d'Etude des Rythmes Cosmiques et Psychophysiologiques, 8 Rue Amyot, 75005 Paris. It should be added that the Gauquelins have 30 or 40 volumes of non-astrological works to their credit, chiefly relating to the field of psychology.

CHAPTER IV

The Work of Michel and Francoise Gauquelin

Part Two: Results

Anyone who sets out to explain a technical or semi-technical subject to the lay reader must, at the outset, entertain some slight misgivings. Can he make clear to those not previously acquainted with the subject the nature of the issues involved? As it happens the work of the Gauquelins rests upon something which is a matter of simple everyday observation and therefore the basis of their work and the character of their findings are, in their essence, easy to understand (at least in their initial import).

Every day the sun rises in the east, culminates in the south and sets in the west (at least in the northern hemisphere). Because this is the result of the Earth turning on its axis from west to east, it follows that not only the sun but the moon and planets also rise in the east, culminate and set in just the same way. This apparent movement of the heavenly bodies across the sky each day is called their diurnal (or daily) motion.

It is the positions of the planets in these, their diurnal circles, which form the basis of Gauquelin's principal studies. In his first book *L'Influence des Astres*, after devoting the first part of the book to a critique of the work of Krafft and Choisnard he sets out to show that at the time of birth of the members of different professional groups there was a statistically highly significant tendency for certain planets to occupy characteristic positions in their diurnal circles.

In order to do this he made large collections of the birth dates of prominent members of the different professions from the standard works of reference and then wrote to the registrars of births in the localities where they were born to obtain a copy of the birth certificate. (In France, as in other European countries, the time of day at which birth took place is registered and appears on the birth certificate.)

Altogether he amassed over 9,000 such sets of birth data from French sources and it is upon a study of these that *L'Influence des Astres* is based, the planetary positions for each person's birth being calculated for the precise time, date and place of birth (using the latitude and longitude of the principal town of the district).

This was a huge undertaking, calling for those qualities of persistence, thoroughness and systemization which characterise all the Gauquelins' work. Needless to say, throughout his studies Gauquelin strictly observes the established rules of statistical procedure; the work or works of reference used are all listed and exhaustively treated in the terms laid down. One thing which Gauquelin realised at an early stage in his work was that his results might be challenged on the grounds of unreliability of data, and therefore he adopted the procedure, from the beginning, of publishing every particle of data and in later works he lists not only all the data used but all the planetary positions derived from them and all other relevant information. Thus sceptics may, if they wish, take samples at every stage of the working and check the data and results for accuracy.

It may be an illustration of the maxim that fortune favours the brave that France is evidently one of the few countries in the world where the law specifically states that the civil authority *must* provide a copy of any birth certificate to *anyone* who asks for it and pays the appropriate fee. Because of this the Gauquelins had very few failures in obtaining their birth data, although the (remarkably few) cases where the birth record could not be traced are duly listed.

Another point which should be mentioned is that, in choosing the professional groups to be studied, Gauquelin specifically sets out to collect, as far as possible, professions where there is likely to be a distinct element of vocation which reflects some definite personal aptitude or inclination. Thus the nativities he studies are those of artists, actors, sports champions, top army officers, leading scientists, outstanding physicians, priests and politicians. Of course it may be argued that those who enter these professions do not always do so by virtue of any special aptitude or personal preference. For example, it used to be a tradition in some families that the sons went into the armed services; but even here a son who was of a gentle or scholarly disposition would be more likely to have been entered for the law or the church. In any case, Gauquelin shows over and over again in his work that those who are most successful in any career, and who are therefore evidently best adapted to it by nature, are those who show the astrological distinguishing marks most clearly.

Now although the basis of the Gauquelin experiments is essentially very simple, as explained at the beginning of this chapter, yet it is true that the astronomical factors involved are by no means as straightforward as they may appear at first sight. However it will be easier to understand the nature of the complications if we first look at some of the results.

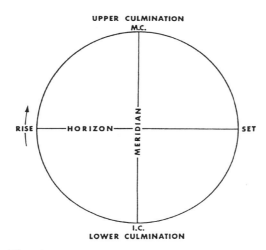

Fig. 2

Every day, as we have noted, the sun, moon and planets rise in the east, culminate at the upper meridian and set in the west, passing below the horizon to rise again next day and this circular movement can be shown diagrammatically as in Figure 2.

In astronomical and astrological parlance the point of upper culmination is known as the MC (Latin: *Medium Coeli*, the middle of the heavens) and the point of lower culmination is known as the IC (*Imum Coeli*, the bottom of the heavens) and we will therefore use these abbreviations if only because they take up less room on a diagram.

In order to study the astrological effects of the planets in these their diurnal circles it is obviously necessary to divide up the circle in some way so that the position of each body in its apparent daily journey 'round the Earth' can be identified. In order to do this, astrologers (as noted in Figure 1) divide the circle into twelve "houses" which they number anti-clockwise. Gauquelin, however, in order to have greater detail, divides the circle first into twelve sectors, then into 18, and finally into 36 sectors, and these he numbers in a clockwise direction (which, since it follows the direction of the daily motion of the heavens, seems more natural).

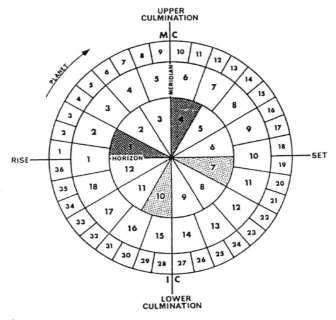

Fig. 3

This diagram (Figure 3) is one to which we shall need to refer from time to time. All three of Gauquelin's division are shown but in most of his writings he confines himself to illustrating his results in terms of the division by 12 or 18 sectors, since in that way the simplest and clearest picture is given. (The shaded areas will be explained in a moment.)

The Thesis

Gauquelin's thesis is that the planet or planets which outstandingly describe, astrologically, the characteristics needed in a given profession, show a clear statistical tendency to occupy sectors 1 or 4 in the division by 12 sectors, that is to say those which immediately follow a planet's rise or upper culmination (these are the areas cross-hatched in Figure 3). The planet is also liable to show some tendency, although less pronounced, to occupy sectors 7 or 10 (that is to say those which follow the setting and lower culmination of the planet, as shaded).

To give an example, the planet Mars is considered to be prompt in action, energetic, hardy, courageous, combative, rigorous and so on. These are the qualities which one would, in a general way, expect to find in the top athlete or high-ranking army officer and which should therefore promote success in those callings. Thus one would expect to find Mars occupying sectors 1 and 4 much more often than would occur by chance at the time of birth of members of these groups.

Conversely there will be some occupations where these qualities are not needed and where, indeed, they might prove something of an impediment to success. For example, one might expect that the typical artist, who must lead a more contemplative life and is called upon to show sensitivity and refinement of perception and touch rather than forcefulness, would not be a man to show the Martian qualities to any notable extent. Thus in the nativities of artists one might expect to find Mars in sectors 1 and 4 only infrequently. (Of course some athletes *are* dreamers and some artists attack their canvasses with aggression, but these are not typical.)

The first set of results

Let us look then at the position of Mars at the time of birth of top sports champions.

It should be noticed, in passing, that Gauquelin insists that, in order for the Mars emplacement to reach a high level of statistical significance, only those sportsmen who have attained the very highest rank should be included and he therefore confines his collection of sporting personalities to those who have represented their country in their chosen sport. Thus 570 sportsmen of international calibre whose birth data were given in two works of reference were taken and their times of birth ascertained. Their nativities were then calculated and the number of times each planet fell in each sector of the diurnal circle was counted. Figure 4 shows the distribution of the planet Mars in terms of the division of the circle by 12. It will be seen that sectors 1 and 4 are both high-scoring.

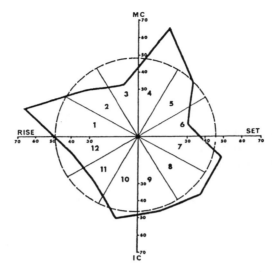

Fig. 4 Mars positions for 570 sports champions.

The circle is divided up in such a way that each planet would, over a period of time, spend an equal length of time in each sector. Thus, if births took place at an equal rate throughout the day and throughout the year, one would expect the score for any planet to be, on average, the same in each sector. As it happens, births do not take place regularly throughout the day and year and therefore the Gauquelins had to take immense trouble to ascertain the correct 'expected' distribution of the planets in their diurnal circles at the time of human births for any given period of time, since it is upon this knowledge that the true calculation of statistical probabilities depends.

This calculation was made in the first place from a thorough study of all the theoretical factors involved but it was confirmed by a comparison of these theoretically derived frequencies with the planetary distributions at the time of birth of a cross-section of over 24,000 births in the population at large (concerning which more later).

On the basis of these observations[1] it is possible to compare the distribution of Mars, sector by sector, in Figure 4 with the distribution which would be expected if there were no presumed astrological factor involved. Thus we give below: in line one, the sectors; in line two, the expected frequency of Mars in each sector; in line three, the observed frequency as shown in Figure 4.

Sectors   1   2   3   4   5   6   7   8   9 10 11 12

Expected 50 50 49 48 47 46 45 45 46 47 48 49

Observed 68 41 34 68 47 31 50 51 48 52 39 41

So we see that at the time of birth of our 570 sports champions, Mars was just past its rise or upper culmination (sectors 1 or 4) 136 times whilst chance would have placed it in those sectors only 98 times (actually 97.8). The odds against such an excess appearing in these two sectors is over 70,000 to one.

Gauquelin also divided his champions up into four main groups: cyclists (99), boxers (135), team games (166) and others (168) and showed that Mars was significantly inclined to sectors 1 and 4 in each group separately.

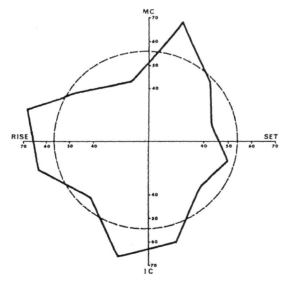

Fig. 5 Mars positions for 676 army officers.

Another group which might be expected to show the martial characteristics is that of the highest ranking officers in the army and navy. Figure 5 therefore shows the distribution of Mars in 676 such nativities and again we see peak totals in sectors 1 and 4. In fact, Mars appears in sectors 1 or 4 140 times against an expected frequency of 115.7. (Chance would give this result less often than once in 100 times.)

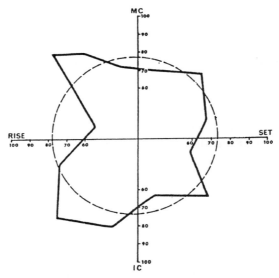

Fig. 6 Mars positions for 906 artists.

On the other hand a group of 906 artists (painters) showed a strong tendency for Mars *not* to occupy sectors 1 and 4 (see Figure 6), indicating that the Mars characteristics tended to be lacking in this group. Here Mars occupies sectors 1 or 4 only 127 times against an expected score of 115.2. (Probability: less than 1:100.)

In the nativities of scientists it is the planet Saturn which shows strongly. This is in conformity with the traditional astrological attributes of Saturn which is considered, among other things, to be careful, thoughtful, exact, introverted, sober, prudent, taciturn and so on. The word 'Saturnine' is significant.

In this group Gauquelin has, in *L'Influence des Astres:*

576 Academicians of Medicine
508 other distinguished physicians given in the chosen
    works of reference
281 Academicians of Science.

(In the writer's view, one should not ordinarily mix physicians with pure scientists for one would not expect the doctor, whose daily occupation is concerned with *people*, to have the same characteristics as the pure scientist whose work is more with facts and ideas. However, in this case it is reasonable to assume that the Academicians of Medicine and perhaps the other renowned physicians were more science orientated than the ordinary general practitioner.)

In these 1365 nativities, Saturn occupied sectors 1 or 4 260 times against an expected total of 219.7 (probability 1:300) and Mars too scores high in these sectors: 281 times instead of 232.9 (P = 1:3000). We may suppose that the doctor, especially perhaps the surgeon, must have something of the soldier's decisiveness, penetration, coolness in critical situations, promptness in action, etc, although these are obviously only one aspect of the ideal physician's temperament.

The planet Jupiter is considered astrologically (at least on one side of its nature) to be extroverted, expansive, self-confident, ambitious, cheerful, affable, optimistic, boastful and so on. The word 'jovial' covers some of these traits. Gauquelin shows that Jupiter is strong (ie significantly tending to sectors 1 and 4) in the nativities of actors, politicians and army officers but "weak" in those of scientists.

The Reaction to Gauquelin's work

There is no need to continue with our illustrations of these results from Gauquelin's first book. Suffice to say that they were impressive enough for Gauquelin to feel confident that they would interest any fair-minded scientist who would examine them.

Perhaps he hoped that these scientific studies of the old astrological conception of a relation between human life and destiny and the stars would cause something of a stir in scientific circles and he was particularly careful to place as much ground as he could between himself and traditional astrological attitudes and assumptions. (Indeed he has been criticised for overdoing this tendency.)

However, if these were his hopes, they were to be rudely shattered. His attempts to interest the scientific world met with almost unanimous outrage and ridicule.

One group whom he approached was the *Comité Para*, a Belgian committee of scientists from various disciplines specialising in the investigation of claims of positive results in the field of the paranormal and who, it would evidently be fair to say, prided themselves on never having failed to expose, to their own satisfaction, the fallacious nature of all such claims.

The *Comité Para* were very resistant to the idea of examining Gauquelin's claims, which they considered absurd, and it was only with much persistence that he prevailed upon them to do so. They studied his results, scrutinized his methodology and discovered something of the problems and complexities of the subject matter. They could find no ascertainable errors but remained unconvinced about some of the (to them) demographic 'unknowns' and for the rest fell back upon the rather curious argument that Gauquelin's results must reflect some unusual feature in the occurrence of French births! If Gauquelin would only follow up his enquiries by repeating his experiments using births from other countries, they said, he would soon discover the ephemeral nature of his superficially impressive results.

It must have been a period of grim re-appraisal for the Gauquelins to find that the results of their very considerable labours were to be so lightly brushed aside. The prospect of having to accumulate fresh data on a high scale from foreign countries must have seemed particularly daunting, for the difficulties, at first sight, were immense.

Nevertheless, with their remarkable resilience, they were soon at work again planning their campaign for the extraction of birth dates and times from foreign sources. First it was necessary to discover in which countries they stood the best chance of successfully acquiring the data they sought and, after a survey of the possibilities, they chose, for various reasons, Germany, Holland, Belgium and Italy.

Then began the difficult search for appropriate works of reference from these countries which would yield data parallel to and comparable with those they had already collected from French sources.

Those who have never tried to make such collections of data will not realise how much labour or how many difficulties can be encountered in such work, yet these were nothing compared with the task which now faced the Gauquelins of acquiring the many thousands of birth certificates needed. Merely to have written to the hundreds of towns involved, politely requesting copies of the birth data when there was no compelling obligation on the local registrars to provide these would have led to wholesale neglect, indifference and refusal.

The Gauquelins set out, therefore, using public transport (!) to travel through the countries concerned. Their standard procedure upon arriving in a new town with their list of notabilities born in that district was first to find digs and then to install Michel in the local library, if any, or in some other convenient place where he could get on with the paper work and calculations involved. Francoise then sought out the office of the registrar of births and, calling upon her fluency in the various languages, attempted (with astonishing success) to extract the copies of birth certificates needed. For this job she was provided with an assortment of documents, letters of introduction and in fact every conceivable aid that ingenuity and impudence could devise, reinforced by her evidently considerable powers of persuasion.

Anyone who has tried to extract information from unwilling civil servants or who has tried to find an obscure government office in an unknown town (even in his own country) or who has endured the frustration of discovering that, when found, it was open only from ten to twelve or on Tuesdays and Fridays will imagine something of the courage required to see this job through. Charles Darwin did not display greater tenacity in his search for specimens than did our two travellers and he must have found amid the flora and fauna of the South Seas more pleasing prospects to delight the eye and sweeter mysteries to cheer the heart than ever the Gauquelins found on the railway platforms or amid the civic offices of Europe's industrial heartlands. It was a piece of remarkable scientific heroism!

When the operation was completed, the data of some 15,000 foreign births of notabilities had been collected to add to the 9000 already acquired in France. These 24,000 births ranged in date from 1794 to 1937, although most were from the second half of the nineteenth century and the first part of the twentieth. They now comprised nine main categories: leading scientists, top sports champions, high-ranking service officers, outstanding politicians, actors, painters, musicians, writers and captains of industry.

For each person in these collections, the Gauquelins keep a file which includes the official documentation of the birth data and the biographical and astronomical details required for their statistical studies. These files are always open to inspection.

With all this information collected, the calculations performed and the data organised into easily manageable form, the way was now clear for the next stage of the Gauquelins' work in which the conclusion based on the French births could be compared with those to be derived from the new data. However, before we proceed to set out the new results, there are a few matters which should be mentioned.

Some explanations and comments

1 **Detailed Evidence**. The perceptive reader, especially if he has a background in statistical studies, may, as he reads this description of the Gauquelins' work, think of queries, criticisms and possible objections of the results which are presented and the methods used to arrive at them.

It is therefore important, perhaps, to emphasise that one could not, in a brief outline such as this, deal with all the countless details which were taken into consideration and explained in the Gauquelins' own writings. Suffice it to say that in the twenty-five years since the publication of his first book, Gauquelin's methods have repeatedly been subjected to close and critical scrutiny and no significant flaw in his methods has been exposed and where legitimate doubts have been raised he has always taken steps successfully to satisfy these and remove anomalies. For full details of his methodology and discussion of the problems involved in his statistical work the original writings should be consulted and details of these are given at the end of this chapter.[2]

2 **Computers**. It may be supposed that in the age of the computer the Gauquelins would have made use of this tool for disposing of the vast quantity of calculations and operations involved in their work. As it happens they had no money for this and all their work has been done "by hand". In any case, and more importantly, Gauquelin has taken the view, as does the present writer, that in all original

research it is better to keep the mind in close contact with the material, for in this way a thousand small details (some of which may be important) are noticed in the actual handling of the material which would not come to light if the work were handed over to a machine.

As anyone who has tried it will readily confirm, this capacity to perform the work of a computer, and at the same time to retain one's sanity, calls for a special kind of mental toughness and resilience, not to say single-mindedness, and one can only view with astonishment the Gauquelins' performance in this respect.

3 **Planets studied**. In preparing his first book, although Gauquelin studied and published the positions of *all* the planets in the solar system at the time of birth of his celebrities, he found that the ones which gave most significant results were Mars, Jupiter and Saturn and he therefore concentrates his attention on these planets. For most of the others he obtained negative results but, as we shall see, with more evidence he was able to include the Moon in his second lot of studies and, later still, Venus.

4 **Control Group and the Study of Planetary Heredity**. One problem which was, to some extent, not fully resolved at the time of Gauquelin's first book was that of the planetary diurnal distributions which would be given by chance in any collection of human births.

The Gauquelins therefore tackled this with all the thoroughness for which they are noted. They addressed themselves to the problem on a theoretical level and Francoise Gauquelin was herself a pioneer in the study of the incidence of human births and the questions relating thereto. But they also decided that they should make a control collection of births from the population at large.

Making a virtue of necessity they decided to combine this work with a study of the heredity factor in astrology.

Astrologers (Kepler is an example) have always maintained that there were similarities to be seen between the horoscopes of parents and those of their children. Strictly speaking this is no more than one would expect given the basic astrological standpoint. If the horoscope is said to describe the person born under it and if children are genetically similar to their parents then it must follow that the horoscopes of parents and children are in some degree alike.

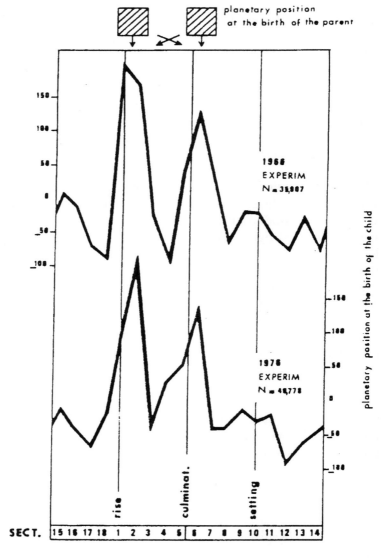

**REPLICATION OF THE PLANETARY EFFECT
IN HEREDITY
MOON AND PLANETS ADDED**

Fig. 7a The Planetary similarity at the births of parents and children; results of the 1966 and 1076 experiments. From *The Truth About Astrology*, Gauquelin (Hutchinson, 1973)

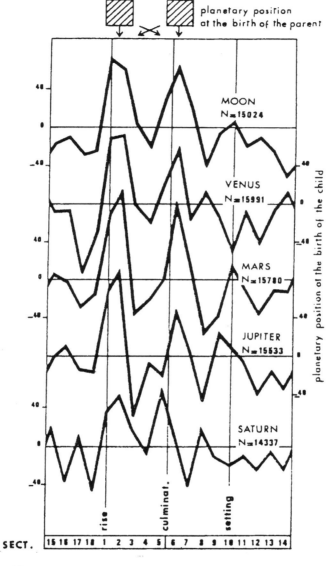

THE   1966 + 1976   EXPERIMENTS
FOR EACH CELESTIAL BODY

Fig. 7b   Increase in the planetary effect on heredity for children whose parents have the same planetary positions: combined results for the five significant plants. (*Ibid.*)

The Gauquelins therefore made a collection (equal in size to the collection they now had of 24,000 notabilities) of the birth data of parents and children. By means of these they were thus able to compare the planetary positions at the time of birth of successive generations in the same family, all the birth data concerned being published in six quarto volumes.[3] In this way they at once provided themselves with a large control group (since the nativities collected were those of ordinary citizens from all walks of life with no common bonds between the thousands of families involved) and at the same time were able to confirm statistically the age-old belief that the nativities of children contain elements in common with those of their parents.

It may be stated here that the original study (published in 1966) was finally based on the data of over 30,000 births. At a later date (1976), in order to demonstrate the replicability of this experiment, the Gauquelins made a further collection from different localities in France of over 37,000 *new* birth data of parents and children and in this way confirmed exactly the findings of the first study.[4]

Briefly stated their discovery was this: following upon the demonstration of the sensitivity of sectors 1 and 4 in the nativities drawn from professional groups, they showed that if one of the parents of a child had Moon, Venus, Mars, Jupiter or Saturn in sectors 1 or 4[†] then there was a clear statistical tendency for the child to have the same planet in one of those sectors.

If *both* parents had the same planet in one of the sectors of the heavens, then the tendency for their offspring to have the same feature in their horoscope was twice as strong. This is in conformity with genetic principles.

Figure 7 shows (on the left, 7a) the overall tendency of the child's Moon, Venus, Mars, Jupiter and Saturn, taken together, to occupy the sensitive areas of the heavens (at, or just after, the rise or culmination) when these areas are occupied by the same planet in the nativities of the parents (top line = 1966 experiment, bottom line = 1976) and (on the right, 7b) the tendency for each planet separately to conform to the position of the parents' planetary position.

This work of the Gauquelins which is concerned with what one might call "astrological heredity" is a most important facet of their work, but the brief outline here given of their results in this field

---

[†] Actually in sectors 36, 1, 2 or 3; or 9, 10, 11, 12 in the division by 36 sectors.

must suffice.   (In the writer's opinion, the hereditary link demonstrated by the Gauquelins represents only a fragment of the true astrological "genetic code" but more will be said about this later.[†])

5 **Medical Interference at Birth**. One of the questions which will occur to anyone considering the work of the Gauquelins is: What about the artificial induction of labour and surgical intervention in the birth process? How does this affect the significance of the birth time?

The Gauquelins have made intensive studies of these questions and show that where artificial interference with the birth process takes place the correspondence between the nativities of parents and their children is, in varying degrees, destroyed.

They also show that since 1945, in societies where the induction of labour has become increasingly common, the general law concerning the sensitivity of the sectors after rise and culmination gradually shows a breakdown. As it happens, virtually all the birth data used by the Gauquelins was of pre-war vintage and therefore results based on their data are not affected. However they insist that in all studies involving post-war births care must be taken to distinguish natural births from those where medical intervention affecting the timing has taken place.

Again, the many issues examined by the Gauquelins bearing on this problem are too complex to discuss in detail here and the original works should be consulted.[5]

6 **A further Astronomical Explanation**. Finally in this section of notes, we must enlarge somewhat, for the sake of completeness, on the brief explanations already given regarding the problem of dividing the diurnal circle. Those who are not particularly concerned to understand the technicalities could omit this note.

The object is to divide the diurnal circle of the planetary motions into equal sectors so that a random collection of planetary positions would not show a built-in bias towards any one sector.

In Figure 8, which is for the northern hemisphere, the horizontal circle represents the horizon at a place on the earth's surface, X. The

---

[†] This subject was not dealt with in the material collected up for this work; but see chapter 20 of *Harmonics in Astrology* (2nd ed. 1996, Urania Trust) for some discussion on genetics and harmonics.

four cardinal points are marked N, E, S, W. The ecliptic (heavy circle) is the sun's apparent path round the earth (actually the earth's path round the sun). It is in this place, approximately, that the planets have their orbits. The circle 'B' represents the celestial equator which always rises due east and sets due west; it represents the plane of the earth's spin.

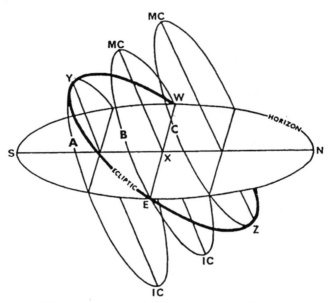

Fig. 8 The diurnal circles of bodies at different points in their orbit.

Since the plane of the earth's spin governs the plane in which all bodies rise, culminate and set, the dotted parallel circles, A and C (or any other parallel circles which lie between them) represent the diurnal circles of the planets at different points in their orbits.

When a planet is at Y in its orbit it is said to have maximum southern declination. It is then near longitude 0° Capricorn and the part of its diurnal circle above the earth (circle A) is a short arc (like the sun in our winter) and the part below is a long arc. When a planet is at point Z it is near 0° Cancer and is said to have maximum northern declination (circle C); its daily journey above the earth is then a long one (like the sun in mid-summer) and its journey below the earth is a short one.

But because the planets are constantly moving between northern and southern declination (the Z position and the Y position) then in the long run (that is to say when the data is spread over a long period as Gauquelin's is) their mean distribution will tend to be equally above and below the horizon as in circle B.

The problem therefore is simply to ensure that the sector divisions are made so that whether a planet is moving in circle A or circle C (or in any intermediate circle), the six divisions above the earth[†] and the six below are equal divisions of time so that a planet does not in the long run spend longer in one sector than another. Thus, in effect, Gauquelin takes the time between a planet's rise and its set and divides this into six equal periods, and similarly between its set and its rise. As it happens, this method approximates closely to the astrological method of house-division of Placidus de Tito (seventeenth century) which is the most common house division used by astrologers today, although Gauquelin did not chose his method for this reason but because it is astronomically free from bias for statistical purposes.

(The difference between Gauquelin's method and Placidus is that by basing his calculations upon the time of the rise and set of a planet he thus takes into account the planet's latitude, whereas the Placidian tables of houses are prepared for positions along the elliptic, without latitude.)

There were other factors which Gauquelin had to take into consideration; for example a slight eccentricity in the orbits of some planets is sufficient to affect the issue, and the distribution of the incidence of births during the daily and yearly cycles, taken together, also have a complex bearing on the matter.

A complete study of all these problems was published by the Gauquelins in 1957: *Methodes pour etudier la repartition des astres dans le mouvement diurne.* This important study is a basic work of reference in which no significant errors have been found since its publication. It contains a foreword by Prof Jean Poile (a sceptic in relation to astrological studies), Administrator of the *Institut National*

[†] Or the nine or eighteen above in the case of the divisions by 18 or 36.

de la Statistique in which he confirms the validity and accuracy of the methods described.

The acid test of the validity of the astronomical and demographic elements allowed for in Gauquelin's theoretical distributions is: do they accurately account for the observed planetary distributions at the time of births among the general population. This they do.

The Second Set of Results

Sports Champions

In Italy, Belgium, Holland and Germany the Gauquelins obtained the birth data of 915 leading sports champions to add to the 570 already collected in France.

The French champions, we may recall, showed a tendency for Mars to be in the sectors 1 or 4 far in excess of chance (in the order of 1:70,000). The champions born in other countries showed a Mars distribution (compared with its expected frequency) as follows:

	1	2	3	4	5	6	7	8	9	10	11	12
Theoretic:	81	79	77	75	74	74	72	74	75	78	78	79
Observed:	99	83	80	92	66	67	66	82	74	52	80	74

Here Mars occupies sectors 1 or 4 191 times against an expected total of 155.5. The probability of such a result occurring by chance is 1 in 700.

Figure 9 shows this distribution of Mars for the 'other countries' and one may compare it with Figure 3 which shows the same effect among French sportsmen. For the 1485 combined births from French and foreign sources, Mars is in sectors 1 or 4 327 times against an expected frequency of 253.4 (P = 1.5 million).

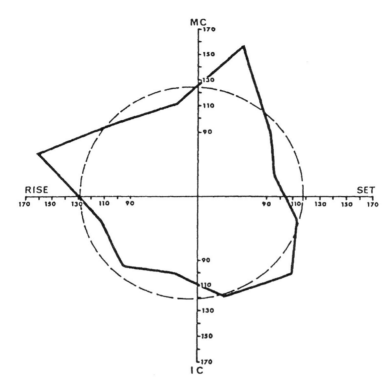

Fig. 9 Mars and (non-French) sports champions.

Scientists

The French studies of the nativities of scientists showed Saturn and Mars strong in sectors 1 and 4:

Saturn: Observed 260; Expected 219.7 (P = 1:300)
Mars: Observed 281; Expected 232.9 (P = 1:3000)

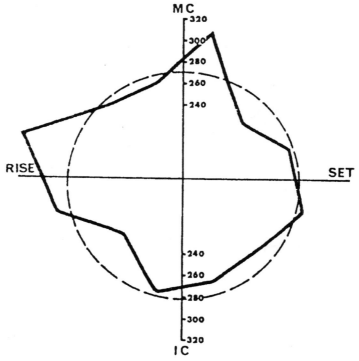

Fig. 10 The diurnal distribution of Saturn for scientists of all countries.

In Italy, Belgium, Holland and Germany 1940 new birth data of outstanding scientists and physicians were obtained. These showed in sectors 1 and 4:

Saturn: Observed 372; Expected 320.7 (P = 1:700)
Mars: Observed 385; Expected 332.7 (P = 1:700)

The total result for all five countries is shown in Figures 10 and 11. Here, Saturn 632 times (against 540.4) and Mars 666 times (against 565.6) yield statistical probabilities of 1:100,000 and 1:500,000.

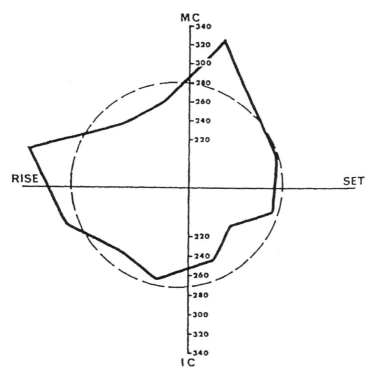

Fig. 11 The diurnal distribution of Mars for scientists of all countries.

High-Ranking Officers

In France a collection of 595 generals and admirals and 81 war heroes (676 in all) showed, in sectors 1 and 4:

Mars: Observed 140;   Expected 115.7   (P = 1:100)
Jupiter: Observed 136;   Expected 113.8   (P = 1:50)

In their foreign travels the Gauquelins made a collection of 2270 comparable high-ranking officers and in the meantime had also acquired 196 further data from French sources, giving a total of 2466

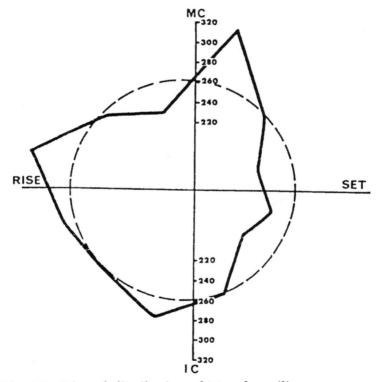

Fig. 12   Diurnal distribution of Mars for military men.

new cases to compare with the original French data. These showed for sectors 1 and 4:

Mars: Observed 494; Expected 419.9 (P = 1:50,000)
Jupiter: Observed 508; Expected 412.1 (P = 1:5 million)

The total collection of 3142 nativities of high-ranking officers now yielded levels of significance for Mars of 1:one million and for Jupiter of 1:50 million. The distributions are shown in Figures 12 and 13.

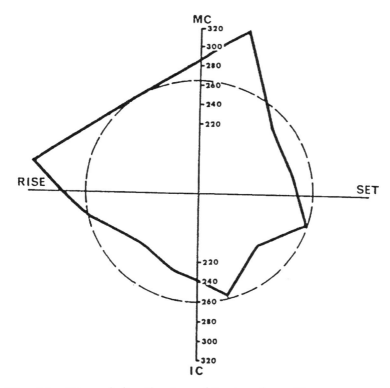

Fig. 13   Diurnal distribution of Jupiter for military men.

Actors and Politicians

In France the extrovert Jupiter had scored highly not only in the nativities of soldiers but also (though less highly) in those of actors and politicians.

These *plus* scores for Jupiter were well confirmed in a collection of 770 actors and 858 political figures in the other European countries.

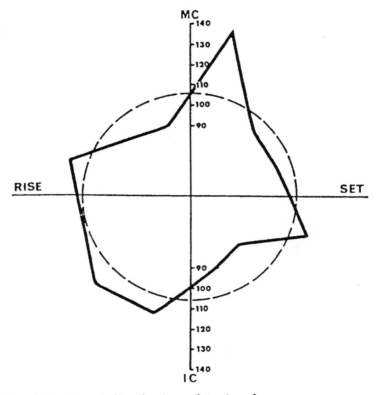

Fig. 14 Diurnal distribution of Jupiter for actors.

Opposing parties (Nazis and anti-Nazis) both showed the power-loving Jupiter strong for politicians; on the other hand, Jupiter yielded significantly low scores in sectors 1 and 4 among French scientists and this again was well confirmed by the other 1940 European scientists. Figures 14 and 15 show the total distributions for Jupiter in the nativities of actors and scientists and the opposite type of distribution is easy to see.

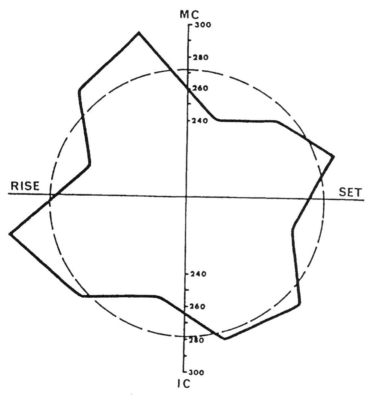

Fig. 15 Diurnal distribution of Jupiter for scientists.

Writers and the Moon

There is no need to multiply our examples of Gauquelin's second lot of studies but mention should be made of the Lunar results. The distributions for the Moon in Gauquelin's first set of results (ie in *L'Influence des Astres*) were given but were considered to be of relatively secondary significance, but in the light of the newly gathered European data they gave a clearly positive result.

The Moon is considered to be sensitive, imaginative and responsive and it was the category of writers which yielded the clearest lunar influence. Moon in sectors 1 and 4:

French: Observed 71; Expected 51.0 (P = 1:800)
Other countries: Observed 109; Expected 86.7 (P = 1:100)
All Writers: Observed 180; Expected 137.7 (P = 1:15,000)

Politicians also showed the Moon strong in sectors 1 and 4, but sportsmen and soldiers were significantly weak in relation to this position.

Summary Result

To sum up the results of the two studies (French and Other Countries), Gauquelin totals the distribution (by 18 sectors) of those instances showing significant planetary peaks (Moon, Mars, Jupiter and Saturn) in the French groups and compares them with the exactly parallel groups from other countries. Figure 16 shows this comparison. (There are roughly 10,000 positions in the French set shown in the upper distribution and 19,000 from other countries in the lower.) The similarity is obvious and is such as would occur by chance only once in 100,000 times. The secondary peaks in sectors 7 and 10 are easy to see.

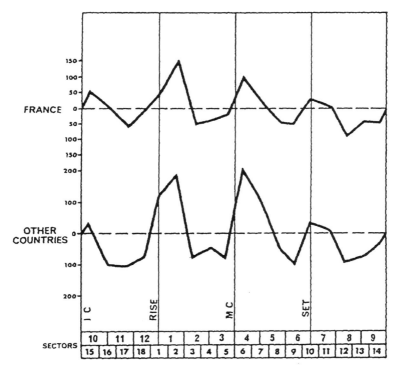

Fig. 16   The diurnal distribution of Mars of two separate samples of eminent sports champions showing the same pattern in the French sample and those born in other countries.

Confirmatory experiments

In addition to the foregoing, Gauquelin also gives the result of a number of secondary experiments which were designed to provide confirmatory evidence.

1   For example, in response to a suggestion by a critic, he takes the names of the sports champions in alphabetical order, as listed, together with their dates, years and places of birth but attributes to them the *times* of birth of those listed in *reverse* alphabetical order, thus shuffling the dates and times. The position of Mars in the set with the real birth-times was, of course, highly significant; in the set

with the fictitious birth-times it showed, of course, a random, non-significant distribution.

2   He performs several experiments along these lines: the 906 painters given in *L'Influence des Astres, who all came from the same work of reference,* were divided into three groups: those with an entry of a measured half-column or more (the 'chefs d'ecole'); those with an entry of between eight lines and half a column (the 'artistes notables'); and those with less than eight lines (the 'artistes obscurs').

Here the strength of the postulated results were significant as in the order given. The first group showed the planetary emplacements characteristic of artists to a highly significant degree, the unknowns yielding a 'chance' result, showing that the higher the attainment in the profession the more definite the astrological indications.

3   Similarly, Gauquelin compares the highly significant Mars distribution in the nativities of sports champions *at international level* with that of 717 footballers from the Italian football league. The result for the latter was very slightly, but not significantly, above chance.

4   Gauquelin also draws attention to some interesting contrasts. For example, two planets of *opposite* nature will show *opposite* distributions in the *same* group of people. Thus, Jupiter and Saturn (whom we might call L'Allegro and Il Penseroso, the lively man and the thoughtful man) show significant and opposite distributions in the charts of scientists, Saturn being often, Jupiter seldom, in sectors 1 or 4.

Similarly, the *same* planet will tend to show an *opposite* result in the nativities of those who are deemed to be of an opposite temperament. Gauquelin illustrates this by comparing the distribution of Mars and Saturn (taken together) in the nativities of various groups of artists (painters, musicians etc) with the distribution of the same two planets in the nativities of scientists and physicians. The statistical contrast between these two distributions (reflecting the difference between two traditionally opposite types, artists and scientists) is too large to register in the ordinary probability tables, but it is such as would occur by chance only once in many thousands of millions of times. Yet the nativities involved are drawn from roughly the same epoch and there is no reason why there should be totally opposing distributions unless there is an astrological factor at work. Gauquelin draws attention to other similar contrasts.

All these results of the Gauquelins are presented without fuss and in a dry statistical form and it is easy enough for anyone with no imagination and a closed mind to shrug them off and to ignore the fact that they represent a heroic attempt to draw attention to a scientific truth of the most far-reaching importance.

Critical Tests

With the results we have described and others like them, Gauquelin was able, after the publication of *Les Hommes et les Astres*, to go back to some of those who had expressed scepticism about his original results, for example, the Comité Para in Belgium.

The Comité Para reviewed the work and, being unable to identify any errors of procedure, were pressed by Gauquelin to perform a repeat of the Mars-Sports Champion experiment (or any other).

They made a new collection of 537 sporting personalities all of whom had represented their country in their chosen sport and analyzed the distribution of Mars in these nativities. Figure 17 shows the two results: Gauquelin's (top line) and the new group collected by the Comité Para (bottom). As will be seen, the two results are almost identical, Mars again showing up strongly (and very significantly) after its rise and upper culmination. The Comité Para constructed several different kinds of control but these only confirmed the validity of the result they had obtained.

More recently a similar repeat of this experiment has been done in the United States. It is interesting to reflect that the famous attack on astrology in the American *Humanist*, and which implied that there was no scientific evidence to support the subject, was published some 15 years after the two books by Gauquelin which we have described.

When Gauquelin challenged the views expressed in *The Humanist*, the correspondence, statements and counter-statements of opinion which followed were long and intricate and served chiefly to demonstrate the complexities of the demographic and astronomical issues involved and, above all, the ease with which these could be misunderstood and misrepresented by those who, unlike the Gauquelins, had not had to grapple with them in a practical way or solve the methodological problems they posed. However, to cut a

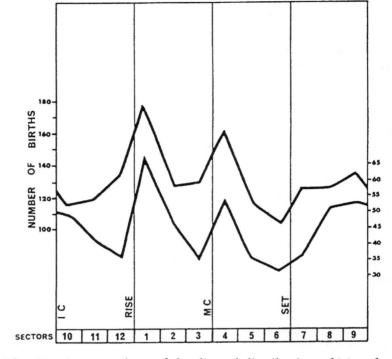

Fig. 17 A comparison of the diurnal distribution of Mars for sports champions, the upper line showing Gauquelin's study, and lower showing those of the Comite Para.

long story short, the Committee for the Scientific Investigation of Claims of the Paranormal (CSICP) under the chairmanship of Prof Paul Kurtz (Editor of *The Humanist* at the time of the attack on astrology) did ultimately agree to repeat the Mars-Sports Champions experiment using American births.

Unfortunately, this experiment to some extent went off 'at half-cock'. In framing the terms of the experiment Gauquelin insisted (1) that the sportsmen included should be of the very foremost rank in their sport and (2) that they should have been born before 1950 and preferably before 1930.

However, the CSICP were not able fully to observe these conditions. A work (or works) of reference was agreed upon and this yielded 605 top athletes, a sufficient number. Unfortunately, the birth data of *only 128* of these proved to be obtainable because only 18 of the States in the US were willing to furnish the data.

More names had to be found but this was achieved by the CSICP *only by lowering the standard of athletic achievement below a level which was acceptable to Gauquelin*. On the strength of this whole sample, the CSICP claimed that the "Mars effect" (so called) was not present to a significantly high degree in these births, although it was undoubtedly present.

In commenting upon this result, Gauquelin found another work of reference: *The World Almanac and Book of Facts* (1978 edition) which listed Olympic Gold Medal winners and other athletes of the highest international reputation, and this gave the date of birth of 87 US star sportsmen born before 1950 who had already been listed by the CSICP and who could be taken to represent the very highest achievers in their samples.

Gauquelin was then able to show - Figure 18 - that the Committee's original sample of 128 (top line) taken by themselves already showed a significant "Mars effect" and that the list of 87 star US sportsmen (bottom line) showed an even stronger and highly significant tendency to have Mars in sectors 1 or 4.

From a number of works of reference used in the whole of this experiment, the only source which failed to produce a significant Mars effect was the one which Gauquelin had rejected as having too low a criterion of sporting achievement.[6]

More recently still, Gauquelin has carried out a further replication of the experiment with 432 European champions[7] not included in previous studies, including 43 from Scotland (where birth times are recorded). This gave a result which was entirely in conformity with earlier results. A point of interest was that this group contained a higher proportion of women than earlier collections had done. It was found that women who reach international standard in sport have an even stronger tendency than men to have Mars in sectors 1 or 4. Gauquelin suggests that this is because it is harder for women to reach the top in sport because there are fewer opportunities.

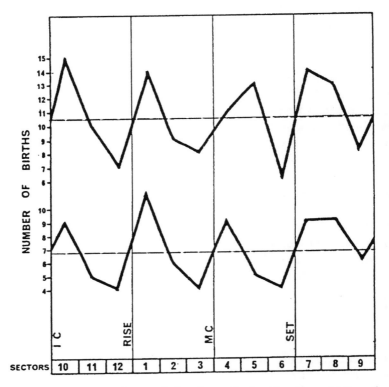

Fig. 18 A comparison of the diurnal distribution of Mars for US sports champions, the upper line from the Comite Para, and the lower those listed by *The World Almanac and Book of Facts.*

The Planets and Human Characteristics

So far the Gauquelins had demonstrated significant correlations between planetary positions in the nativity and the tendency to belong to a certain profession. But the question remained: did this relationship reflect the attraction to a certain profession *as such* or did not the planetary positions indicate, rather, certain innate characteristics which in turn equipped the native for success in a certain kind of activity, since it is obvious that the athlete, the scientist or the actor would tend to have certain characteristics which would fit him for his calling?

It is fairly clear that, from the outset, Gauquelin assumed that the planetary position probably correlated directly with innate characteristics as such and only indirectly with the profession. But how was he to demonstrate this?

He solved the problem in this way: he sought out identifiable sources of biographical material which gave not merely the bare bones of where educated, degrees, qualifications, posts held, books published, etc, but information of a more discussive kind which gave some assessment of the personality, aptitudes and general character of very many of the people already featured in his collections of notable nativities.

Using such sources the Gauquelins were able, with help, to go through the biographies of their subjects, in each case extracting the *character trait words* which were applied to those people already included in their collections of professional nativities.

As usual with all their work the Gauquelins published in detail the information derived from this exercise. For example, in the actors collection, Maurice Chevalier is listed as having the following characteristics in one of the two reference sources used:

"CHEVALIER Maurice 171 (21)

Wants to flee - popular - famous - successful - personality - irresistible - dynamic - irresistible - unexpected - ease (with) - simplicity - tender - laughing - not generous - popular - likes money - cold - miser - likes money - likes money - likes money. (Fond Rondel Ro 15908)."

After the name appears Chevalier's reference number in the actors collection (171) and the total number of words applicable (21) - *this is what I call hereafter the 'word count'* - and at the end of the list the reference number (15908) of the work consulted: La Fond Rondel (Ro = variety and music hall actors) in the Bibliotheque de l'Arsenal in Paris.

Where a phrase or metaphor was used as a character description some single synonymous word was entered for the sake of brevity and simplicity. It will be noticed that where a characteristic is mentioned several times ('likes money') it was as far as possible repeated in the list of characteristics so that the total "word count" for each person included such repetitions. The significance of this will be seen later in the way in which the data were treated.

In this way the Gauquelins were able to compile a huge vocabulary of character trait words - words which had been applied to those people for whom they already held details of planetary positions at their birth, and this gave them a very flexible tool for the study of personal characteristics in relation to planetary position.

This is not really the place to enter into a discussion of the precise value, limitations or problems of this technique of using biographical material in this way except to say, first, that it had been used successfully before; secondly that the ascriptions of characteristics had been made by experts (sports writers writing about sportsmen, theatre and literary critics writing about actors and writers, scientists writing about scientists) and thirdly that, despite certain limitations (for example the tendency of biographers to say complementary rather than derogatory things about their subjects) the method must have a general validity. Even the presumed tendency to give a favourable slant to descriptions of characters - to describe someone as 'firm' rather than 'obstinate', or as 'conscientious' rather than 'fussy' - does not invalidate the general method since such qualities are in each case of the same *type*.

The professional category which the Gauquelins first tackled in this way was that of sports champions and this yielded a total word count in excess of 6000. As they became more experienced at this job, the word count tended to rise; thus scientists yielded a word count of over 9000, actors nearly 18,000 and writers over 19,000 (these were the four groups used in this experiment) giving a total word pool of over 50,000 applications of character trait words to those men and women for whom they held birth data and therefore planetary positions. Armed with these data the Gauquelins were thus able to carry out the following experiments.

First Character trait Experiment

Their first step was to enquire whether the planetary positions correlated with the profession as such or with a certain type of personality profile which tended to promote success in that profession.

In order to do this they first set out to discover what were the typical characteristics of the four groups being studied: champions, scientists, actors and writers. This they did in several ways; they examined what had been written by specialist writers about the characteristics of typical representatives of the different professions and what qualities promoted success in that field. They made use of studies of such groups which, in some cases, had been made by psychologists and they also asked 'educated members of the public' (university graduates) to complete questionnaires in which they were invited to choose from a list of character-traits which ones they thought typical of the members of this profession or that.

In this way they were able to obtain a considerable degree of unanimity as to what personal qualities were typically shown by the top athlete, the successful scientist and so on. From these they took for each profession a short list of key words (or 'centre words' as the Gauquelins called them) descriptive of the essential characteristics of each group. For example in the case of the scientists' temperament the short list of words derived from a choice made by the 'educated public' is as follows:

Austere, without ceremony, discreet, gentle, methodical, detailed, not in fashion, modest, obstinate, precise, prudent, retired within oneself, dreaming, scientific, scrupulous, silent, studious, tenacious, timid.

A similar list of centre words is derived from a study by the psychologist, R B Cattell, of the typical traits of the scientific researcher; another list is given by Eysenck and Rachman and another again by Anne Roe in a study of the scientific temperament. (These assessments are treated separately and provide a check on each other.)[8]

Starting, then, from their centre words the Gauquelins referred to a dictionary of synonyms and extracted *all* the synonyms given for each of the words. Each of *these* words was then treated in the same way, yielding a 'second generation' of synonyms, so that in all they were able to list several hundred words said to be typically applicable to each professional group. We will call this 'List A'.

Next they took a dictionary of antonyms and, starting again from their key words, they carried out a similar process and in this way acquired a large vocabulary of words descriptive of the *opposite* type of quality to that typical of each profession. Let us call this 'List B'.

Returning to their biographical data the Gauquelins were now able to go through the character-traits for each person and for each time that one of that person's characteristics appeared in List A their planetary positions counted once as correlating with that characteristic. (Each profession and each planet was of course treated separately.)

The process was then repeated with List B. (In each case where a certain characteristic was attributed to a person more than once their planetary positions counted so many times. This had the effect of weighting the result so that the positions of those who showed the characteristic most strongly counted most often.) The end result of these operations was a pool of planetary positions associated with the words typical of the professional group (List A) and another pool associated with the opposite type of characteristic (List B).

In each professional category there was, of course, a predominance of those described by the words typical of that profession. But in each group there were also many who did not conform to the characteristic type and it was thus possible to compare the planetary distributions associated with the two opposite sets of characteristics.

On the following pages the four diagrams (Figure 19) show:

a The distribution of the combative planet Mars at the time of birth of athletes who had the typical champions' temperament and for those with the opposite temperament;

b the distribution of the introverted Saturn at the time of birth of scientists with the typical scientists' temperament and for those with the opposite characteristics;

c the same for the extrovert Jupiter and actors; and

d for the sensitive Moon and writers.

(Needless to say, several thousand comparisons are involved for each set.)

In each case it will be seen that the planet which characteristically shows the qualities typical of the professional activity tends to show a high distribution in sectors 1 and 4, whereas the opposite type of characteristic shows a low score in those sectors. Sectors 7 and 10 also tend to show the same contrast though less obviously.

It will thus be seen (as the Gauquelins set out to show) that the planetary positions correlate *not with the profession as such but with the personal characteristics*, since members of the same profession tend to show opposite characteristics in accordance with their planetary positions.

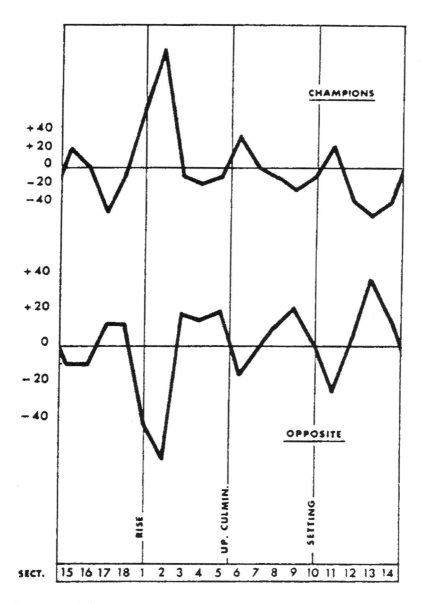

Fig. 19a The 'Mars' temperament and its opposite in sports champions. (Turn this and the 3 subsequent diagrams sideways to appreciate fully.)

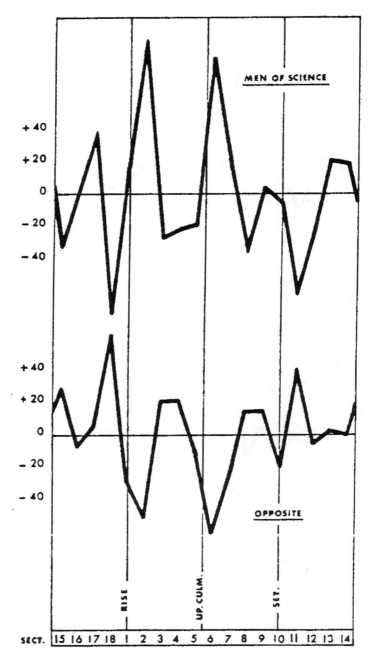

Fig. 19b The 'Saturn' temperament and its opposite in scientists.

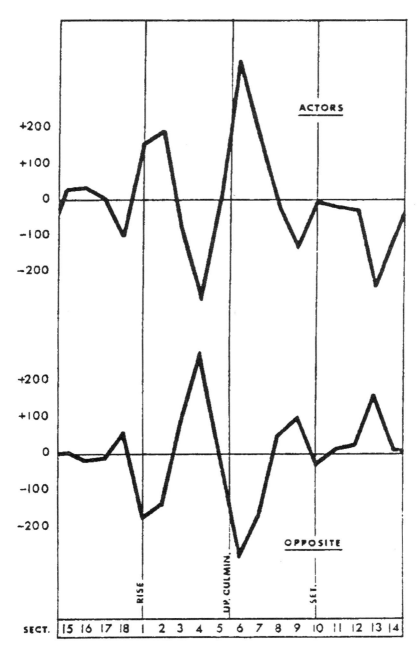

Fig. 19c The 'Jupiter' temperament and its opposite in actors.

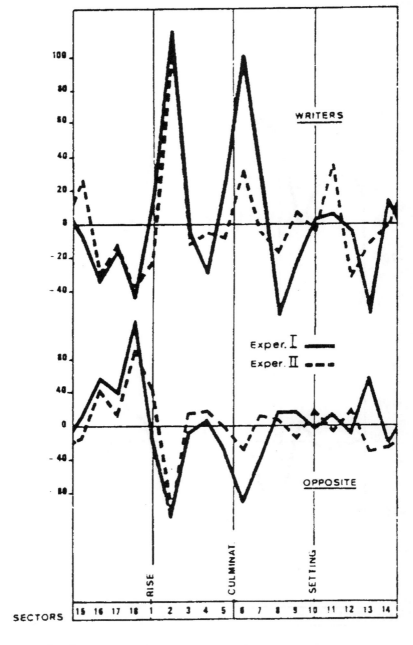

Fig. 19d The 'Moon' temperament and its opposite in writers.

Second Character-trait Experiment

In order to reinforce the demonstration in the first experiment that the planetary positions correlate directly with the personal qualities (and not with the profession) the Gauquelins asked the following questions.[9]

Did the scientists and actors[†] who were described by the words typical of the sports champions (competitive, determined, energetic etc) show the same Mars distribution (with peaks in sectors 1 and 4) as for the champions? Did actors and champions described as having the characteristics of the typical scientist show the same Saturn distribution as for scientists? Did scientists and champions described by the actors' words show the same Jupiter distribution as for actors?

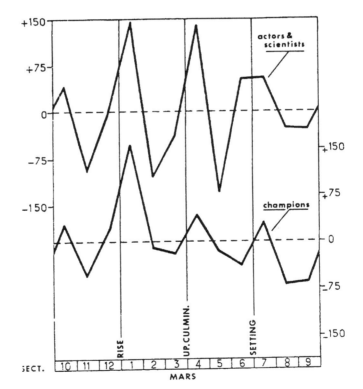

Fig. 20a

The diurnal position of Mars in champions, actors & scientists displaying 'Mars' qualities.

† Work on the writers' collection had not been completed at the time of this experiment.

The answer to these questions is shown in Figure 20 where it can be seen that it does not matter what actual profession was being followed; the planetary positions again show a clear correlation with the characteristics attributed to them by astrologers regardless of the profession itself.   Mars tends to fall in sectors 1 and 4 for the atypically forceful actor or scientist just as much as for the typical champion.   Jupiter verges towards sectors 1 and 4 for the extrovert scientist or champion just as much as for the actor, and Saturn is just as often in these sectors for the reserved type of actor or champion as it is for the typically introvert scientist.

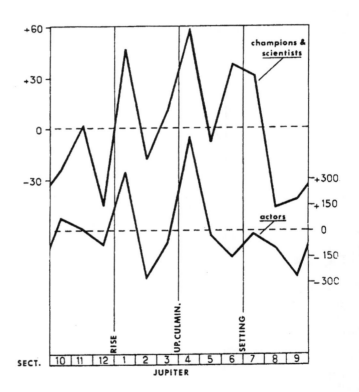

Fig. 20b

The diurnal position of Jupiter in champions, actors & scientists displaying 'Jupiter' qualities.

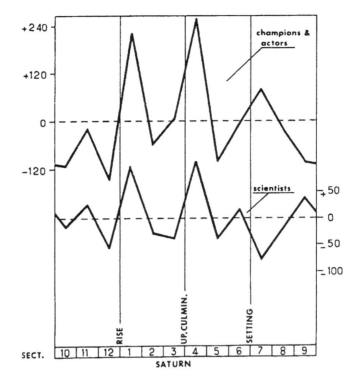

Fig. 20c

The diurnal position of Saturn in champions, actors & scientists displaying 'Saturn' qualities

Summary and General Assessment

In the foregoing pages we have given an outline of the principal researches of Michel and Francoise Gauquelin. Concerning these, H J Eysenck, Professor of Psychology at the Institute of Psychiatry of the University of London has said: "I think it may be said that so far as objectivity of observation, statistical significance of differences, verification of the hypothesis and replicability are concerned there are few sets of data in psychology which could compete with these observations. Full details of all the persons included in these studies are included in the voluminous publications of the Gauquelins and I have checked a small random sample of easily accessible ones; the Comité Para, of course, have completely checked their own choices. Should one even consider the possibility of fraud, it must be rejected; there is no possibility of fraud entering into the picture. However much it may go against the grain, I think we must admit that there is something here which requires explanation."[10]

Professor Eysenck has a reputation as a strict empiricist who is not to be satisfied by scientific evidence which is less than adequate to the occasion. His judgment on the Gauquelins' work is therefore high praise. But he continues: "Whether that explanation would be along astrological lines is of course another question - indeed, astrology really does not furnish us with an explanation at all; it simply asserts the facts (or something very much like the facts) actually found. To say that the stars and planets influence us in some mysterious way is of course no explanation; an explanation would have to state in a testable manner just how the planets, or stars, influence us. This astrology has, so far, failed to do and it is probably this failure which aligns it with ESP and which is responsible for its complete neglect by most scientists."

As to this part of Eysenck's judgment, we would only say that in our view it is not true that astrologers do not furnish an explanation of astrology. The fact that the explanation they do furnish does not satisfy today's scientists could be due to the inadequacy of the explanation or it could be due to the scientists having taken their stand upon too narrow a ground and that the type of explanation they require would prove, if it were forthcoming, to be no explanation at all. Apart from that, we would only point out that all the evidence suggests that scientists do not reject astrology because they have no explanation for it but that they have no explanation for it because they reject it. *Two completely different things.*

Of course, during the 30 years of their investigations, the Gauquelins have produced many secondary studies, of one kind or another, bearing upon astrological concepts. These have usually been related, directly or indirectly, to their main researches and they may be examined in the appropriate publications. However there are two aspects of Michel Gauquelin's writings which should perhaps receive specific mention before we attempt a summary judgment of his work.

These are, first, his writings about astrology itself and secondly his attempts, with his wife, to provide some kind of description of the chain of causes and effects at work behind the phenomena he has studied (whether one calls these phenomena "astrological" or something else).

So far as the latter is concerned it might be true to say that *as long as one is satisfied with an explanation in terms of the mechanisms of the process*, Gauquelin comes as near as anyone to offering a more or less intelligible account of what lies behind the association between cosmic conditions, the time of birth and the temperament of the native.

He begins by showing[11] that the latest scientific studies of what determines the onset and progress of labour point to the *foetus itself* as the initiating and regulating agency. He also points out that there is now a firmly established body of evidence that living things (and not least, man) are sensitive to weak changes in the earth's magnetic field which is turn is in a constant state of flux in response to changes in cosmic conditions.

Since he himself has demonstrated a clear link between the strength of the "astrological" heredity effect (referred to on page 31) and fluctuations in the earth's magnetic field, Gauquelin is able to produce an outline chain of causes and effects, starting with solar disturbances, thence via the solar wind to repercussions among the planetary bodies including the Moon, producing, in turn varying intensities of terrestrial magnetic perturbations to which the foetus responds *selectively* in accordance with its genetic make-up. This foetal response, Gauquelin shows, is probably hormonal, impinging on the maternal organism, triggering the onset of labour and regulating the uterine contractions and the general progress of parturition.

Gauquelin would be the first to admit that this outline of events, to which he has evidently given much careful study and thought (but which we have been able to describe in only the most sketchy fashion), still leaves much to be explained. However, anyone who looks carefully at the details of Gauquelin's explanation may well feel that he has probably isolated some of the mechanisms involved.

This is the kind of explanation of astrology that a modern scientist would look for and to which Eysenck refers in the quotation given above.

Its weakness is that it deals with the issue only in phenomenal terms. In the same way one would say that a piano sonata was caused by certain digital agencies which depress certain ivory keys which cause rods to move hammers which strike wires and set them vibrating, causing sound waves which are received by the ear and so on. All quite true, but is that all we want to know about the origin of the sonata? It is an explanation which might satisfy a mechanic but it will not a satisfy a true philosopher *and it ought not to satisfy a scientist.*

The fact of the matter is that several *different kinds* of explanation are called for in the case of astrology if we are to get at the truth and it is the author's view that no one should dismiss out of hand an explanation which is uncongenial to him simply because it starts from an unfamiliar viewpoint. We shall have much more to say about such topics in later chapters.

Turning briefly to Gauquelin's references to traditional astrology it should be said that he had tended, in such works as *Astrology and Science*[12] to be very scathing about the foolish, trivial and unscientific elements in the astrological world of which there is no shortage of examples in its long and chequered history.

It is easy to understand that a man who has, in effect, devoted his life to the restoration of scientific astrology should wish to dissociate himself firmly from the follies and abuses which are so widely paraded in the name of astrology and no-one, least of all a lover of astrology, would dispute that many of his strictures on pop astrology are well deserved.

The criticism one has to make, however, of this aspect of Gauquelin's writings is that he seems to make too little attempt to distinguish between what is good and what bad, what true and what false, in the history of astrology. This seems rather curious for he is himself very much a part of astrological history and his tendency to cast a slur over the whole subject seems out of place.

We have indicated in our opening chapter that although astrology has sometimes been taken up by the ignorant and credulous and even, though more rarely, by the unscrupulous, such men have never been the true custodians of astrological thought and practice and have never made any contribution to its development. The real exponents of astrology have been quite a different class of men, but Gauquelin often seems content to pass over this distinction and to blur an issue of fundamental importance in such a way as to make it more difficult for most people to see what kind of thing astrology really is.

We do not propose to say more about this aspect of Gauquelin's writings; it seems the least admirable side of his work.

Some people might argue, and some astrologers have argued, that the contribution of the Gauquelins to the understanding of astrology has been slight, for the light they have thrown on the workings of the laws and principles of astrology, as such, has to date been limited.

The notion that the "nugget of gold" in the astrological tradition handed down from the past consists largely in the power of a planet immediately after its rise or culmination to colour the personality in a martian, jovian, saturnine or suchlike way is, to say the least, totally inadequate - *inadequate even to account for the results of their own investigations when these are carefully examined* (as we shall show).

Likewise their attempt to explain the chain of causation linking the nativity to the cosmic scheme is of a somewhat tentative nature although it provides a good starting point for some (but only some) lines of enquiry and leaves untouched most of the larger philosophical issues which lie at the heart of the astrological problem.

However such a judgment on the value of the Gauquelins' contribution to this field of study is certainly not one that we could accept.

Science as a whole should be at the service of mankind but where great prejudices or errors of thought prevail in the scientific world, all the individual scientist can do, if he is to carry scientific opinion with him and harness the intellectual, moral and material resources of science to his own field, is to take scientific opinion *as he finds it*, deal first with the prejudices and misconceptions, and then to show the reasonableness, coherence and utility of the knowledge he seeks to propound and its relation to other aspects of science.

From this point of view, two things were and are needed vis-a-vis astrology. The first is the breaking down of the extraordinary barrier of prejudice against the subject existing in the sphere of scientific orthodoxy (and this in itself is a Herculean labour). The second is the purification and integration of astrological teachings themselves and the exposure of their conceptual foundations.

Of these two objectives, the contribution of the Gauquelins to the second has indeed been strictly limited and it is almost in the nature of what they set out to do and, for that matter, in the nature of the position of astrological studies at the time they began their work, that that should be so.

But their contribution to the first objective (that is to the breaking down of scientific prejudice) has been heroic in the highest traditions of scientific endeavour and devastatingly successful.

The hostility of scientific opinion to astrology has been profound, uncompromising and almost unanimous, springing from the most deep-seated distortions of thought in the foundations of the modern empirical tradition. This hostility will not be removed without a full and clear account of how and why astrology is true, but such an account *will not even be listened to* unless it can be shown in the first place that it *is* true and that its rejection by science is based on false assumptions.

How to achieve such a demonstration? It is no use to do as many astrologers are content to do: to stand on one's own ground and shout rude names at the opposition; it is just such conduct that they deplore in others.

What then was needed and what was it the Gauquelins had to do?

First they had to find a simple clear-cut issue which went to the root of the problem, which showed unequivocally the relationship along astrological lines between planetary positions at birth and human characteristics and which was statistically accessible and susceptible of indefinite replication.

They had to acquire data on a massive scale (since it was clear that nothing short of overwhelmingly convincing numbers would carry the necessary weight) and show by obtaining birth certificates for every case (at their own expense and if necessary by foreign travel) that all this data was duly authenticated.

They had to solve the problems of calculation and record-keeping in relation to these huge quantities of data, and to find the means of publishing, again from their own pocket, some twelve quarto volumes of birth data which also showed the distribution, sector by sector, of the planets in their diurnal circles so that anyone who had misgivings about the accuracy of the foundation material could check samples of the data and the calculations based on it.

They had to grapple with the complex astronomical and demographic issues affecting the exact assessment of statistical probabilities, overcoming the sometimes extraordinary difficulties in obtaining the information required for such assessments, sometimes having to find it for themselves from hospital records or suchlike sources and publishing original studies in specialist periodicals as necessary preliminaries to their main researches.

Needless to say they had to acquaint themselves with a wide and variegated literature in the fields relating to their work - in psychology, biography, gynaecology, demography, biology, statistics, geophysics and the like, not to mention astronomy and astrology.

They had to learn to view with equanimity the scorn and derision (the imputations, even, of dishonesty) of scientists who did not like their astrology and the obtuseness of astrologers who did not like their empiricism; they had to spend precious time from their work in answering,[13] patiently and often necessarily at length, the objections and criticisms of those who, as a rule, understood but imperfectly the nature of their work, the technicalities involved or the larger issues at stake. And of course they had to contend with the same obstructionism by official and scientific bodies with which most researchers in this subject are familiar.

They had to find the means to publish every step and detail of their experiments in six further large volumes and numerous smaller ones and, in order to make all their work available to the widest scrutiny, to translate the whole corpus of material giving French and English texts on facing pages!

Finally, they had one other small problem: how, having no private means, to stay alive for 30 years while they were doing all this work which very few people wanted to know about and which therefore could not possibly pay for itself, let alone support them. This problem they solved, firstly, by making it a firm rule to take 'outside' work, providing them with a modest income, *only in the mornings*, keeping the afternoons and evenings free for their research and, secondly, by living frugally and, among other things, by doing without heating in the house for the first ten years; in the winter time they put on their overcoats and perhaps kept warm by laughing at the pompous letters they received from those who assured them they were wasting their time.

The story of the Gauquelins is a story of the most extraordinary courage, tenacity, intelligence and industry. It will be seen in time as one of the great scientific undertakings. Never again will scientists be able to close their eyes to one of the primary truths about man's relationship to the cosmos with all its far-reaching consequences.

And yet, if my old friends will forgive me for saying so, it will not do. It will not do. *It will not do at all!*

As a demonstration of the underlying truth of astrology and a counter to 'scientific' prejudice, the work of the Gauquelins is masterly. As an explanation of what astrology is, how it works and its underlying principles, it is totally inadequate and a close examination of *their own results* will quickly show that those results are far more interesting than they appear on the surface, and that they tell a very different story to that which the Gauquelins would have us believe.

CHAPTER FOUR - NOTES

1   It might be argued that in his first book, *L'Influence des Astres* Gauquelin does not sufficiently expose all the issues involved in determining the theoretical or expected distributions, although they are implicit (possibly because they depended upon a mass of work which at that time had only just been done and may not have been fully digested). We therefore give, in the resume which follows, the figures and levels of significance as re-stated in his second work.

2   A full list of the Gauquelins' publications would be too lengthy to give here, but *Birth and Planetary Data,* series C, Vol 1 (see III below) gives a list of some 88 publications of the Gauquelins which was up to date at that time (1972) and which should be consulted for special aspects of their work. However, some of the principal works relating to their astrological studies are as follows. (His first two books - see notes 8 and 9, Chapter Two - are not included here. They have not been translated into English.)

All are published by the Laboratoire d'Etude des Relations entre Rythmes Cosmiques et Psychophysiologiques, 8 Rue Amyot, 75005 Paris, France.

I   Birth and Planetary Data, Series A: Professional Notabilities. Volumes 1 to 6 give respectively the birth data (with sources, sector positions etc) of -

(1) 2089 Sports Champions
(2) 3647 Scientists and Physicians
(3) 3439 Military Men
(4) 2722 Painters and Musicians
(5) 2412 Actors and Politicians
(6) 2027 Writers and Journalists

(All 1970-71)

II   Birth   and   Planetary   Data, Series B: Heredity Experiment. Volumes 1 to 6 give the birth data of the subjects used in this aspect of the Gauquelins' work. (All 1970-71.)

III Birth and Planetary Data, Series C: Psychological monographs. (Five Volumes) -

(1) Profession - Heredity. Results of Series A & B (1972)
(2) The Mars Temperament and Sports Champions (1973)
(3) The Saturn Temperament and Scientists (1974)
(4) The Jupiter Temperament and Actors (1974)
     (5) The Moon Temperament and Writers (1977)

IV   Scientific Documents Series (Six Volumes to date) -

(1) Planetary Factors in Personality: Their permanence through four professional groups (1978)
(2) Replication of the Planetary Effect in Heredity (with a resume of the first experiment) (1977)
(3) Statistical Tests of Zodiac Influences (1978)
(4) The Venus Temperament (1978)
(5) Diurnal Positions of Sun, Mercury, Uranus, Neptune and Pluto. (Supplement to Series C, Vol 1) (1978)
(6) The Mars Effect and Sports Champions: A New Replication (1979)

V   Semi-popular works translated into English include:

(1) The Cosmic Clocks, Avon, New York (1969)
             Peter Owen, London (1969)
(2) Cosmic Influences on Human Behaviour, Stein & Day, New York (1973) and Garnston Press UK (1974), Futura Publications (1976)

3   See note 2(II) above.

4   See note 2[IV(2)] above.

5   See note 2[IV(2)] and [V(2)] above.

6   There were a number of unsatisfactory features of this study and it should be recorded that Dr Elisabeth Scott, Professor of Statistics at Berkley University (and one of the original 186 signatories of the document against astrology) could not accept the negative findings of the CSICP but was unable to obtain publication of her views.

7   See note 2[IV(6)] above.

8   For full details of all this aspect of the Gauquelins' work, including all references to works used and methods employed, see Note 2[III(2-5)] above.

9   For full details of this work see Note 2[IV(1)] above.

10   H J Eysenck quoted from New Behaviour, Vol 1, No 6 (29 May 1975), New Science Publications, London.

11   See, for example, Note 2 above [IV(2), pp 34-35] for full details.

12   Originally *Astrology devant la Science* (1965). Trans *Astrology and Science*, Peter Davis, London (1970). Paperback: Mayflower (1972).

13   Michel Gauquelin's tenacity in replying to criticisms of his work reminds one that he was, at one time, one of the ten or twenty best tennis players in France, a game in which the object is to return the ball to one's opponent's court!

CHAPTER V

The Harmonics of Cosmic Periods

My own researches began in 1955. Like Gauquelin (of whom I heard little and knew less for another ten years or more) my intention was to show that astrology had a demonstrably true basis and was capable of being studied and developed in a scientific manner. I believed that in order to begin to do this I had only to collect appropriate data and show that the astrological effects postulated by the traditional rules of horoscopy could be seen to apply.

My viewpoint and attitude to the subject were, in certain respects, very different from Gauquelin's (and remain so), yet my initial experiences were like his in that I found myself unable, in the studies I made, to confirm the validity of the traditional concepts. It was not that they appeared to be <u>totally</u> wrong and I could, of course, have convinced myself that all was well. But I wanted to stand on firm ground and the fact was, or appeared to be, that something somewhere was amiss. A new insight of some sort was evidently required.

The picture which eventually came into view was that at the heart of all astrological concepts, behind all the traditional rules of horoscopy, to be seen in different forms in different astrological traditions and techniques and, above all, plainly visible in my own experimental results, was the idea of the HARMONICS OF COSMIC PERIODS.

What are we to understand by a 'cosmic period'? We mean the interval measured out by any regularly recurring circle or cycle of movement or activity in the heavens.

Although this may seem such a simple and straightforward concept, it is important that we should pause here and look carefully at just what it implies.

Anyone who knows that the Earth turns on its axis, giving us night and day, and that the planets move in regular orbits round the Sun, may conclude that the number and variety of cosmic periods (say, within the Solar System) is quite small: perhaps a few dozen. This, of course, is not at all the case. On the contrary, cosmic periods are of an almost endless diversity and the principal reason for this is that everything in the heavens is moving in relation to everything else.

This produces a situation in which each apparently simple cycle of any cosmic body becomes *many different cycles* when viewed in its ever-changing relationship with other phenomena. Thus, for example, we are all familiar with the idea of a month - a lunar revolution, as we may sometimes call it. The idea seems simple enough, yet it is not.

The month we usually think of (leaving aside the calendar month) is the synodic lunar cycle. A synod is a meeting or coming together and in this case it is the meeting or conjunction once every 29.53 days of the Moon with the Sun. This synodic lunar cycle whereby the Moon moves from the conjunction of the Sun (new Moon) round to the opposition (full Moon) and back again to the conjunction is, of course, what gives us the familiar phases of the Moon. But it is not by any means the only lunar revolution.

The Moon goes round the Earth and back to its starting place among the fixed stars once every 27.32 days (a sidereal month) but because the Sun has moved on, so to speak, since the Moon was last in that part of the sky, the Moon has to 'catch up' with it and this takes another two days, hence the difference between the two cycles: 29.53 and 27.32 days.

But there are a number of other lunar cycles. For example, the Moon's orbit is inclined to the plane of the ecliptic (the plane in which the Earth circles the Sun) and the ascending and descending points at which the Moon crosses this plane are called its nodes. But the relationship between these two planes is such that the nodes are continually regressing round the Earth, yielding another lunar period (the nodal or Draconic month), this time of 27.21 days. (Incidentally, this period is distinctively connected with the eclipse cycle, which is said to be measured off by some megalithic stone circles.)

The interval between two successive occasions when the Moon is at its closest to the Earth (perigee) is called an anomalistic month (27.55 days) and again a tropical month is like a sidereal month except that it discounts the so-called precession of the equinoxes and so is very slightly longer. The difference between them is only 6.8 seconds yet they are two distinct cycles and must be seen as such.

But continuing to use the Moon as our example, we have so far considered only its monthly synod or conjunction with the Sun. It has, too, a meeting each month with every other planet and since these are all moving at different speeds, this yields a fresh crop of lunar synodic cycles. Thus, starting from *one single orbital movement* (that of the Moon round the Earth) we quickly find that we can identify fifteen or twenty different periods, even without changing our terrestrial point of view.

But this is only for the Moon. Each planet, separately, has its own set of periods, broadly speaking analogous to those we have mentioned, yielding (especially if they are considered heliocentrically as well as geocentrically) several hundred more cosmic periods.

Then there are diurnal periods such as those in which the Gauquelins have specialised in their astrological studies and concerning which we shall have more to say shortly.

Of course, we could add other cycles within the solar system (such as the Sun-spot cycle and others of a similar order), but if we were to go *outside* the Solar System we should find ourselves in a sea of cosmic periods (and not only revolutionary periods, but periods of luminosity, radioactivity and the like) so vast as to baffle thought. But perhaps this great panorama is a distraction: let us keep to the homely confines of our own Solar System.

Yes, even in our own 'small' system we could easily identify hundreds of cosmic periods, yet this number must be multiplied many times when we come to think in terms of the *harmonics* of cosmic periods.

What do we mean by this term?

We mean not only the circles or cycles of activity measured off by the whole length (duration) of each cosmic period, but also the sub-rhythms of activity which recur and are exactly completed *within* each period and *which therefore must have a duration based on the division of that period by a whole number.*

Figure 21 shows the concept in diagrammatic form. Here we have the 3rd, 4th, 5th, 8th and 15th harmonics of a circle. The circles represent any cosmic period; the harmonics are simply rhythms which are exactly completed *within* each period.

The highest numbered harmonic we have shown is the 15th, but there is no theoretical upper limit to the number of harmonic divisions into which the circle could be divided.

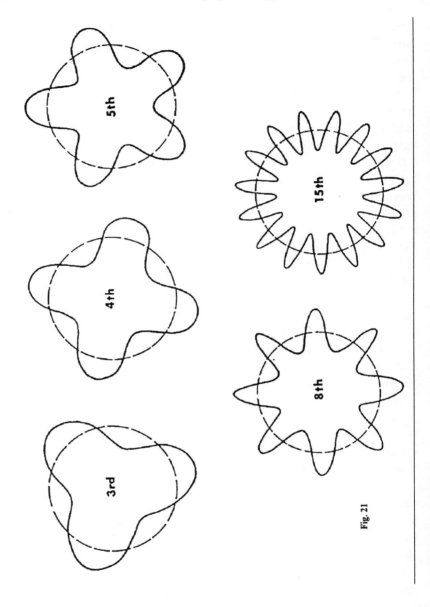

Fig. 21

Just to keep our feet on the ground, let us have a few simple examples of natural phenomena based on the harmonics of cosmic periods. It has been found[1] in the United States that the intensity of rainfall precipitation in that country shows a second harmonic of the synodic lunar cycle. Thus Figure 22 shows heavy rainfall in the US over 50 years plotted against the lunar period - new Moon to new Moon - and it is easy to see that there is a twofold rhythm at work 'phased' (note the semi-technical term) so that the two 'peaks' or rainfall maxima occur in the week following the full and new Moons and the two 'troughs' (low rainfall) in the week before. Thus we can say that rainfall in the US follows the second harmonic of the synodic lunar period (though not necessarily that alone).

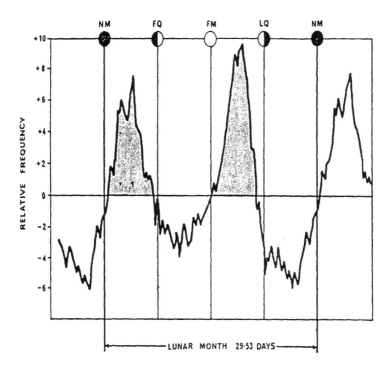

Fig. 22 US rainfall plotted against the lunar period.

How is this rainfall graph (Figure 22) obtained? Obviously, the rainfall figures for every synodic month from 1900 to 1949 have been collected up and, as it were, superimposed or added together so that one can see the general pattern of rainfall *during that precise period* of 29.53 days. There would be over 600 synodic months during those fifty years and it is obvious that the second harmonic rainfall pattern would not necessarily be discernible in any one particular month; there would be wide variations from month to month and it is only when we isolate the exact lunar synodic cycle and examine the recurring rainfall pattern during *that* precise period that the second harmonic can be seen.

Obviously it would be no good treating the rainfall figures for the *sidereal* month (27.32 days) in that way and expecting to see this second harmonic pattern because that feature relates strictly to the synodic period.

However, we *can* look at a natural rhythm based on the sidereal month. For over twenty years, in Germany, Maria Thun has conducted experiments in the relationship between plant growth and the lunar cycle, her work being inspired by some of the teachings of Rudolf Steiner. Without going into details of the history and methodology of her work, it can be said that one of the most interesting *and consistent* of her results is that she observes a large variation in crop yields *according to the time during the Moon's sidereal period that sowing takes place.*[2]

In broad terms, she divides plants, for the purpose of her experiments, into four categories[3] according to whether they are intended to yield (1) root crops (eg potatoes), (2) leaf crops (eg lettuce), (3) seed or fruit crops, or (4) flowers. If it is desired to maximise root growth then the crop should be planted at one time in the sidereal lunar cycle, if leaf growth then at another time and so on (see Figure 23). The regulating factor, this time, is the *third* harmonic; in other words there are, in each month, three periods (of just over two days) when one should plant each type of crop if one wishes to obtain the highest yield.

As an example of Maria Thun's results in this field, Figure 24a[4] shows the average weight when lifted (in kilograms per 100 square metres) of potatoes planted at regular intervals (as indicated above) in the sidereal month. The figures given are the mean totals for five consecutive years of planting, 1965-69 inclusive. Earlier and later plantings gave similar results.

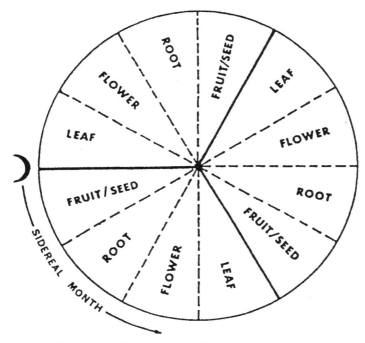

Fig. 23 Plant growth during the lunar month.

This third harmonic feature in the yield of crops planted at different phases of the Moon's sidereal period has been abundantly confirmed by Maria Thun over more than twenty years and has been reproduced by other gardeners and with a variety of crops. For example Figure 24b shows the result of a similar series of experiments with regular plantings, this time of *lettuce*, done by Colin Bishop[5] of Cardiff in 1976 and we can see the higher yield by weight of plantings made during the 'leaf crop' phase of the sidereal cycle. Further experiments by Bishop the following year confirmed this result.

In these examples of the germination and growth of lettuce and potatoes (as of other crops studied in the same way) we evidently have a clear instance of the operation of the third harmonic of the *sidereal* month.

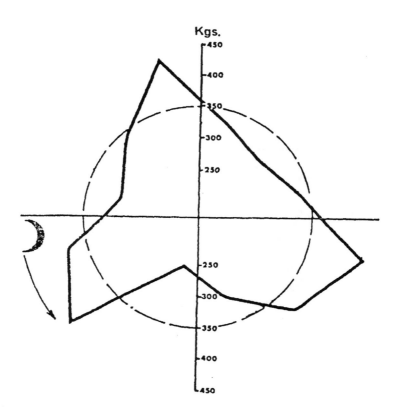

Fig. 24a Crop yield (potatoes), from the Maria Thun experiment.

If it should be asked how we can be sure that the cosmic period involved is not really the tropical month - rather than the sidereal - we should have to admit that we cannot in fact be sure. The difference between the sidereal and tropical months is, as we have said, only 6.8 seconds, so that during the twenty years or so during which this cycle has been under investigation in this context, the 'shift' between the two cycles is only 30 minutes and neither the work of Maria Thun nor of any of her followers is in any way attuned to distinguish such a small difference. In the circumstances, it seems best simply to note that Thun has evidently identified a very interesting manifestation of a third harmonic of either the sidereal or tropical month and one which is revolutionary in its potential usefulness.

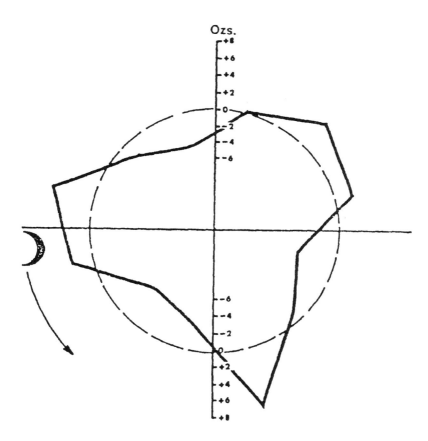

Fig. 24b Crop yield (lettuce), from the Colin Bishop experiment.

But in case anyone should think that, in drawing on this somewhat esoteric example, we are short of good illustrations of natural phenomena as related to cosmic rhythms, it should be said that it is now well recognised that most aspects of plant life respond to lunar rhythms of one sort or another. Oxygen absorption, the uptake of water and nutrients, electrical activity and other phenomena of plant life (and animal life, too, for that matter) have long been known to reveal rhythms which are harmonics of lunar and Solar periods.[6] Frank Brown of North Western University, Evanston, Illinois, among others, has been a great pioneer of such studies for some 30 years.

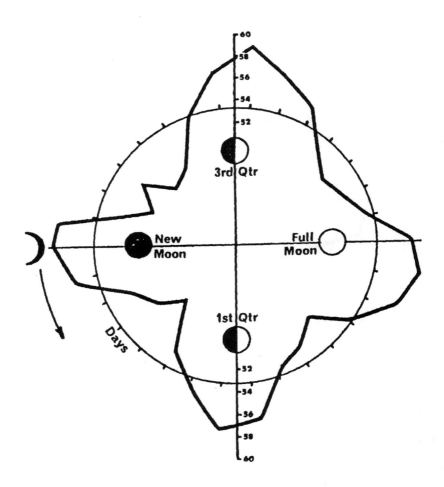

Fig. 25 The uptake of water by beans in the synodic lunar cycle.

A typical specimen of Brown's results (in this instance in collaboration with C S Chow) is given in Figure 25 which shows the uptake of water by dried beans in relation to the synodic lunar cycle. The fourth harmonic variation can be clearly seen. (The weight of water absorbed is expressed as a percentage of the beans' dry weight and daily measurements were made in a series of concurrent experiments extending over 8 months and involving almost 8000 separate measurements. Figure 25 shows a typical result of one test series).[7]

Brown and Chow conclude from this and other evidence that this "lunar quarterly response" (ie the response to the fourth harmonic of the Moon's synodic period) *must be "widespread among plants and animals"* (our italics). The response, they say, is to "some subtle, pervasive and normally uncontrolled, geophysical variations" which they believe must belong to the "electro-magnetic family of forces".

Before leaving this topic of the relation between natural phenomena and the harmonics of cosmic periods, we ought to draw attention to a contrast illustrated by our last two examples.

In the first case (Maria Thun) the subsequent growth of the plant was seen to depend upon *the time the seed was put in the ground* and this was shown by a *third harmonic*. In the second case (Brown and Chow) the realisation of the bean's potentiality for growth depended upon *its absorption of a necessary ingredient (water) from its environment* and this was shown by a *fourth harmonic*. The first case refers to something which takes place once at a particular time, the second to a continuing process. We shall refer to this again.

We have now explained and illustrated what we mean by the idea of the harmonics of cosmic periods. In a nutshell, they are the rhythms and sub-rhythms of periodic phenomena in the heavens.

But what has this to do with astrology? We began, indeed, by saying that it was this concept which evidently lay at the heart of all astrological teachings and held the first key to their significance; we have implied that astrology had, over the centuries, lost its way precisely because it had failed to understand and to keep in sight the central position of this principle.

In order to appreciate this situation more clearly, let us return to the work of Michel and Francoise Gauquelin.

CHAPTER V - NOTES

1 Bradley D and Woodbury M A: Heavy Rainfall Precipitation and the synodic lunar period. *Science* (USA) Vol 137 (1962) pp 748-9.

2 Works describing the experiments of Maria Thun can be obtained from The Biodynamic Agricultural Association, Woodman Lane, Clent, Stourbridge, W Midlands, DY9 9PX.

3 These four categories are linked by this school of thought to the four traditional elements: Earth, Water, Air, Fire, represented in the signs of the Zodiac.

4 The data presented in Figure 24a are taken from *Anbauversuche über Zusammen hange zwischen Mondstellungen im Tierkreis und Kulturpflanzen*, Vol II, by Maria Thun and Hans Heinze (Biologisch-Dynamische Wertschaftsweise) p 78.

5 Bishop C: Moon Influence in lettuce growth: Northern Hemisphere. *Astrological Journal* Vol XX, No 1, Winter 1977-78. Also Kollerstrom, Nick: Zodiac Rhythms in Plant Growth: Mercury Star Journal, Vol IV, No 1 (1978) (Editor: Robert Powell, 35 Park Road, London NW1 6XT).

6 Kollerstrom, Nick: Plant Response to the Synodic Lunar Cycle: A Review. *Cycles* Vol XXXI, No 3 (1980). Also Best S and Kollerstrom N: Introductory Essay in *Planting by the Moon* (1980-81) Pub W Foulsham Ltd, London.

7 Brown F A and Chow C S: Lunar Correlated Variations in Water Uptake by Bean Seeds. *Biological Bulletin*, Oct 1973 pp 265-278.

CHAPTER VI

Harmonics as a Foundation Concept in Astrology

In this chapter we shall try to establish a *prima facie* case for supposing that the key to Gauquelin's results and to astrology as a whole lies in the concept of the harmonics of cosmic periods.

I began the last chapter by referring to my own attempts, over the past twenty-five years, to re-examine the foundations of astrology and it would seem natural, now that I come to explain what I conceive to be the fundamentals of the subject, to begin by describing some of my earlier researches.

But there are certain advantages in taking, as one's 'demonstration model', data which have been collected by someone else. In this way the suspicion is avoided that one is dependent upon material specially selected to support a particular viewpoint or hypothesis.

The datum collected by the Gauquelins is of high quality in itself: sufficiently accurate, objective (supported in every case by the time given on the birth certificate), copious, versatile and well adapted to the illustration of the principles of astrology. It has also been comprehensively published and is available to students everywhere.[1] Therefore, in using the Gauquelin data to illustrate my thesis, I ensure that the information upon which it is based may be readily scrutinised and my results compared with other studies of the same material.

But in thus using these data I must make it clear that the interpretation I place upon them and the theme of my exposition, *which centres upon the idea of the harmonics of cosmic periods*, is my own and that the principles enunciated hereinafter were, in a broad way at least, framed in the days before I was acquainted with the work of Michel and Francoise Gauquelin.

And now a warning. It is my hope that this work will be read by students from many and varied backgrounds. Some, indeed, may already have studied astrology from the text books of the day; some may have a background in the natural sciences; others may approach the subject from the direction of philosophy or psychology or from other standpoints. But I must caution the reader that his difficulties with the book are liable to be in direct proportion to the degree in which the material in it looks familiar to him (and that applies as much or more to astrologers as to others). He may too easily assume that because he recognises the type of material, the kind of result, which is being presented, then he is on his own ground. This will not necessarily be the case and the reader must be on his guard *for there is nothing harder than to see something with which one is already partly familiar, but in a different light and with new eyes.* And it is with new eyes that the reader must regard the results set out in this work.

When we approach astrology we shall be trying to observe how the principles which substand the cosmos achieve expression; we shall be trying to see how the unmanifest becomes manifest and how noumena take on form and produce phenomena. How hard this is today! Our vision has become adjusted to phenomena. A phenomenon is an *appearance.* Men have become enamoured of appearances; scientists have become enamoured of appearances and, in doing so, have led the world into an intellectual blind alley.

Harmonics of "Planetary Days"

We saw in the last chapter - what indeed is well known - how readily natural phenomena tend to exhibit rhythmic characteristics. We also saw that some at least of these rhythmic features correlate with the harmonics of cosmic periods. This too is well known if only because most natural phenomena are linked to the daily and yearly cycles both of which are 'cosmic periods'. However, the examples we gave, and which could have been multiplied many times, were not seasonal in any conventional sense and were unrecognised say 30 years ago, and this suggests that the link between cosmic periodicity and natural rhythms in terrestrial phenomena may be widespread and is only just beginning to be recognised.

Does this throw any light on Gauquelin's work and on the character of astrology? After all, nature is the very realm in which astrology operates and that must include man on his natural side.

If we look at the graphs derived by Gauquelin from his studies of planetary distributions at the time of birth of different professional groups, the most obvious thing that strikes us is their tendency to display what appears to be a 4th harmonic distribution - a 4th harmonic, that is, of a particular planet's daily cycle. One has only to look at, say, figures 5, 6, 10 or 15 to see this or, better still, at figure 16 which provides a summary picture of many results, and to compare these with, say, figures 25 or the theoretic pattern of 21b in order to appreciate this point.

To take a specific case, scientists tend to be born after Saturn has crossed the horizon (rise or set) or the upper or lower meridian, more than at other times (see Figure 10). Of course it is not scientists *as such* who tend to be born at these times, but people of a certain temperament, as Gauquelin has shown in his character trait studies.

What *exactly* does this mean?

The sun, moon and planets rise, culminate and set each day as the earth turns on its axis, *but the diurnal period of each body is different.* The earth takes an average of 24 hours exactly to turn once in relation to the sun, so the *mean solar day* is 24 hours in length. But the sun is moving against the fixed stars so the earth takes just over 23 hours and 56 minutes to turn once in relation to *them* - a mean *sidereal day*. Similarly a mean *lunar day* is about 24 hours and 50 minutes in length and a *Saturn day*, a *Jupiter day* and a *Mars day* etc are, again, all different and each constitutes a distinct cosmic period. The difference between these different kinds of 'planetary' days may be very small (falling, as they do, in length, between the mean sidereal and solar days) for they are all 'circadian', that is, 'about one day'; but the difference, small as it may be, accumulates and in due time becomes an important variation.

So when we say that the scientific type tends to be born in accordance with (among other things) the 4th harmonic of the Saturn day (phased so that the planet has just passed one of the four 'cardinal points' of the diurnal circle at the time of these births) we are simply noticing that, as Saturn rises, culminates and sets each day, there is a tendency for the scientific type to be born at times when it is at or near one of the points A, B, C or D in Figure 26.

Furthermore, *and this is important*, if we are dealing with a 4th harmonic pure and simple, then the scientific type births will tend to cluster at the points A, B, C and D *equally*, that is without showing a preference for any one of the four points, producing a distribution of such births during the day like the regular fourfold wave in Figure 21b.

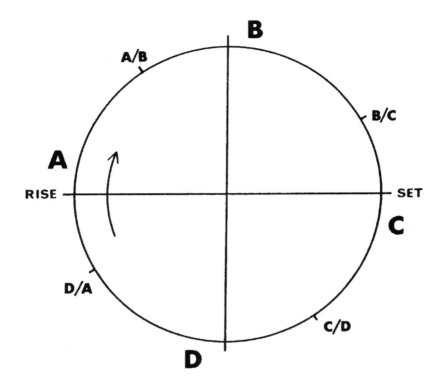

Fig. 26 Points of the 4th harmonic.

Similarly (and at the risk of labouring the point) we can say that those who are - in some particular respect at least - opposite in temperament to the typical scientist will tend to be born when Saturn is half way between A and B, B and C, C and D or D and A (shown in Figure 26 as A/B, B/C, C/D and D/A).

Now it so happens that what we have just said about the birth of the scientific type in relation to the Saturn day is true of the same type in relation to the Mars day. (Both Saturn and Mars may be considered in this context and in a broad way to have, as a common characteristic, *strictness*.)

We can show all this diagrammatically. Thus Figure 27 shows (heavy black line) the distribution of Mars and Saturn together at the time of birth of scientists (1095) and physicians (2552) - a total of 3647 positions for Mars and the same for Saturn, 7294 positions in all.

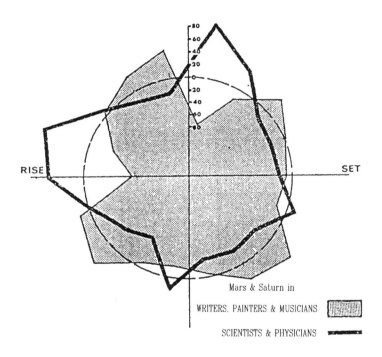

Fig. 27 Saturn & Mars distribution comparing different professions.

The same diagram also shows (shaded area) the distribution of Saturn and Mars combined at the time of birth of writers (1352), painters (1473) and all musicians (1249). This time therefore we have a grand total of 8148 planetary positions and these three groups we may take as representative of the 'artistic' temperament as opposed to the scientific.[2]   (In both graphs in Figure 27 the observed distribution is shown as above or below the expected distribution, so all purely astronomical factors have been eliminated.   We have superimposed the two graphs so that the opposite phasing of the two 4th harmonics can be clearly seen and such a degree of dissimilarity of distribution would occur by chance only once in many hundreds of millions of times.)

Now these two graphs bring some of the vital issues into focus; with their help we can begin to see what it is we need to ask ourselves if we wish to throw light on our problems.

One can see clearly that Mars and Saturn do verge towards the points A, B, C and D (Figure 26) in the diurnal circle in the case of the scientific temperament and we can see that they verge towards the mid-points A/B, B/C, C/D and D/A in the case of the opposite, artistic, temperament.

But whereas the graph for the artists does in fact show four more or less equal arms of a regular 4th harmonic, that for the scientists does not, but shows a much larger preponderance of births at A and B than at C and D, a feature which, as we have shown, Gauquelin often finds.

So there are two questions we need to ask:

1   If we are really dealing with a 4th harmonic, why is it that in some cases Gauquelin obtains a more or less *regular* fourfold wave and in other cases a very lopsided one (with the lopsidedness usually favouring points A and B or, in other words, sectors 1 and 4 by Gauquelin's twelvefold division of the diurnal circle)?

2   What is the significance of the contrast in the *phasing* of the 4th harmonics illustrated in Figure 27, one showing peaks at A, B, C and D and the other showing peaks half way between these points?

We cannot really tackle this second question concerning the significance of the phase until we have satisfied ourselves about the first.   Are we really dealing with a true 4th harmonic effect and, if so, why the lopsidedness?

There is one simple answer to this question and there is every reason to suppose that it is the correct one in this case, as we shall show.   The reason for the lopsidedness sometimes observed is quite simply that we are usually dealing, *not with a 4th harmonic only, but with a combination of harmonics.*

We must proceed carefully here for it is a mathematical fact that any distribution pattern such as those we have been looking at can *always* be accounted for in terms of a combination of regular wave forms. In other words we have to show that a certain harmonic of a certain phase correlates *consistently and significantly* with a certain kind of characteristic, even though it may be involved in a complex of harmonics from which it must, so to speak, be disentangled.

The use of harmonic analysis

Let us consider, for example, the much discussed case of Mars in the nativities of sports champions. Figure 4 shows the distribution of Mars at the time of such births as collected in France and Figure 9 shows those collected in other European countries. For ease of comparison we will put these one above the other (Figure 28) when it will be clearly seen that they show pronounced similarities. Both have 'highs' in sections 1 and 4 and a less pronounced one in sector 8. Furthermore we may recall that the Comité Para in Belgium made a similar collection of athletes' nativities and obtained an exactly similar result as unmistakably shown in Figure 17. If asked to describe the general shape of this distribution, one would be hard put to it to say whether it was primarily a square or a triangular type of figure. But in any case such guesswork will not suit the occasion; we need to *know* exactly what the harmonic constitution of this Mars distribution is. How can we find out?

As it happens there is a mathematical technique, known as harmonic analysis or Fourier analysis (after the mathematician of that name) by means of which any series of totals of the kind we are dealing with can be broken down into its harmonic components. It is a somewhat laborious mathematical process but a suitably instructed computer can make short work of it and it is to this technique of harmonic analysis that we may have recourse to discover how any of our planetary distributions is made up harmonically.

At this point it is proper that we should go slowly with our explanation in order that even those readers who are entirely unfamiliar with this kind of problem should understand, at least in a general way, what is being done.

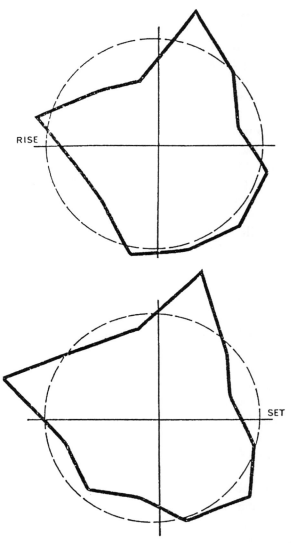

Fig. 28 Mars and sports champions: a comparison of the positions of 570 French (see fig. 4), top; and 915 non-French (see fig. 9), bottom.

The position is that we have noticed in three separate samples of champions' births a markedly similar and highly significant diurnal distribution of Mars. If, then, there are consistent features common to them all, there must be consistent forces at work shaping those distributions, and since it is our avowed purpose to discover the nature of these forces, it will obviously be best to obtain as comprehensive a picture of this Mars distribution as possible.

As we know (see Chapter IV) Gauquelin gives us the breakdown of his planetary distributions by 12, 18 and 36 sectors, so in order to obtain the clearest picture possible we shall take the distribution by 36 sectors and subject these 36 totals to harmonic analysis. And since it will be as well in the first place to have not only the *most* totals but also the *highest* totals available, we will combine the totals for French and other European countries.

We will show the result of the harmonic analysis of these totals first and explain what it means afterwards. Here, then, is the analysis of the distribution of Mars in the diurnal circle at the time of birth of top athletes. We omit the first harmonic as that is affected by astronomical factors.

Harmonic	Amplitude %	Peak Phase
2	8.3	95
3	12.4	356
4	12.1	56
5	6.8	122
6	4.6	78
7	4.3	27
8	4.8	170
9	4.9	248

This analysis gives us two items of information: it shows (1) the *amplitude* of each harmonic and (2) the *phase* of each harmonic.

1 <u>Amplitude</u>: Figure 29 shows two examples of a 3rd harmonic. There is no difference between them except that the one on the left has a lower, and the one on the right, a higher, amplitude. In other words the amplitude tells *how much the wave rises and falls above and below the mean*, so it may be conveniently expressed as a *percentage*

of the mean. If the mean is 100 in Figure 29 the harmonic on the left has an amplitude of 10% (ie it rises to 110 and falls to 90), the one on the right 25%.

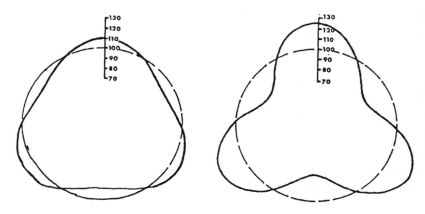

Fig. 29 Examples of the third harmonic with differing amplitudes.

Thus it is obvious that the higher the amplitude of a particular harmonic the greater will be its importance as a determining factor in the distribution under consideration. *A high amplitude equals a vigorous presence.* It will be seen that in our harmonic analysis of Mars for champions there are two harmonics which are markedly stronger than the others: the 3rd and 4th harmonics both have amplitudes of over 12%. As it happens we have nothing, at this stage, with which to compare this figure; however it may be stated that when the distributions of the Moon, Venus, Mars, Jupiter and Saturn in our champions' nativities are subjected to harmonic analysis (from the 2nd to the 9th harmonic in each case, 40 harmonics in all), these two harmonics, the 3rd and 4th of Mars, are the *only two* to reach double figures in amplitude, and since we already know that this Mars distribution has been shown to be highly significant, we may tentatively presume these amplitudes to be significant too.

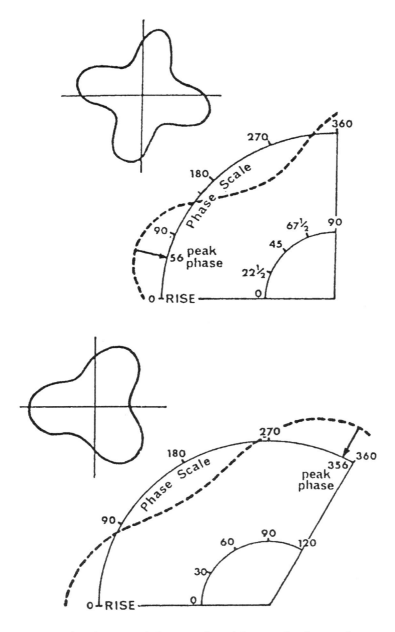

Fig. 30a (top) Fourth harmonic with a peak phase of 56°.
Fig. 30b (bottom) Third harmonic with a peak phase of 356°.

2 <u>Phase</u>: The phase of a harmonic tells us *whereabouts* in the circle the high and low points of the wave fall. For this purpose, obviously, we must have some kind of *scale of measurement* in order to fix the position. This is done as follows.

Every wave form represents one complete cycle or circle. It is like a circle which has been partly straightened out. Thus we can treat each wave as if it were - for the purpose of determining the phase, *but not for other purposes* - 360° in length, like any other circle.

In the case of harmonics in the diurnal circle we always start our measurement from the planet's *point of rise* and we measure to the point where the wave reaches its highest and call this the 'peak phase'. Thus, Figure 30a shows the scale of the 4th harmonic. We know that this harmonic divides the circle into four and so repeats four times at regular 90° intervals, so we need to illustrate only a quarter of the circle. We have marked (on the outer quadrant) the phase scale from 0° to 360° and we have drawn in (dotted line) the 4th harmonic wave (peak phase 56°) as indicated in the Mars analysis. (In order to remind ourselves that the scale of phase measurement is not the same as that by which we measure the full circle, we have drawn an inner quarter-circle with the usual scale of 90° marked.)

In the case of the 3rd harmonic there will be three equal and regular waves in the full circle so each will occupy 120°; thus our phase scale of 360° will now be stretched over a third of the circle - see Figure 30b where we have also drawn in the wave with a peak phase of 356°, exactly as shown in the harmonic analysis of the sports champions.

(Before proceeding, we should note that this principle of phase measurement applies to all harmonics. The 5th harmonic occupies 72° of the full circle and so the phase scale, in that case, is stretched over 72° of the circle, and so on with other harmonics.)

We are now in a position to see exactly how the two most important harmonics in our harmonic analysis (ie those with the highest amplitudes, the 3rd and the 4th) do in fact combine to produce the kind of distribution shown in Figure 28. Thus we can draw, in Figure 31a, the 3rd harmonic (dotted line, phase 356) and then *superimpose on that* the 4th (solid line, phase 56) when it will be seen that these two harmonics together do provide a good description of the general distribution of Mars in the diurnal circle at the time of birth of all sports champions (Figure 31b).

It is the author's belief that the true distinguishing characteristics of all Gauquelin's planetary distributions are thus to be observed through the *harmonic* elements of those distributions and indeed that the individually significant elements of meaning, the symbolic "words" of the language of astrology, are to be arrived at through these harmonic terms.

In the case of Mars in the nativities of sports champions it is evidently common (though not invariable as we shall show) to find in such people two distinct sets of characteristics linked to the diurnal position of Mars and these are shown by the 3rd and 4th harmonics thereof.

We shall show what these characteristics are and exactly how they are indicated astrologically in the next chapter. In the remainder of *this* chapter we shall first illustrate once more, using a different example, how harmonic phase is the key to the results of Gauquelin's planetary distributions and, secondly, we shall further justify our insistence that it is not merely the strength and phase of the *fourth* harmonic which is important (nor Gauquelin's sectors 1 and 4) but that a careful examination of *Gauquelin's own results* (quite apart from other evidence we may uncover) justifies us in believing that other harmonics besides the 4th play a significant and meaningful part in accounting for his planetary distributions and providing us with an intelligible scientific basis for reading the astrological meaning of planetary positions.

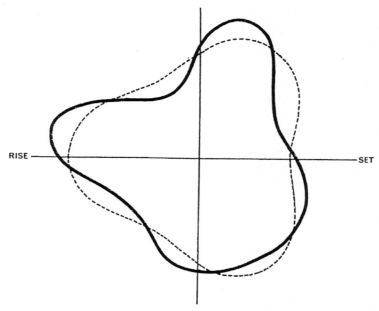

RISE

SET

Fig. 31a The 3rd harmonic (dotted line, phase 356) and superimposed the 4th (solid line, phase 56).

A harmonic contrast: artists and scientists

Consider then the distribution of Saturn and Mars in the nativities of writers, painters and musicians illustrated in the shaded part of Figure 27. As it happens no birth data of musicians were collected outside France but for the other two groups we can compare the births collected in France with those collected in other European countries. Thus that graph is actually made up of *ten separate sets* of planetary positions; it shows the distribution of Mars for writers and painters, each from two different sources, and again for musicians - making five groups, and then the same again for Saturn. If we submit these ten sets of planetary positions, separately, to harmonic analysis, we obtain results (just to remind ourselves of what we are dealing with) such as the following. (We again use Gauquelin's observed distribution by 36 sectors and we will omit the first harmonic since that is the only one affected by purely astronomical considerations.)[2]

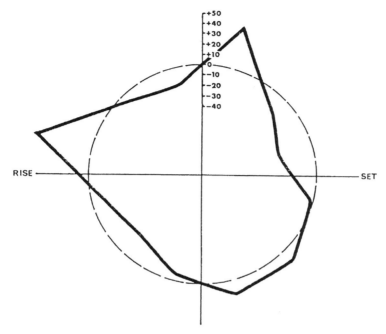

Fig. 31b Distribution of Mars in the diurnal circle at the time of birth of all sports champions.

Saturn: Painters

France (1133) (Avg per sector 31.5)			Other countries (340) (Avg per sector 9.4)			Combined (1473) (Avg per sector 40.9)		
Harm	% Ampl	Peak Phase	Harm	% Ampl	Peak Phase	Harm	% Ampl	Peak Phase
2	7.5	125	2	11.6	326	2	3.4	108
3	7.6	247	3	13.3	310	3	7.7	268
4	**16.3**	**253**	**4**	**16.5**	**245**	**4**	**16.3**	**251**
5	2.1	192	5	14.4	331	5	2.3	304
6	3.8	47	6	22.9	207	6	2.7	187
7	5.9	199	7	13.1	184	7	7.5	193
8	2.3	14	8	6.8	63	8	3.0	37
9	2.6	245	9	7.9	162	9	2.9	206

Mean 6.0   Mean 13.3   Mean 5.7

We have chosen to give this example because it illustrates an important point: the effect of sample size in harmonic analysis. There were 1133 nativities of painters from France or an average distribution of 31.5 Saturn positions for each of the 36 sectors of the diurnal circle. Such a total will normally give a reasonably stable result and one can see that the 4th harmonic (amplitude 16.3%) stands out. But from the other European countries there were only 340 nativities (an average distribution of only 9.4 per sector) and such a relatively small total will produce a much less stable result. When the mean distribution per sector is so small, random elements obtrude more into the result and we tend to get a collection of high amplitudes from which the important 4th harmonic no longer stands out so clearly.

But notice that it is the agreement of *phase* which is so important. Where there is no such agreement between the two sets, even such a high amplitude as the 22.9% (for the OC 6th) is cancelled out when it is combined with the larger group of French nativities with a different phase.

Despite this problem of some rather small samples, if we now give the results of the analyses of these ten sets we shall see that they do show a high measure of agreement. Rather than give a mass of figures it will be better to present the results diagrammatically and this we do in Figure 32. Remember that it is the agreement of *phase* we look for first and foremost, for phase describes the quality or characteristic which these nativities have in common. Amplitude only tells us how strongly the particular sample of nativities exhibits that characteristic.

In this diagram (Figure 32), we see that the peak phase of the 4th harmonics of Saturn and Mars in the ten sets of writers, painters and musicians tends strongly to cluster in the region of 220, the sole exception coming from the smallest sample (Mars: Painters: other countries) which is therefore likely to give the least reliable result.

The agreement as to phase is matched by amplitude strength, the 4th harmonic being over all, easily the strongest of the harmonics from the 2nd to the 9th.

We have drawn a single representative wave with a phase of about 220.

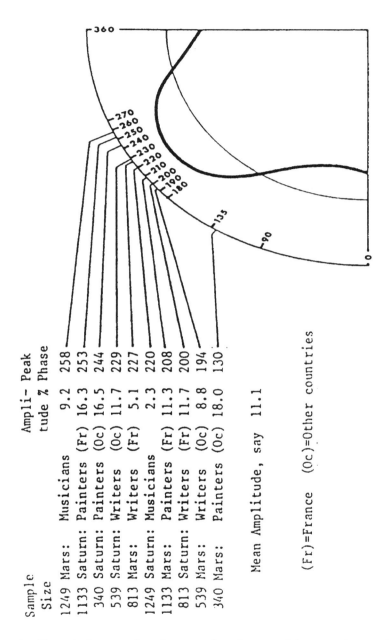

Fig. 32 Fourth harmonic phase angles for musicians, painters & writers.

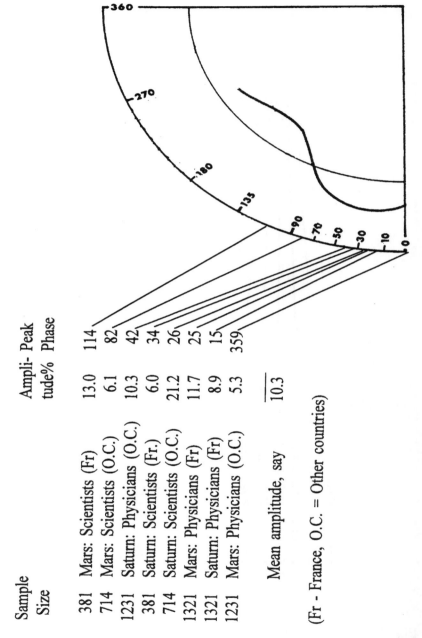

Sample Size		Ampli-tude%	Peak Phase
381	Mars: Scientists (Fr)	13.0	114
714	Mars: Scientists (O.C.)	6.1	82
1231	Saturn: Physicians (O.C.)	10.3	42
381	Saturn: Scientists (Fr.)	6.0	34
714	Saturn: Scientists (O.C.)	21.2	26
1321	Mars: Physicians (Fr)	11.7	25
1321	Saturn: Physicians (Fr)	8.9	15
1231	Mars: Physicians (O.C.)	5.3	359

Mean amplitude, say   10.3

(Fr - France, O.C. = Other countries)

Fig. 33 Fourth harmonic phase angles for scientists and physicians.

We can compare this 4th harmonic distribution of Mars and Saturn in the nativities of writers, painters and musicians (Figure 27) with that for scientists and physicians. In the latter we have eight separate sets of nativities as shown in Figure 33, and we see again not only the clustering of phase angles of Mars and Saturn in these nativities, not only that the only major disagreement as to phase (that for Mars: French Scientist: 114) comes from the smallest (least reliable) sample, and not only that the amplitude is again outstanding, but that the mean peak phase for *this* group of "scientific" nativities (say about 40) is approximately 180° away from the mean phase (roughly 220) of the "artistic" nativities, indicating the opposition of the two types of characteristics. (It is recognised that the terms "artistic" and "scientific" in this context are not satisfactory - after all, the physicians are practising an art too - but their general meaning will be understood and this is not perhaps the place for a full discussion of the correct distinction to be made.)

We have now shown (what indeed is implicit - in terms of the *fourth* harmonic at least - in the work of the Gauquelins) that harmonic *phase* is one of the keys to the astrological interpretation of planetary position (though we have not shown exactly *how* it is the key), but we still need further to support our contention that it is not only harmonic phase but also *harmonic number* which must be considered in arriving at an interpretation.

The importance of harmonic number

We have indeed already indicated in the case of sports champions that it is the 3rd harmonic just as much as the 4th which gives to Mars its characteristic distribution and we could, as it happens, say something similar of the scientists and physicians for they, like the champions, show the same lopsided distribution of Mars and Saturn that the champions showed for Mars (albeit with a slightly different emphasis) so that Figure 27 (Scientists) shows much higher peaks after the rise and upper culmination than after the set and lower culmination.

Thus this feature is again chiefly due to the presence of a certain combination of the 3rd and 4th harmonics, this time of Mars and Saturn in the nativities of scientists and physicians. The agreement of phase in the 4th we have already seen in Figure 33; the agreement of phase in the 3rd we can now show in Figure 34.

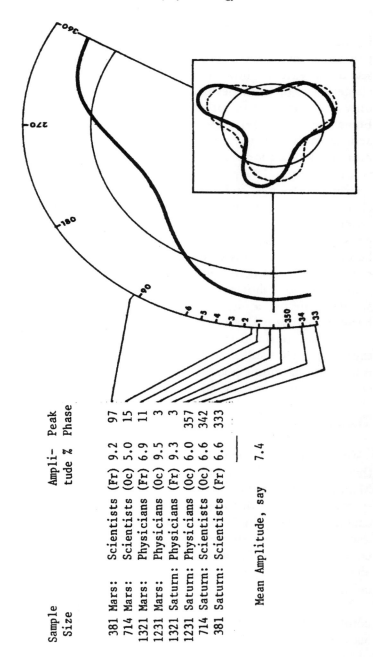

Fig. 34 Third harmonic phase angles for scientists and physicians.

But in order to show that it is not by any means always the 4th harmonic which is the only, or even the dominant, factor in Gauquelin's planetary distributions we have only to examine his own published results.

For example in Chapter IV, under the heading 'First character trait experiment' (p. 54), we have told how Gauquelin compiled a large vocabulary of words which were characteristically descriptive of the temperament of the typical scientist, and another list of words which described the *opposite* type of temperament to that of the scientist. We explained that he did the same for champions, actors and writers too and was able, in each case, to show that the planetary distributions in the nativities of those who were described by the one set of words were opposite to those described by the other set.

Figure 19 shows some of those results in diagram form and an inspection of the four sections of that figure will reveal an interesting fact, namely that whereas the three sections illustrating the distribution for Mars for the champions' type of personality and its opposite and the same for Jupiter/actors and Moon/writers - these all show a clear 4th harmonic both for the temperament in question and its opposite, *yet in the case of Saturn and the characteristics of the typical scientist and his opposite we have a 5th harmonic and not a 4th.*

If the reader will look at the appropriate part of Figure 19 he will easily see the five peaks and troughs in the Saturn/scientists distribution, but it is not until one draws the same diagram in circular form that it becomes unmistakably obvious that we are dealing with a true 5th harmonic distribution both for the scientific type and its opposite (see Figure 35).

It is a necessary characteristic of an odd-numbered harmonic that when drawn in circular form there will always be a peak opposite to a trough and a trough opposite to a peak - see for example the 3rd and 5th harmonics in Figure 21. Thus in Figure 35 (where we have numbered the peaks and troughs) the first peak for the scientific temperament (1) is exactly opposite to the trough at 6 (where, in an even-numbered harmonic such as the 4th, there would be a peak); the peak at 3 is exactly opposite the trough at 8 and so on round the circle, showing two five-pointed star formations.

But why is it, the reader will ask, that when the distribution of Saturn in the actual nativities of scientists shows a clear *fourth* harmonic, the distribution of Saturn which is related to the *alleged characteristics* of the typical scientist is dominated by a *fifth* harmonic?

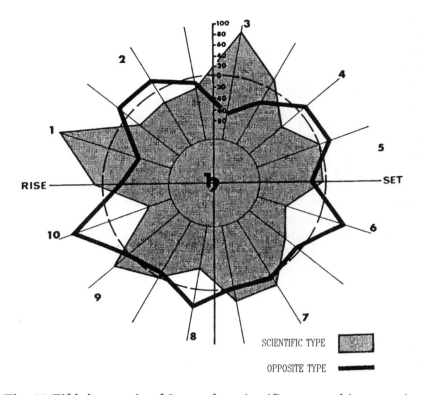

Fig. 35 Fifth harmonic of Saturn for scientific type and its opposite.

Similarly one could ask: why is it that when the champions themselves show a very strong *third* harmonic in their Mars distribution (as well as a 4th), the distribution of Mars which is related to the *alleged characteristics* of the champion is clearly dominated by a 4th harmonic only (Figure 19a)?

There can really only be one answer to these two questions, namely that those who were asked to say what the characteristics of the champion and the scientist are, erred in that they correctly predicted one set of qualities but largely ignored another set.

We shall return to the 5th harmonic in the case of the scientists in a later chapter (it is sufficient to notice at this stage that we have here a well indicated 5th); for the present let us take a closer look at the case of the champions.

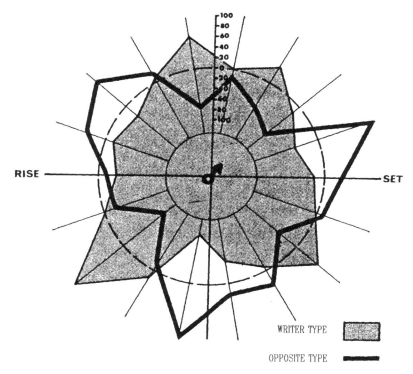

RISE

SET

WRITER TYPE

OPPOSITE TYPE

Fig. 36a Third harmonic of Mars for typical writers characteristics and their opposites.

The position is this: in the sets of champions collected in Europe by Gauquelin (one set in France, one in other countries) the 3rd harmonic is clearly as important as the 4th. The same is true of the champions collected by the Comité Para in Belgium. So the qualities indicated by that particular phase of Mars' 3rd harmonic are evidently just as relevant to the champions' temperament as those shown by the 4th. Yet, when Gauquelin investigates the temperament and character traits of the typical champion, the "experts" (leading sportswriters, articulate top athletes and members of the educated public) pick out *one* set of characteristics - those indicated by the 4th harmonic - and ignore those shown by the 3rd. The ones they fasten on are the tough, self-assertive characteristics: determination, aggressiveness, competitiveness and so on.

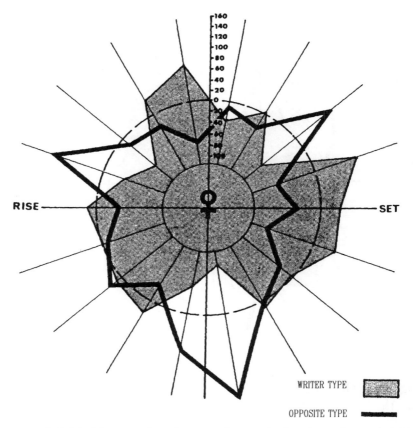

Fig. 36b Third harmonic of Venus for typical writer characteristics and their opposites.

What are the ones they ignore? Whatever they are - and we shall be able to answer this question shortly - it is of interest to note that the nativities of champions collected in the United States (see Figure 18) exhibit strongly the 4th harmonic qualities but not the 3rd.

Before leaving this topic let us look at two more clear-cut cases of 3rd harmonic distributions which we can find in Gauquelin's results although, if he notices them, he does not draw attention to them.

Figure 36a shows the distribution of Mars for the typical personality of the writer and for the opposite type and 36b shows the distribution of Venus for the same two types.[3] In these two figures we see perfectly clearly the complementary triangular formations of oppositely phased 3rd harmonics; *they do not leave any room for doubt that other harmonics besides the 4th play a significant role in describing astrologically the characteristics revealed in the nativity.*

Summary

In this chapter we began by explaining that just as a mean solar day (of 24 hours) consists in a single revolution of the earth in relation to the sun, or a lunar day (of 24 hours 50 minutes) in a single revolution of the earth in relation to the moon, so the period taken by the earth to turn once in relation to Mars or Jupiter (or any other planet) can be called a Mars day or a Jupiter day and so on.

Such 'planetary days' are simply cosmic periods which are variations on the earth's diurnal period and all natural rhythms based on such planetary days are in the nature of circadian rhythms.

We then suggested that all Gauquelin's results (which are, in effect, studies of the incidence of different classes of human births in relation to the diurnal period) can best be considered as deriving their significance and intelligibility from the way they reflect the harmonics of those cosmic periods which we have just designated 'planetary days'.

We then illustrated the nature and use of harmonic analysis in this context and showed that in three sets of nativities of sports champions collected in Europe the distribution of Mars was dominated by a certain phasing of the 3rd and 4th harmonics of the 'Mars day', these two harmonics showing much the greatest strength (highest amplitude) and consistency of phase.

We illustrated this concept in much greater detail in relation to the nativities of painters, writers and musicians on the one hand and scientists and physicians on the other, showing that in ten separate sets of nativities of the former and eight separate sets of the latter the 4th harmonic in the diurnal distribution of Mars and Saturn revealed an outstanding amplitude strength and consistency of phase.

Because the peak phase in the nativities of artists was opposite to that in the nativities of scientists we concluded that contrasting temperamental qualities in the two groups were indicated by the contrasting harmonic phase and as a general law, therefore, that *phase = quality* and *amplitude = intensity.*

But in order to identify quality, it is not enough, we argued, to consider phase only, for each harmonic is evidently related to a different range of qualities; therefore when we examine Gauquelin's results we find that it is not only the harmonic *phase* of planetary distributions but also the harmonic *number* to which we must have regard.   Thus we were able (Figure 35) to point to the complementary distributions of Saturn in the 5th harmonic as describing the qualities identified as those of the typical scientist and his opposite.   Similarly we illustrated instances (Figure 36) in which opposite and complementary *3rd harmonics* were the distinguishing feature in the comparison of opposite characteristics.

We have now shown that harmonic phase and harmonic number are evidently the key to Gauquelin's results in particular and to the astrological significance of planetary positions in general.

But what are the principles by which characteristics and qualities are related to harmonic phase and number in this context? This will be the next step in our enquiry.

CHAPTER VI - NOTES

1   Every self-respecting university library should now have a complete set of the scientific publications of the Gauquelins as listed in the notes of Chapter IV, 2, I to IV.

2   All totals are from *Birth and Planetary Data*, Series C, Vol 1: *Profession and Heredity*. Diagram 27 shows the difference between the observed and expected distributions. The harmonic analyses are based upon the observed totals but these show bias due to astronomical factors only in the first harmonic. The 'mean amplitudes' given in the tables and in Figures 32, 33 and 34 are approximate in that they are not adjusted for the differences of sample size; however they provide a fair comparison.

3   The totals are taken from *Psychological Monographs*, Series C, Vol 5: *The Moon Temperament and Writers*, Tables IX and X (pp 106-107) distribution by 18 sectors. To obtain the distributions shown in Figure 36 it is necessary to deduct the theoretical from the observed frequencies.

CHAPTER VII

The Concept of the Spectrum of Qualities

In the last chapter it was argued that the most scientifically satisfactory way of identifying Gauquelin's significant planetary distributions was via harmonic phase and harmonic number. This approach, it was implied, was both more comprehensive and more flexible, being adapted to the comparison and interpretation of a wider variety of results including those which did not conform to Gauquelin's commonest type of finding and, furthermore, offering the possibility, where more than one quality or characteristic was being exhibited in a particular sample of nativities, of separating these one from another and identifying each.

We must now take the argument a step further by clarifying the nature of the principles involved and illustrating their operation. In order to do this we must make use of Gauquelin's 'character trait' method, and although some account of this technique, as used by the Gauquelins, has been given in Chapter Four, we must take a few pages here to recapitulate briefly, to offer a few needed explanations and comments and to tell the reader where he may find fuller details about the data and methods employed if he wants them.

Because they had found that the typical planetary involvements observed in their results related not to profession as such but to character and temperament, the Gauquelins set out to explore the psychological affinities of the planets they had found to be most outstandingly significant in their results.

In conformity with astrological tradition, Saturn was the planet which showed up most strongly among scientists, Jupiter among actors, Mars among champions and the Moon among writers; so the Gauquelins concentrated their attention on these four groups.

For each of the four groups they set themselves the rather difficult task of finding a homogeneous source of biographical reference which provided not merely a dry catalogue of facts and events for those listed in their compilations of birth data but a rounded portrait which put flesh on the bare bones and gave at least *some* assessment of what the living person was like.

For example, in the case of actors, the Gauquelins made use of the Bibliotheque de l'Arsenal in Paris, a library specialising in information about the stage and cinema.

Here they found two sources of reference which suited their purpose. First, Francoise Gauquelin systematically extracted all the character trait words and descriptive phrases applied to actors in the *Dictionnaire des Comediens Francais*. ("This remarkable work gives short but lively and homogeneous biographies of actors of the 19th century".)[1]

Secondly, a team working under Michel Gauquelin performed a similar feat by examining the biographies contained in the Fond Rondel in that library. ("The Fond Rondel is the most important French source of documents on the theatre and motion pictures . . . . It contains information on all kinds of actors, French and foreign, contemporary and otherwise . . . . The texts are written by specialists of the stage, dramatic critics, theatre historians, journalists, etc. The psychological judgements about actors are free and varied . . . (providing) . . . good materials for our purpose.")[1]

Using these two reference sources for actors and other parallel ones in the case of champions, scientists and writers, the Gauquelins listed all the character trait words that were applied to each person who appeared both in their collections of nativities and also in their sources of biographical reference. In this way they built up a very large vocabulary of character trait words of all kinds and they already had the planetary positions of all the people to whom each trait was applied.

In evaluating this method of assessing the personal characteristics of individuals, it must be acknowledged first, one would suppose, that the proof of the pudding is in the eating and it is undoubtedly true (as we shall have good cause to recognise hereafter) that the Gauquelin character trait studies show a quite remarkable internal consistency as between one set of results and another and between one group of people and another. Thus, the method is revealed in practice to be extraordinarily sensitive and this is perhaps its best justification.

Of course, a characteristic will occasionally be mis-attributed to someone but taken by and large we are dealing with assessments of personal characteristics by good and responsible judges who know their subjects and are likely, in four cases out of five, and perhaps nine out of ten, to be pretty close to the mark.

To appreciate what is involved the reader may imagine that he has been asked to write a short appreciation, for his firm's magazine, of a colleague who is leaving after, say, 20 years. In such circumstances, one is quite free to pick out the qualities which strike one as interesting and worthy of note. One does not have to attempt to score the subject for every conceivable sort of tendency or aspect of character; there may be some sides of the person one is not sure about or which one has never got to know - well, then, there is no obligation to mention those things and the natural tendency will always be to refer to the traits one has observed and considers to be truly applicable and *as a rule* one will be right.

Of course, there are those who assert that there are no such things as stable individual qualities of this sort and that everyone is constantly veering about in his behaviour according to the ever-changing circumstances of the moment. Such a view is certainly contrary to commonsense and those who subscribe to it are usually as ready as anyone else in practice to sit down and write a testimonial saying that Mr X is hardworking, tactful and reliable, or whatever the case may be.

Later we shall have some further comments to make about the character trait method as a scientific tool but let us leave these theoretical considerations and come to its practical application.

In general terms the method is simple: we have a large number of people whose planetary positions are known (and have been published) and whose characteristics, culled from impartial biographical sources have been duly listed and published.[2] We can, therefore, take any character trait and give the planetary distributions (in the diurnal circle) for those people who are described as having that characteristic.

Furthermore, as we are dealing with four separate groups of people (champions, scientists, actors and writers), we shall be able to compare the results for consistency as between the groups. For example, do the scientists and champions who are described as, say, 'merry' show the same planetary distributions as the actors and writers who are so described, and do those people who are described as 'solemn' (whatever their group) show an opposite distribution?

This is the general idea. In practice its application must rest upon a mass of data and upon precise rules and methods of treating those data. Most readers will not need to know all these details but it is important that we state here where they can be found and it is hoped that all readers will briefly examine this information so as to get the overall picture of how the evidence has been assembled.

WHERE THE DETAILS ARE TO BE FOUND

1 The Raw Data

All the original data come from the works of Michel and Francoise Gauquelin as listed in the notes to Chapter Four, particularly in Note 2, Sections I and III: *Birth and Planetary Data*, Series A (Professional Notabilities) and Series C (Psychological Monographs). The former provides birth data, the second character trait data.

2 The Words Used

Gauquelin, in his studies, builds up a vocabulary of between two and three thousand different words and in his statistical methods he uses as many of these as possible. For reasons to be explained later, we favour a "paring down" method so that we use a limited vocabulary of only the most commonly applied character trait words.

In the near future we hope to have available on CD-ROM a list of all the words we use listed in alphabetical order (English-French and French-English) together with the number of times each word was applied to someone. We also explain there why and how we have divided the list of words into three groups according to their frequency of use.

3 The Gauquelin Character Trait Methodology

Also on the CD-ROM we explain how Gauquelin calculates the distribution (through the 36 sectors of the diurnal circle) of each planet for each word. He is able to show what the *expected* distribution is per sector for any word and the observed distribution is shown as plus or minus that figure. His methods, which we accept and follow, are ingenious and carefully devised so as to avoid statistical bias in the results.

4 My Own Methods

Finally, on the CD-ROM I explain in detail my own method of treating the Gauquelin data and give a specimen page of the computer printout resulting from that treatment which shows the information at my disposal in setting forth the evidence.

I also there acknowledge my great indebtedness to Neil Michelsen and Tom Shanks of Astro-Computing Services for their generous and expert help in dealing with the specialised treatment of the data I needed.

It is perhaps worth saying here that Michelsen and Shanks started from the foundation data of the Gauquelin material, taking for each person the given date, time, latitude and longitude of birth and calculating the birth positions with even greater accuracy than the Gauquelins did or could have done on such a scale. Therefore, all the calculations for my own work (except the final stage) are performed by the computer (after I had spent several years exploring the precise requirements) and are based on this matrix of original birth data. Thus, my own contribution has been simply to arrange the statistical evidence so that its implications can be seen for what they are.

5   *In Volume Two of this work* [which is to be produced on CD-ROM] are given harmonic analyses of planetary distributions for every character trait in the Gauquelin collection which is attributed more than a certain number of times.

Also set out in Volume Two are character trait 'spectra' (to be explained later in this Chapter) for each harmonic of each planet, harmonic analyses of Gauquelin's professional groups and other data referred to in this work.

6   *Deposited with the Astrological Association's Data Section* and available for specialist research are two copies of the detailed analyses of the Gauquelin data as used by the writer and described in Appendix notes.

So what are the Characteristics of the Champion?

In our last Chapter, we posed a question. We found that there were two consistent and outstanding features in the distribution of Mars in the nativities of European sports champions; one of them was the strong 4th harmonic with a peak phase around 56, the other a 3rd harmonic with a peak phase about 356. (See Figures 30a and b.) We wish to know what kinds of characteristics are shown by these two features.

In order to answer such questions the author asked for an exact harmonic analysis of the planetary distributions for the 199 most frequently used character trait words in the Gauquelin vocabulary.

This statement raises two questions: Why *only* the most frequently used words and why 199 in particular?

The total 199 is the result of stipulating a certain minimum usage in order for a word to be included. The reason for taking only the most commonly used words is this: The number of actual biographies is *relatively* small (about 1718 different people) in comparison with the number of *different* character trait words (roughly in the order of 2500) and the total number of actual attributions (about 50,000). Thus a person who is described as, say, courageous (a word of major usage) is quite likely also to be described as bold, fearless, valiant, brave and/or unflinching (words of minor usage). Yet if we count *all* these words we are simply using the same person's planetary positions over and over again. Thus, since there is a relatively small pool of different planetary positions, it seems wisest to use only the major word or words for each type of characteristic, for in this way we avoid the possibility of introducing distortions into the results due to multiplying one set of positions.

Here, then, is an example of how our harmonic analysis of each character trait works.

Among the four groups of Gauquelin's professionals, the word ENERGETIC was attributed to 187 *different people* (94 champions, 34 scientists, 42 actors, 17 writers).

But with some of these 187 people, the biographer was so impressed by their energy that, in describing them, he used the word energetic more than once. Thus the word is actually attributed 258 times (champions 125, scientists 45, actors 70, writers 19).

We can, therefore, take the position of, say, Mars in the diurnal circle at the time of birth of all these 187 energetic people and subject the resulting planetary distribution to harmonic analysis. This we call the 'single count' method. The planetary position of anyone described as energetic counts once, and once only, no matter how many times he may be described as energetic. This has also been called the one-man-one-vote method.

Alternatively, if we wish to 'weight' the planetary distribution in favour of those who are described as energetic more than once, and who may therefore be presumed to be even more energetic than average, we can have an harmonic analysis of the planetary distribution counting the planetary position once for each time the word energetic is attributed. This is called the 'multiple count' method. We consider the single count method to be less spectacular but more conservative and reliable and it is the single count method we use throughout this book, keeping the multiple count to provide additional evidence where needed.

We can now give the actual harmonic analysis of the distribution of Mars in the diurnal circle for the characteristic 'energetic' by both the single and multiple count methods. Here they are:

Energetic (Energetique)   MARS   Single 187. Multiple 258.

Single Count			Multiple Count		
Harmo-nic	Ampl %	Peak Phase	Harmo-nic	Ampl %	Peak Phase
1	13.4	241.1	1	10.8	290.3
2	9.5	307.8	2	9.0	297.5
3	6.9	347.3	3	5.4	340.4
4	31.4	37.4	4	46.5	42.1
5	7.6	336.6	5	14.8	330.9
6	7.1	150.9	6	7.3	127.7
7	4.2	349.0	7	1.7	0.5
8	29.2	151.9	8	30.8	131.1
9	20.8	65.4	9	24.8	63.9
10	8.5	139.2	10	10.1	134.3
11	14.6	164.7	11	15.8	170.5
12	9.4	158.4	12	9.4	102.6
13	11.8	197.3	13	17.4	177.6
14	24.8	205.5	14	24.1	226.4
15	5.1	114.4	15	5.2	86.2
16	5.7	267.9	16	12.5	60.1
17	19.4	202.7	17	20.6	211.8
18	16.4	235.4	18	21.5	258.2
19	13.0	167.7	19	9.5	203.9
20	6.0	357.7	20	9.8	117.1
Mean	13.2		Mean	15.4	

We see from these analyses that the highest amplitude (the most vigorous presence) by both the single and multiple count methods is the 4th harmonic and the second strongest is the 8th. The mean amplitude is shown at the foot of the amplitude column and it will be seen that the 4th and 8th are over twice the mean by the single count method and thrice and twice the mean by the multiple count. It will also be seen that the results of the two harmonic analyses are basically similar (not surprisingly) and that the peak phase for the 4th is, in both cases, about 40 which, incidentally, places the word very much in the category of those characteristics typical of the sports champion.

But now, having at our disposal these harmonic analyses of the planetary distributions for each word, we can answer some of the questions we have been asking. We can now tell what *are* the qualities which correlate most strongly with, say, Mars in the 4th harmonic at about the phase shown by the champions *and at every other phase of the 4th too*.

Likewise, we can show what are the qualities shown by that 3rd harmonic position of Mars which appears so consistently in the nativities of top athletes.

In order to do this we have only to go through our harmonic analysis and note which words score strongly (show a high amplitude) for any harmonic which interests us.

For this we shall need to have rules for deciding what strength of amplitude qualifies a given word to be accounted relevant. The methods we have adopted are explained in detail in [a future publication] but it is sufficient here and for general purposes to say that our list of 199 most-used character trait words have been divided into three groups: (1) those which are applied to at least 130 different people (these mostly have a multiple count of over 200); (2) those which are applied to between 50 and 129 people; and (3) those which, although applied to less than 50 people have yet a multiple count of at least 50.

The third group is the least reliable; the numbers are rather too small for comfort. Nevertheless, the 'qualifying mark' for group (3) words to count as significant has been set high and it is true that they are much more often apt than not and they are sometimes useful in throwing light on a certain harmonic when other evidence is thin. The first group is normally a very reliable one and the second is normally reliable too. So as to be able to deal with these three groups of words together, we have biassed the scoring of the words for reliability so as to give most value to group (1) words, less to group (2) and least to group (3).

How to read the Harmonic Spectrum of Qualities

We can now perform our first exercise in examining a specific harmonic of a specific planet and the natural place to start seems to be the 4th harmonic of Mars. Going through our harmonic analyses of the distribution of Mars for each characteristic we note which words show a high amplitude (a vigorous presence) in the 4th harmonic and we note the *phase* of all such words and enter them upon what we shall come to recognise as *a spectrum of qualities*, as shown for this example on page 124. Remember that in making our spectrum we always use the single count analysis.

Every harmonic is measured *in terms of phase* from 0° to 360 but since the 4th harmonic occupies a quarter of the circle - 90° - we give both scales of measurement - phase along the top, degrees of quadrant position along the bottom. (In each case the measurement is from the point of rise or set, MC or IC.)

Note that those words which score very highly appear in capital letters; those which are least certain are shown in brackets. Any word where the 4th is the strongest of the twenty harmonics given in our analyses (as with the word 'Energetic' in the example given above) is marked with an asterisk. Under our system of value-weighting, group (3) words (those applied to fewer than 50 people) can never appear in capital letters and *a line is drawn to separate them from the other words.*

Sometimes we shall find it convenient in the interests of simplicity to omit group (3) words and words in brackets from our examples but as this is our first example of a harmonic spectrum of qualities we give the full result. The top part of the page is the result by the single count analysis (one-man-one-vote), the bottom part shows the result by the multiple count. The spectrum is divided into nine columns of 10° each or, in terms of phase, 40°. Figure 30a should help to make the position clear. Thus, those characteristics which are listed in column one of the spectrum (0°-10° of diurnal motion or 0°-40° of phase angle) are the ones which appear when Mars is within 10° past one of the "angles". (The four "angles", as astrologers call them, are the MC, IC, and points of Rise and Set.)

Needless to say, our division into nine columns is arbitrary and they do not represent watertight compartments. The peak phase for the 4th harmonic of Mars in sport champions is 56, which falls in column two - that is, so to speak, the high point for the characteristics of the champion in the 4th (ie 14° past the angle or 56 divided by 4), but we shall naturally expect columns one and three to have some relevance too.

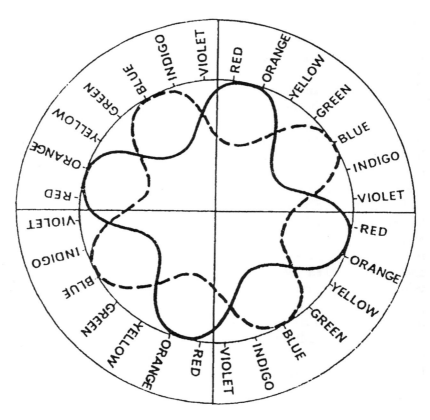

Fig. 37

We can now clearly comprehend the idea of the spectrum of qualities. The type of spectrum most familiar to us is that of the colour spectrum, so we can illustrate the concept, using colours to represent psychological qualities. Figure 37 shows the idea. Let us suppose that the qualities of the champion (as shown by Mars) are represented by the colour red-orange - then we should naturally expect that a collection of people who share that specific quality would show a distribution of Mars at their times of birth as shown by the (solid line) 4th harmonic wave in Figure 37, and that is exactly what we have found (although we have also found a 3rd harmonic element and we shall come to that soon).

If we wish to find the qualities which are opposite to those of the champion, we shall look from columns one and two to column six and those adjacent. Here, (referring to both the single and multiple count schemes) as the opposite of Frank, we find Discreet; as the opposite of Hard we find Indulgent and Charming; opposed to the Man of Action we find the Dreamer; against Courageous we find the French word Timide of which the nearest English equivalent is perhaps Timorous or Diffident but which we translate by the more common word, Shy. So too with other terms; they are not always exact opposites, but we do need to produce exact opposites to justify our thesis; the general opposition of the two lists of words is obvious. The qualities of column six and those adjacent are, of course, the ones indicated as being prominent among painters, writers and musicians. The distribution of Mars in *their* case will be shown by the dotted line wave in Figure 37.

Some people have argued that the contrast between the two groups of characteristics we have just been discussing is the only point of interest in this spectrum. They argue that the truly Martian qualities appear after Mars has crossed the angle (columns one and two in the spectrum) because that is where Mars is strong, and that the qualities which appear at column six are there not, so to speak, in their own right but merely because that is where Mars is weakest. But if this were the true position then it would be a simple contrast between black and white and in that case the qualities given in columns three and four *would be the same shade of grey* as those given in columns seven and eight. *But this is not so.*

The characteristics of columns three and four are unmistakeably lively and outgoing (brisk, verve, gay, successful, amusing, optimistic, authoritative) - this is the extrovert phase of Mars' 4th harmonic; but those of columns seven and eight are deeper and more thoughtful and withdrawn (silent, reflective, likes country life, dreamer, unsociable, calm, quiet hobbies) - this is the introvert phase of Mars' 4th.

There is as much of a contrast between *these* two groups of words as there is between those mentioned earlier: *we are dealing with a true spectrum of qualities.*

A simplified spectrum of the 4th harmonic of Mars, not necessarily using the actual words given in our vocabulary, would evidently go something like this:

Forceful	Vigorous	Brisk	Charming	Temperate	Withdrawn	Precise
Tough	Active	Lively	Good	Shy	Thoughtful	Realistic
Self-Assertive	Courageous	Imagina-tive	Discreet	Sensitive	Brooding	Smould-ering

At the end of our detailed (full-page) spectrum there is a curious dearth of characteristics - only one (Realistic) appears there and even that is a 'Group (3)' word. We must remember that the end of the spectrum *must link up*, psychologically, with the beginning and one has the impression that as a result of the penultimate phase, which is obviously one of withdrawal, and concurrently with the tendency towards a deepening and intensification of thought, there is an interior clarification of the springs of action and a growing determination to go out into the world, warrior-like, to set things to rights in the life of action which bursts out after the planet has crossed the angle. Therefore, I have suggested the word Smouldering as *one aspect* of Mars in this position. (It may sometimes be characteristic of the man or woman who broods upon wrongs or errors of some kind and has to spend part or much of his life 'crying in the wilderness' before he is heeded. Indeed it may be that it is not until the end of his life or even after his death that his message is understood and the appropriate action taken.)

To return then to our champions we can now see clearly what characteristics they draw from the 4th harmonic emplacement of their Mars - basically those of columns one and two in our spectrum. By consulting our harmonic analyses and the distribution of Mars for the words involved we can actually draw out the distribution of Mars for the ten most strongly shown qualities in this part of the spectrum and this result is shown in Figure 38.

The characteristics thus shown (single count) are: Active, Ardent, Combative, Courageous, Energetic, Enthusiastic, Frank, Hard, Self-willed and Vigorous. (One could add more words from that part of the Spectrum, but they would, in effect, only duplicate the qualities already shown and increase the technical significance of an already crystal-clear result.)

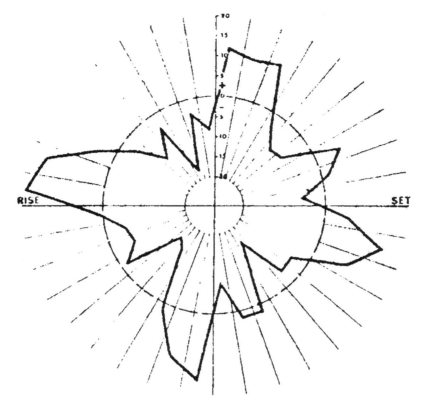

Fig. 38 Mars distribution of 4th harmonic qualities.

The striking thing about this distribution of Mars (Figure 38) is that we can now see that once the *pure 4th harmonic qualities* (active, energetic etc) *are abstracted* from the other characteristics in the nativities of the champions there is no longer any tendency for there to be stronger peaks after the rise and upper culmination; *all four angles are more or less equal in strength.*

In order to see why the champions *themselves* show much bigger peaks in the distribution of Mars after its rise and upper culmination and little or none after its set and lower culmination, we must look at the qualities given by the appropriate phase of the *third* harmonic.

Referring to our harmonic analyses and the third harmonic spectrum derived from them we can list the characteristics associated with that phase of Mars' 3rd which is indicated as being typical of the sports champion. This was given as phase 356 in our analysis, but we can say roughly phase 360° or 0°, and so we take the qualities which show a peak phase within 30° of this point, (ie between 330° and 30°) in the third harmonic.

The qualities derived in this way from our spectrum (omitting group (3) words and those in brackets†) are: Simple, Modest, Intelligent, Enthusiastic, Noble, Disinterested, Humane, Subtle, Vitality and Traveller, and the distribution of Mars for these characteristics is shown in Figure 39 both by 36 sectors and by 12.

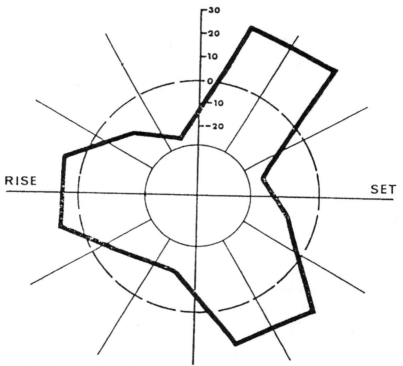

Fig. 39 Mars position for those possessing character traits phased at 360° ± 30°.

---

† The words omitted are Sporting, Straight and 'Seeks the Truth'.

Apart from the word Traveller, which has no particular relevance in this context (although we shall deal with it in its due place), we can see that the characteristics picked out by this phase of Mars' 3rd harmonic are entirely apt. The five qualities - Simple, Modest, Intelligent, Noble and Enthusiastic - account for more than two-thirds of the sample. Are these the qualities of the supreme sports champion? One must admit that in a general way they are, yet they are a very different set of characteristics from those shown in columns one and two of Mars' 4th harmonic. It is because, and only because, the champions *combine* these two sets of qualities that the peak distributions of their Mars are *enhanced* after rise and upper culmination and *flattened* after set and lower culmination - see Figures 31a and b.

What, broadly speaking, is the difference between these two sets of characteristics? We shall discuss this more fully when we come to deal with the character and significance of the different harmonics, but in general terms it may be said that the 4th harmonic, which perhaps plays a dominant role in astrological results of the kind we have been studying, evidently relates to what might be called the constitutional type - one might even say the physical temperament - whilst the 3rd harmonic introduces a more ideal element.

It will sooner or later be obvious, if it is not so already, that we shall inevitably be drawn, in these studies, into a consideration of the significance of Number. Of course, one realises that, to many people, any suggestion of the attribution of meaning or symbolic content to Number is anathema and one sometimes even finds the term "number mysticism" used almost as a term of contempt or abuse. But it must be obvious that the whole world of nature with its endless marvels and mysteries is constructed on numerical principles and to ignore this fact or to sweep it aside as meaningless constitutes a closing of the avenues of discovery which will hardly appeal to the real truth-seeker. The fact that a great deal of nonsense has been talked and written about this subject does not preclude the possibility of an intelligent and scientific approach to it based upon strict empirical evidence as well as upon sound philosophical principles - for in practice both are needed. "Nothing in the history of number symbolism" says one writer, surveying the world's literature, "is so striking as the unanimity of all ages and climates in regard to the meaning of a certain few number symbols", and among these the number Four is consistently found to express the idea of objective manifestation, precipitated existence, or something closely analogous, and without stopping here to examine the niceties of meaning involved, we will only suggest that the 4th harmonic evidently relates to what we have referred to above as the constitutional type. Thus we see, in the first phase of Mars' 4th harmonic, something like the classical *choleric humour* of former times - Bold, Hardy, Rash, Courageous, Energetic and so on.

But if the number four is associated with the outward, manifest and material aspect of things, the number three is commonly associated with their inner, formal and ideal side. Thus, if the 4th harmonic spectrum represents a scale or range of 'humours' or physiological temperaments, it would seem that the 3rd harmonic presents us, in the same way, with a range of *motivating ideals.*

The trouble with many (perhaps most) schools of modern psychology is that they are too ready to draw conclusions about human psychology and conduct from a study of the behaviour of animals in wire cages, ignoring one of the absolutely central differences between man and animals, namely, that man is motivated by ideals whereas animals never are.

We shall deal with these issues much more fully later but as a tentative interpretation of this phase of the 3rd harmonic of Mars, I suggest that it represents what we may call the 'Olympic Ideal' - that of being willing to sacrifice all else in order to strive for the highest, not in the spirit of winning at all costs but in accordance with what is strictly a spiritual ideal of (in this application) perfect sportsmanship. This ideal is well expressed in its higher meaning by a famous passage in Iamblicus: "For not by mortals whose thought is of body are things divine attainable but by those who, stripped like athletes, speed upwards to the heights." It is an ideal of complete dedication to the disciplines required for the highest attainment whilst at the same time setting a higher value upon the manner of doing it than upon the result, concerning which a measure of detachment or disinterestedness is preserved. This, of course, is what used to be regarded (and no doubt still is in some quarters) as the 'amateur ideal' in sport - the quaint old English idea of 'playing the game'.

In terms of satisfaction one might say that the qualities of the 4th harmonic are such as tend to look for, and produce, tangible results; the 3rd looks for a certain formal attractiveness which is more satisfying spiritually.

Summary and Conclusions

In the last chapter we asked several questions. We wanted to know what were the principles whereby qualities were related to harmonic phase and harmonic number.

We have now demonstrated the idea of the *spectrum of qualities* by virtue of which the successive phases of each harmonic unfold a series of qualities which constitute (like the colour spectrum) one complete circle of effects, the end of each spectrum joining up again with the beginning. It is easy to see how this principle answers (in part at least) our question of what determines phase.

We have also given some indication of how harmonic number is related to quality (and how, therefore, each harmonic will be found to embody the spectrum of a different set of qualities) and we illustrated this through the differences between the 3rd and 4th harmonics. This does not explain the principles behind the Numbers, but to embark upon *that* problem, at this stage, would be out of place. We hope to tackle the question of Number and its meaning in Volume Three of this work; at this stage we must be content to give some piecemeal indication of the ideas involved, but only insofar as the results call for some measure of explanation.

Again, in our last Chapter we noted that Gauquelin's 'experts', when asked to say what were the characteristics of the sports champion, all chose the qualities derived from the idea of will-power and the determination to win. We can now answer the question of what were the qualities ignored by the experts, and these we can now see to have been the ones given by the appropriate phase of the 3rd harmonic and described above.

Again, we raised the question of why the nativities of sports champions collected in the United States showed a very strong 4th but very little 3rd (see Figure 18). The conclusion one might reasonably draw here is that in the United States there is a much higher premium than elsewhere on sheer competitiveness and the ability to produce results and much less on being a 'graceful loser'.[6]

(One of the revolutionary things about the foregoing techniques is that they provide an objective, scientific means for identifying the characteristics and tendencies in a given population and for observing changes therein. The capacity to do this would be valuable in many fields of research, for example, in psychology and medicine. There is some suggestion that the more recent collections of successful sporting nativities continue to show a powerful 4th but not such a strong 3rd and this might suggest that modern conditions favour the extreme competitiveness of the 4th harmonic element, but are less favourable to what one might call the gentlemanly sporting ideal.)

The sceptic who has read this chapter may have reservations. Is it really true, for example, in relation to Figure 38, showing the distribution of Mars for the qualities of the champion and showing consistent peaks after all four angles - is it really true that this type of distribution is equally indicated in the nativities of writers, actors and scientists as well as champions? And if it is and we thus have a consistent pattern in all four groups, is this effect not due to some other (non-astrological) cause? Where, in short, is the control group?

These questions are understandable even though anyone thoroughly acquainted with the work of the Gauquelins would understand why a control group is not needed or, rather, is provided for in the basic methodology. Therefore, in order to remove these doubts and to get a clearer grasp of the idea of the harmonic spectrum of qualities, it is desirable that we should spend a little longer and look a little closer at the 4th harmonic of Mars (for to understand one harmonic is to understand the principle of them all) and this will be our first job in the next Chapter.

CHAPTER VIII

The Fourth Harmonic

The graphs of the distribution of a planet for specific characteristics or groups of characteristics (such as those in Figures 38 and 39) show the frequency with which the planetary position occurs above or below the theoretical or 'expected' distribution.[†]

This ensures that any consistent patterns of planetary emplacement to be found in the results *must* stem from a consistent relation between a specific class of characteristics and a specific type of planetary position - *and from that alone*. The most effective way of demonstrating this is to show how, *from the same pool of nativities*, different, and even opposing, distributions are yielded - *and consistently yielded through the four professional groups* - according to the class of characteristic involved. In this chapter we shall carry out this exercise in terms of the 4th harmonic for Mars, Jupiter, Saturn and the Moon.

The object is partly to show more convincingly the clear and consistent nature of the results and also to look more closely at the concept of the harmonic spectrum, revealing the naturally consecutive character of the phases thereof and how each harmonic spectrum represents a true circle of psychological effects.

Before we proceed to present the results of this study, there is one explanation that is called for. When graphs are drawn showing the distribution of a planet for certain characteristics, so long as the graph is drawn in terms of the *whole circle* (as in Figures 38 and 39), it is impossible to exclude the visible intrusion of other harmonics which are relevant to those characteristics. The reason of course is that *all* harmonics precipitate into the full circle. One can often go some way to cutting out short (that is higher 'frequency') harmonics by reducing the number of sector totals to be used. Thus in Figure 39a there are 36 totals, in 39b there are 12. Both graphs are of the same third harmonic distribution of Mars but, in the second drawing, some of the 'interference' near the MC has been eliminated by taking fewer sectors.

[†] Addey intended to include the distribution for each character trait in a major set of appendices: this has not proved feasible in this edition. These distributions will be made available in CD-ROM image format, once the CD is prepared.

But the best way to cut out those harmonics which one does not wish to see is to illustrate the distribution in terms of the exact length of the harmonic one is dealing with - that is to say, in this chapter where we shall be dealing with the 4th, ninety degrees (90°).

In order to do this, of course, one must divide the circle into four parts for the 4th harmonic (five for the 5th, six for the 6th etc) and superimpose the totals for the four parts of the circle.

To make the method quite clear, one is dividing the 36 sector-totals of the whole distribution into four - Figure 40 - and superimposing the four quarters of the circle so that one total is given for all sectors 'a', one total for all sectors 'b' and so on for the nine sectors in each quarter-circle.

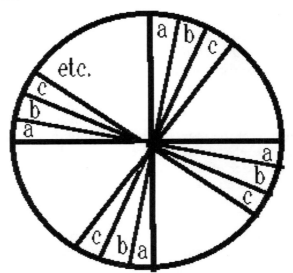

Fig. 40   How the sectors for the fourth harmonic are arranged.

Apart from concentrating all one's planetary positions into the precise harmonic length we wish to examine (instead of spreading them thinly round the whole circle), this method has the effect of eliminating all harmonics except those which fit exactly into a quarter-circle. If there is a 4th harmonic present, it will now show up as one wave of 90° in length and when the result is drawn diagrammatically we shall get the best *visual* picture obtainable of the amplitude and phase of the harmonic.

Because the 8th harmonic will also fit exactly into the quarter-circle (45° x 2) and also the 12th (30° x 3), it may be possible to see *them* too in our diagram if they are relevant to the qualities under consideration. (This we will illustrate shortly.)

In the following pages we give a necessarily *brief* outline of the character of each phase of the planetary 4th harmonics and illustrate, by means of graphs, the consistency of the main character traits through the four professional groups. Of course, the difficulty at all times is to see what lies within and behind a particular group or combination of characteristics, to penetrate the bare list of traits and see the living type. Sometimes this is reasonably obvious; at other times the exercise has called for long reflection in which it has been useful to be able to draw upon a long acquaintance with planetary psychology and also, of course, to be able to examine individual examples in greater depth.

Mars

We have already noted in outline the psychology of the 4th harmonic of Mars. We observed the idea of the spectrum of qualities but we found that although one quality merged into another, it was convenient to distinguish four principal phases.[1]

The first, which reached a peak about 10° or 12° past the angle, could be described as action-oriented; the second phase was markedly extrovert; the third phase (typical of the so-called artistic temperament) was of a mild disposition and could be described as contemplative as opposed to active; and the fourth was markedly introvert. It is normally sufficient to take ten or twelve of the principal words from each phase of the spectrum to illustrate its character and the agreement of the evidence between the four professional groups. Thus the words used for the graphs in this and subsequent chapters are, in each case, designed simply to illustrate the qualities of that phase as clearly as possible.[2] Figure 42 shows how the four phases fall in the quadrant for Mars and Saturn.

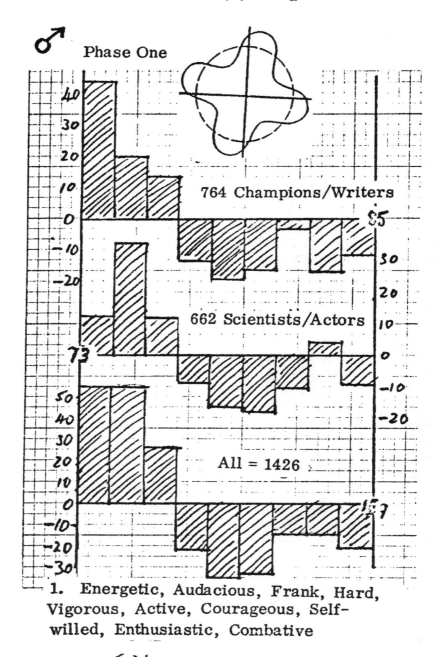

1. Energetic, Audacious, Frank, Hard,
Vigorous, Active, Courageous, Self-
willed, Enthusiastic, Combative

Fig. 41a Mars, phase One of the fourth harmonic.

Phase One (Figure 41a)

Indicated characteristics: *Energetic, Audacious, Frank, Hard, Vigorous, Active, Courageous, Enthusiastic, Self-Willed, Combative.* (1426 applications of these words)

This is the famous "Mars effect" phase typical of the sports champion (and indefatigably argued over by those who would like to reject Gauquelin's work) in which the traditional Martian qualities emerge in full force. The whole tenor of this phase is towards the capacity for prompt, effective and, if necessary, drastic or ruthless action. In our spectrum we find a plethora of action-oriented characteristics at this phase and our graph (Figure 41a) shows the distribution of Mars on a 90° basis for ten of these characteristics. Each of the four professional groups shows a similar distribution but from considerations of space we add the group whose members are *most* often described by these words (champions 515 times) to the group *least* often so described (writers 249), comparing these two together with the distribution for scientists (310) and actors (352) taken together.

Phase Two (Figure 41b)

Indicated characteristics: *Authority, Intelligent, Successful, Imaginative, Influences others, Common sense, Optimistic, Gay, Amusing, Brisk, Dynamic, Seductive.* (1033 applications)

The sheer strength and forcefulness of phase one is here softened into a lively outgoing phase, by no means lacking in vigour and firmness (*dynamic, authority, brisk*) but characterised now as much by thought as by will (*intelligent, common sense*) and above all distinguished by a much lighter tone (*gay, amusing, seductive*). This is an obviously extrovert phase of cheerful vigour.

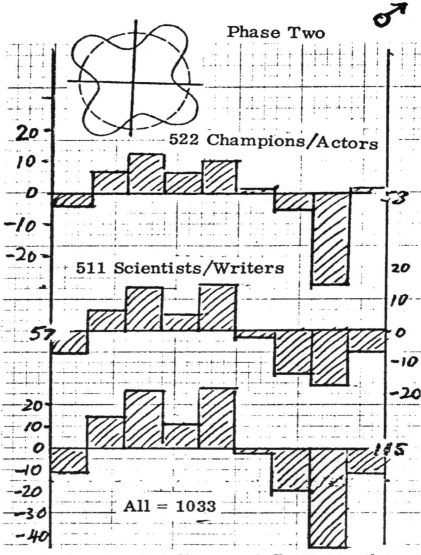

2. **Authority, Intelligent, Influences others, Common sense, Optimistic, Brisk, Imaginative, Successful, Dynamic, Seductive, Amusing, Gay**

Fig. 41b Mars, phase Two of the fourth harmonic.

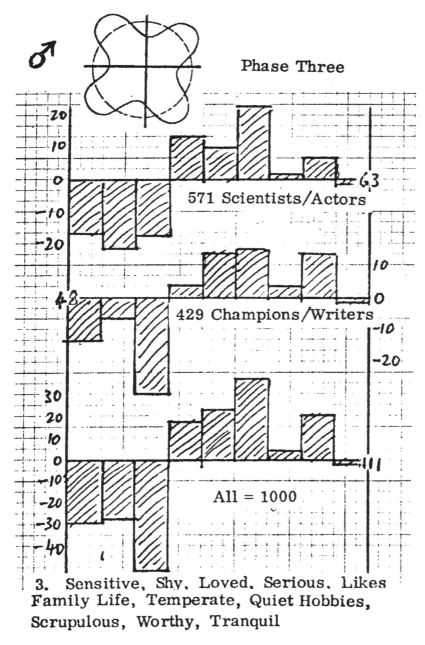

Phase Three

571 Scientists/Actors

429 Champions/Writers

All = 1000

3. Sensitive, Shy, Loved, Serious, Likes Family Life, Temperate, Quiet Hobbies, Scrupulous, Worthy, Tranquil

Fig. 41c Mars, phase Three of the fourth harmonic.

Phase Three (Figure 41c)

Indicated characteristics: *Sensitive, Shy, Loved, Likes family life, Serious, Temperate, Scrupulous, Quiet hobbies, Worthy, Tranquil.* (1000 applications)

As we have seen, this is the position of Mars most strongly in evidence in the nativities of writers, painters, musicians and no doubt other exponents of the fine arts. Every harmonic moves from a thesis, through an antithesis and offers the possibility of a new and higher synthesis. In the 4th harmonic of Mars the main opposition is evidently between action and contemplation, strength and gentleness, the hard and the yielding. Phase three embodies, in broad terms, the latter quality in each of these pairs.

Phase Four (Figure 41d)

Indicated characteristics: *Precise, Calm, Reflective, Unsociable, Silent, Likes country life, Moving, Observant, Intellectual curiosity, Realist.* (718 applications)

Phase four is as markedly introvert as phase two is extrovert. Such words as *silent, unsociable, likes country life* and *reflective* speak for themselves, but a certain spirit of watchfulness is also suggested by the words *calm, observant, realist* and even a capacity for depth of feeling by *moving.*

Of the four phases of Mars' 4th this is the one which is at first hardest to understand. The type of activity or passivity appropriate to the first three phases seems obvious, but what happens in phase four?

It would seem that this is a phase of withdrawal, of deep reflection (we have earlier suggested the word brooding) of a kind which is the prelude to action. The intense outburst of powerful activity which follows (that is in phase one) *cannot come out of nothing* - it *must* follow upon a phase of deep thought and intense feeling. Thus I believe it is the lot of those with Mars in this phase to have to give long and deep thought to wrongs or errors in society (or, on a smaller scale, in their own limited environment) with a view to setting them to rights. Such people are sometimes called upon to spend many years 'crying in the wilderness' before they are heeded and it may be that it is not until late in life or even after their death that their purposes are realised.

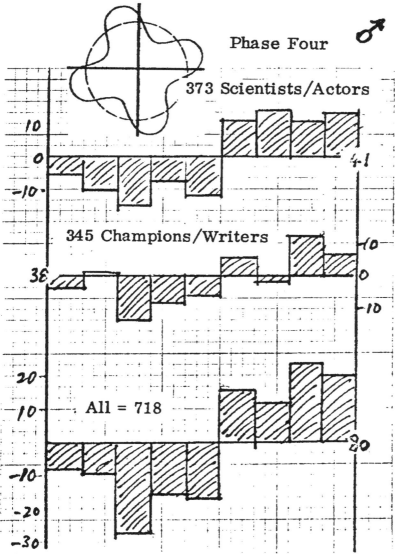

Phase Four ♂

373 Scientists/Actors

345 Champions/Writers

All = 718

4. Precise, Calm, Reflective, Unsociable.
Likes Country Life, Silent, Moving,
Observant, Realist, Intellectual curiosity

Fig. 41d Mars, phase Four of the fourth harmonic.

Winston Churchill had Mars in this phase becoming Prime Minister at the age of 60 to lead his country against an enemy of whom he had warned for many years. In Germany, Conrad Adenauer was put in a concentration camp by Hitler but became Chancellor at the age of 72 and for nearly 14 years led his country in its post-war reconstruction. In Italy, Alcide De Gaspari fulfilled the same role; imprisoned by Mussolini as early as 1926 he fought with the Italian resistance movement during the second world war and became Prime Minister when he was 64 to give purpose and cohesion to his country's post-war recovery. The very similar role played by De Gaulle in France during and after the war is well known. All four of these men were obliged to spend years in eclipse, years in which they seemed to gather the inner force to fight victoriously against a great wrong. All four of them had Mars between about 5°-15° before an angle, that is to say, in the midst of phase four.[3] (It may seem paradoxical that the same may also be said of Hitler who, imprisoned in the early days of the Nazi party, there wrote *Mein Kampf* as the expression of his own broodings upon what he conceived to be old injustices.) But it is not the precise form of destiny which is important (and Mars in this phase does not at all preclude early successes in life as most of the above men show), but the emphasis upon a *certain interiority of the Mars function.*

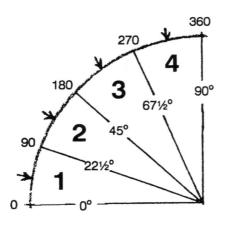

Fig. 42 Showing where the four phases of the fourth harmonic fall for Mars and Saturn. They are most typical at about 11°, 34°, 56° and 79° past the angle.

Before leaving Mars and passing on to Jupiter, there are two points which might be noticed. The first is that the so-called "Mars effect" so much debated and questioned by sceptics in relation to Gauquelin's studies of the nativities of sports champions is really only one of four identifiable phases (all of them "Mars effects" of one sort or another) and is not significantly stronger than the other three phases.[4]

The second point is that in Figure 41a the high "Mars effect" score after the angle is only partly the result of a strong 4th harmonic. As often happens, some of the qualities shown in one harmonic (in this case the 4th) are echoed in a subharmonic (in this case the 8th). Thus all ten words used for graph 41a have a broadly similar phase in the 8th harmonic as well as a closely similar phase in the 4th. But since, as we explained earlier in this chapter, the 8th and 12th harmonics cannot be prevented from showing up in the 4th, Figure 41a really consists of a strong 4th plus a fairly strong 8th, as shown in Figure 43.

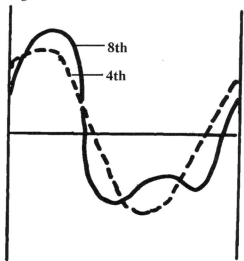

Fig. 43 The 8th harmonic of Mars superimposed on the 4th.

Jupiter

The 4th harmonic of Jupiter follows the same general pattern as that of Mars but with certain interesting differences. A first phase of powerful outward activity is followed by a markedly extrovert phase of good cheer which might be seen as the enjoyment of the fruits of phase one. This is followed by a phase of quiet simplicity which seems to signal a certain disillusion with worldly satisfactions and in which religion or some form of idealism usually plays an increasing part, and finally there is an introvert phase of inner renewal in which deepening inner convictions pave the way for a vigorous resurgence of outward activity at phase one.

The first *difference* between Mars and Jupiter is that whereas, for Mars, phase one *begins* at the angle, for Jupiter it is evidently centred at the angle (see Figure 44).

Fig. 44 The four phases of Jupiter's fourth harmonic. Phase One is centred at the angle.

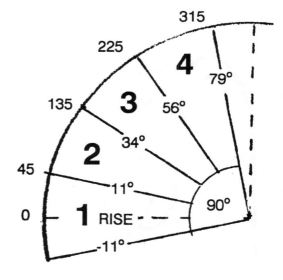

Psychologically the differences are that whereas at phase one Mars seeks to exercise the *strength* to resist what is harmful, purge what is defunct and break down or sweep away the old order, Jupiter seems more distinctly to lead the way towards what is good. At phase two Mars verges more to the enjoyment of action, while the enjoyment of Jupiter is directed more towards the good things of life; at phase three, Mars, interestingly and unexpectedly, tends to turn to the arts (possibly because of the greater sensual element to be found therein) as shown in Figure 32, whereas Jupiter tends to religion and philosophy, being more interested in ideas. At phase four, although this, the introspective phase of both Mars and Jupiter, is in the nature of a precursor of renewed outward activity, yet Jupiter's introversion is more tinged with religions, theoretical or idealistic considerations, whereas with Mars it is practical and strategic measures which tend to dominate the thinking.

Phase One (Figure 45a)

Indicated characteristics: *Personality, Organiser, Original, Audacious, Authority, Self-willed, Director, Methodical, Proud, Merry, Experimenter, Violent.* (1326 applications)

This phase is much concerned with the exercise of power (*authority, organiser, director, personality*). It shows the Jupiterian unwillingness to be bound by convention (*original, audacious, experimenter*) and the tendency in the undeveloped type to go to excess and to become overbearing (*proud, self-willed, violent*).

Some might consider the last group of qualities to be out of place in relation to the beneficent Jupiter and so they are, as a rule, for Jupiter is normally a good leader, cheerful, liberal and disposed to exercise his rulership for the good of the ruled. Yet every experienced astrologer knows how easily Jupiter runs to excess or extremism and one has only to remember Gauquelin's results showing Jupiter prominent among members of the Nazi hierarchy, in this phase and the next, to realise what may, in rare circumstances, happen where there is so much self-confidence combined with power.

But the essential nature of the closely angular Jupiter lies in its tireless, ever-hopeful, forward-looking enthusiasm. It is this which inspires everyone and makes it a natural leader (even against its inclinations for it is not keen on the burdens and responsibilities of leadership and much prefers to be freelance, an aptly Jupiterian term). Furthermore, Jupiter *in this phase* must actually *do* something progressive and it is this which makes phase one so strongly orientated to externals; indeed, both this phase and the next are so orientated, the first in terms of progressive activity, the second in terms of enjoyment and gusto.

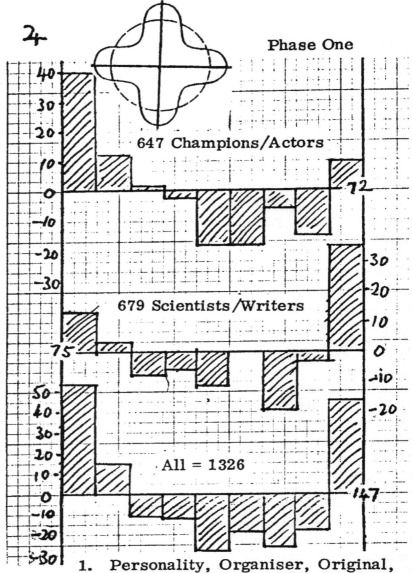

Phase One

647 Champions/Actors

679 Scientists/Writers

All = 1326

1. Personality, Organiser, Original,
Audacious, Authority, Clear, Self-willed,
Director, Proud, Merry, Experimenter,
Violent

Fig. 45a Jupiter, phase One of the fourth harmonic.

An interesting sidelight on this phase is to be found among the abundance of graphs of planetary distributions thrown off by Gauquelin (many of them relatively unstudied). One of these, Figure 46, shows the distribution of Jupiter for the characteristics of the typical writer. There it will be seen that Jupiter on an angle does not favour writers. Why is this? The answer is fairly obvious: most forms of writing call for a willingness to forsake outward activity for reflective thought. The writer needs to spend part of his time leaning over five-barred gates, lying on his bed staring at the ceiling or sitting at the street-side cafe tables and watching the world go by.

This kind of thing is not for Jupiter on an angle - he must be up and doing. Of course not all writers are typical; some gather their material from the observation of externals - the travel-writer for example or, indeed, journalists generally who *do* tend to have Jupiter on an angle; and where your angular Jupiter can write spontaneously and without deliberation the results are usually entertaining, racy and full of interest. Or again, one could hardly wish for a better instance of an angular Jupiter than Michel Gauquelin himself. Anyone who surveys his research and data-gathering activities must conclude that he is a man who must be up and doing - and magnificently so - but there is a case, too, for thinking that if he had been less eager to be ever pressing forward, Jupiter-like, with the next experiment and had been more disposed to go to bed for a day or two (does he ever go to bed?) and think about his results, he would surely have penetrated their significance more deeply.

Phase Two (Figure 45b)

Indicated characteristics: *Gay, Successful, Energetic, Enthusiastic, Witty, Lively, Elegant, Amiable, Brisk, Ironic, Malicious, Good-tempered.* (1324 applications)

Here we see Jupiter at its most expansively extrovert. It is as if the activity of phase one was designed to produce a period of peace and plenty and phase two represented the enjoyment of the fruits thereof. It would be quite wrong to give the impression that this phase of Jupiter's 4th was simply a playboy, yet it does verge strongly towards a lively and cheerful outlook, towards laughter and good fortune and good living. An examination of the words in this phase of Jupiter's 4th harmonic spectrum, of which we give only a dozen, will explain why, once Jupiter has crossed the angle and for another 30° or so, this phase has given the word *jovial*, or its equivalent in other languages, to the terminology of popular psychology in Europe.

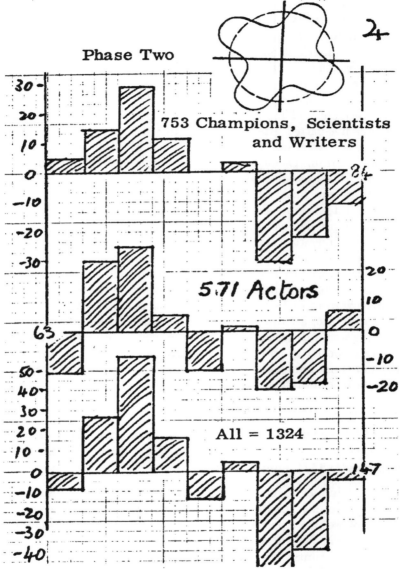

2. Gay, Successful, Energetic, Enthusiastic, Witty, Lively, Elegant, Malicious, Amiable, Brisk, Ironic, Good-tempered

Fig. 45b Jupiter, phase Two of the fourth harmonic.

Nor is it only in Europe. A writer in *The Astrological Magazine* (India) who certainly knew nothing of Gauquelin's researches has this to say of Jupiter just after it has risen:

> "It is a common proverb in East Godavari District in the delta area of Konaseema (where, even to this day, the ancient Vedic love and knowledge is preserved) that Jupiter in the twelfth house is a good sign and that such an individual shall have all-round good fortune and enjoyment. This has been accepted so freely and without any reserve that a person wielding influence and throwing his weight about and around himself is referred to [by a local proverb] which, when rendered into English, means: 'Jupiter for him is in the twelfth house; there is no means of controlling him'."

It may seem strange that the word "malicious" features in this phase but on the contrary it is entirely apt. Jupiter in this position is, above all, expansive and seeks yet more expansion and one way to make oneself look bigger is to make others look smaller. This is the phase of Jupiter's 4th so common among actors and the bitchiness which is sometimes found in the species (among many virtues of course) is proverbial. The term "to up-stage" someone (which is to place oneself in a favourable light - whilst placing others at a disadvantage) is a theatrical metaphor.

Phase Three (Figure 45c)

Indicated characteristics: *Gentle, Modest, Simple, Generous, Cultivates friendships, Tender, Deep, Devoted, Sincere, Disinterested* (1586 applications)

It is important not to lose sight of the fact that the successive phases *gradually* merge into each other. Phase two starts off full of bounce but in its later stages moves steadily into the direction of the above characteristics. It is as if, to express the change picturesquely, the attractions of the bright lights and the expense account lunches gradually (or suddenly) palled. It is the beginning of a change (to be found in many if not most harmonics) from the values of the outer to those of the inner life.

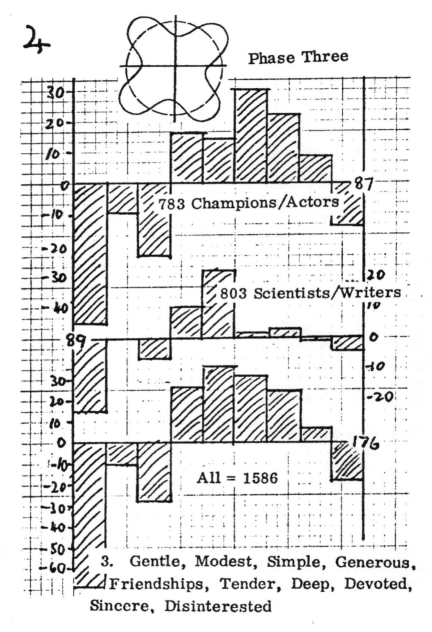

Fig. 45c Jupiter, phase Three of the fourth harmonic.

In his remarkable work *The Astrological Aspects*[5] Charles Carter, most perceptive of English astrologers, says that those with the benefic aspects of Sun and Jupiter "prefer to live peaceably, often in circumstances of natural simplicity rather than the opulent state that tradition had led us to suppose. Their wants are few and moderate and their pleasures are generally intellectual . . ... I have known Sun trine Jupiter men who lived cheerfully in poverty, possessing almost nothing except books, good spirits and moderate health. It is the least personally ambitious of any configuration and can even be shy . . ... It has no restlessness. Such journeys as it likes are of a mild sort, to take a little rest or visit friends. It can be very conventional. It is morally sound, having neither the desire nor the daring to commit crime and being, moreover, kindly disposed to all."

This conveys well the tone and temper of this phase of Jupiter at its best. Of course it is too idealised a picture adequately to cover the range of manifestation which the phase must represent but it clearly shows the *type* of effect we are dealing with.

The single most relevant "key" word which Gauquelin found for the position of Jupiter which, in our classification, falls broadly in the midst of phases one and two was *pride*; thus by the same token the central characteristic which falls between phases three and four is humility - *so far as worldly things are concerned* - but there is the danger of a growing spiritual pride.

Phase Four (Figure 45d)

Indicated characteristics: *Discreet, Calm, Solitary, Worthy, Solemn, Chaste, Religious, Pure, Naive, Quiet hobbies, Passion of his Art* (724 applications)

Just as phase one is the most active and phase three the most contemplative, so phase two is the most worldly and four the most other-worldly of the phases of Jupiter's 4th.

The natural simplicity of phase three paves the way for the deepening convictions and the more withdrawn inner life of phase four; in fact the whole lesson and message of this harmonic is about, first, the growth and expansion of the outer life (with the consequent contraction of the inner) and secondly the expansion and growth of the inner life (and the withering away of the outer).

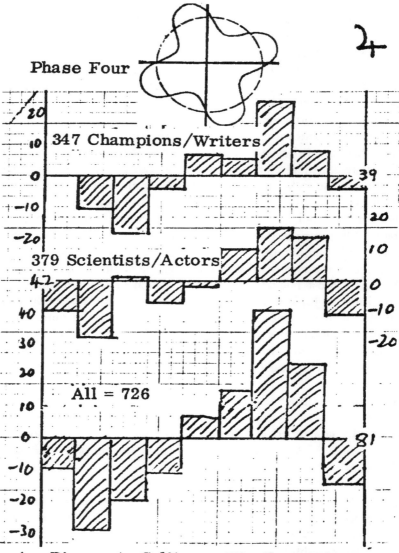

Phase Four

347 Champions/Writers

379 Scientists/Actors

All = 726

4. Discreet, Solitary, Worthy, Solemn,
Chase, Calm, Quiet, Hobbies, Pure,
Religious, Naive, Violent, Passion of
his Art

Fig. 45d Jupiter, phase Four of the fourth harmonic.

The story of Jupiter's 4th harmonic in its loftiest form is the story of all the saints who turned in disillusion from the riches of the world to the riches of the spirit; and then sought again to realise in the world the vision of the ideal.

The danger at phase four of course lies in the very zeal and ardour which is inspired at this stage and which so easily becomes fanaticism. The excesses of the outer life at phase two are matched by the excesses of the inner life at phase four. The word *violent* which we have included among the phase one words actually falls on the border of phases four and one and that is probably where it belongs. Even when expressed in the religious life proper the fervour engendered in the later part of this phase can so easily lead to violence and extremism but among those who are more or less dead to the inner life and who must therefore find another 'religion', say Marxism or football, there too the tendency to extremism and even violence is liable to manifest. It is noteworthy that one of the characteristics thrown up at this phase is embodied in the phrase *passion of his art*, which is applied in Gauquelin's biographies to actors or writers who are deeply inspired and dedicated to the vision of what the practice of their art stands for in its highest expression.

However, one must not over-emphasise the extremist or rebellious side of this phase; the list of characteristics thrown up speak for themselves and reveal the natural goodness and even piety of Jupiter's final phase at its best. Another feature is the trusting innocence often observed at this phase.

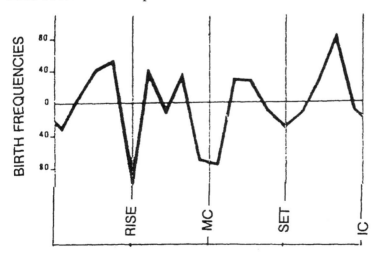

Fig. 46 The distribution of Jupiter for the characteristics of the typical writer.

Saturn

Jupiter and Saturn have always been regarded as opposite and complementary factors in astrology. Jupiter represents growth and expansion, Saturn limitation and consolidation. These two principles must work side by side in all life-processes; Jupiter by itself would be like a balloon, swelling and swelling until it lost not only all substantiality but, indeed, all sense of identity or sameness and permanence; Saturn by itself would ossify, losing the capacity for growth, change and adaptation.

Jupiter *by itself* always represents growth but we have just seen, in examining the 4th harmonic of that planet, how there can be a purely Jupiter cycle: it must be a cycle which fosters first *outward* growth (while the inner development 'lies fallow' as it were) and then *inner* growth (while the outward life ceases to be the focus of attention).

Complementary to this the cycle of Saturn seeks (in psychological terms) to ordinate, consolidate, define and make secure alternately the inner and then the outer life.

In the sequence of phases, Jupiter starts off full of self-confidence, drains the cup of worldly experience and success, is sated, turns to the inner life, expands its vision of underlying realities and returns to the world to actualise that vision.

Saturn, on the other hand, begins at phase one (which like that of Mars starts *at* the angle - see Figure 42) with the extreme of self-doubt and isolation. At phase two it begins to discover itself through service and the assumption of responsibilities. At phase three the ego-consciousness reaches its strongest; there is ambition, self-confidence, a degree of worldly status and a developing sense of power. Phase four is concerned with the way in which that power is used and sustained.

Phase One (Figure 47a)

Indicated characteristics: *Deep, Solemn, Solitary, Religious, Scrupulous, Worthy, Noble, Reflective, Independent, Cold, Severe.* (790 applications)

The characteristics thrown up at this first phase of Saturn's 4th harmonic give an almost perfect description of the classical idea of Saturn. This is Milton's 'Il Penseroso', Durer's 'Melancholia' and many another fabled embodiment of Saturn. Lest the qualities should appear too chilling one should add that the multiple count method also yields, for example, *faithful* and *gentle* both of which can be true qualities of the type, especially the former.

At this phase Saturn tends to be deeply introverted; it seeks to know the foundations of its being by looking within. In worldly terms it tends to be indifferent to success and is frequently called upon to endure deprivation of some sort (financial, affectional). Some degree of isolation or feeling of isolation is likewise a feature of the phase.

It is as if the native of this phase must be driven back from all dependence upon outward things and made to see wherein his selfhood really lies and wherein his true security is to be found. It tends to be borne in upon him that his wisest and safest recourse is to the strict path of duty.

Phase Two (Figure 47b)

Indicated characteristics: *Cultivates friendships, Generous, Frank, Common sense, Good, Natural, Devoted, Humorous, Popular, Imaginative.* (1189 applications)

This is the most attractive phase of Saturn's 4th harmonic. As the sense of duty leads to the assumption of responsibilities and the entering into bonds of service and mutual affection, there is a thawing of the winter of self-doubt, and the deep sense of restraint gives place first to simplicity and modesty and then to an increasing measure of warmth which can afford, by degrees, to be open, generous and natural, whilst the sense of humour is enlisted to help ward off the slings and arrows of outrageous fortune.

It is as if the person with Saturn in phase one had asked: 'How do I know that I exist until I have produced an effect?' At phase two the effects begin to be produced; modest recognition and acknowledgement by others is the result and in this recognition and, ultimately, friendship the native begins to know himself and to believe in his capacities. Thus, all through this phase there is a steadily growing self-confidence but one which is not yet too sure of itself.

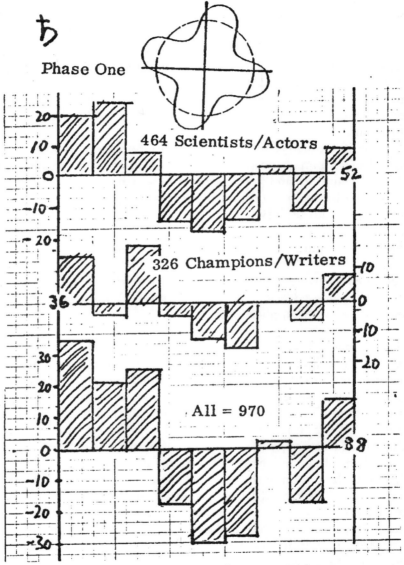

1. Deep, Solemn, Solitary, Rigorous, Scrupulous, Worthy, Noble, Reflective, Independent, Cold, Severe

Fig. 47a Saturn, phase One of the fourth harmonic.

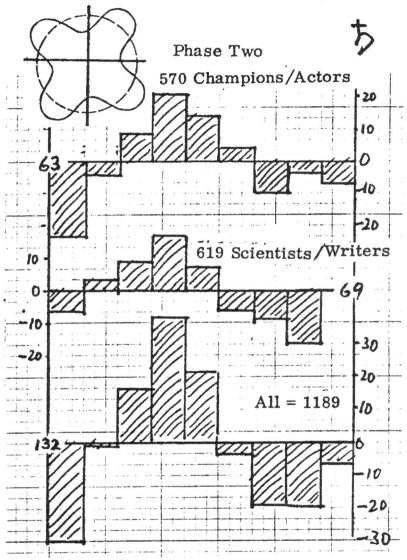

Phase Two
570 Champions/Actors

619 Scientists/Writers

All = 1189

2. Generous, Frank, Common sense, Friendships, Good, Natural, Humorous, Devoted, Popular, Imaginative

Fig. 47b Saturn, phase Two of the fourth harmonic.

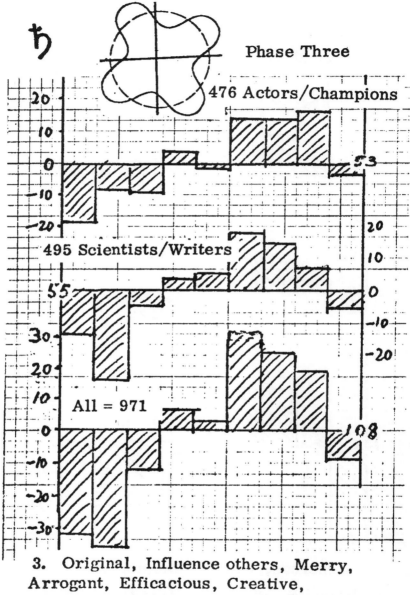

Phase Three

476 Actors/Champions

495 Scientists/Writers

All = 971

3. Original, Influence others, Merry,
Arrogant, Efficacious, Creative,
Ambitious, Seductive, Smiling, Self-willed,
Hon. Distinctions

Fig. 47c Saturn, phase Three of the fourth harmonic.

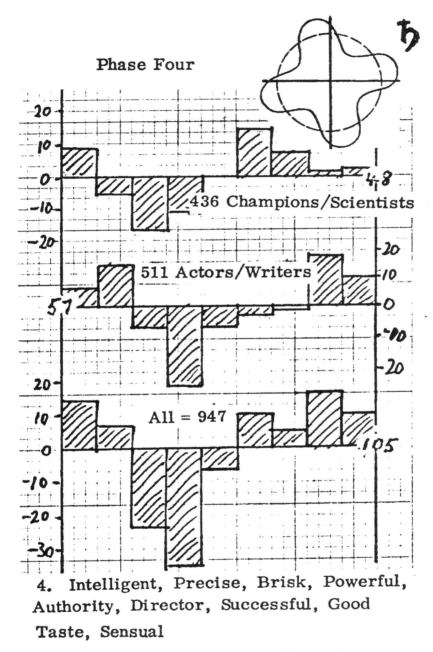

Phase Four

436 Champions/Scientists

511 Actors/Writers

All = 947

4. Intelligent, Precise, Brisk, Powerful, Authority, Director, Successful, Good Taste, Sensual

Fig. 47d Saturn, phase Four of the fourth harmonic.

Phase Three (Figure 47c)

Indicated characteristics: *Original, Creative, Efficacious, Ambitious, Self-willed, Arrogant, Influences others, Smiling, Seductive, Merry, Honourable, Distinctions.* (971 applications)

The impulse to make one's mark, to assert one's identity and to be assured, as it were, that one is a unique individual with a unique contribution to make to society - the impulse born in the self-doubt of phase one and fostered in the dawning realisation in phase two, that the world is not entirely hostile and might be influenced, 'won over' and controlled by persistent effort - this impulse is here carried to its logical conclusion. The self-assurance swells, the powers of effective action are released (*original, creative, efficacious*) and those with Saturn in phase three must reach out for the highest, asserting themselves to the utmost *(ambitious, self-willed, arrogant, smiling, seductive)*.

We have said before, but it is worth repeating, that no planetary phase is 'better' than another; each has its virtues and vices, each plays a necessary part in the unfoldment of soul-life. If it were not necessary for the soul to have contact with objective reality and to seek to master it and assert its authority over it there would be no need for the principle of body. Thus this phase of Saturn's 4th simply represents the ineradicable impulse innate in each person to establish a degree of mastery over his own proper sphere of influence.

There is evidently some tendency in the latter part of this phase and the next to become the heavy authority, verging towards the overbearing, especially (perhaps because of other harmonics) in the north-east quadrant.

Phase Four (Figure 47d)

Indicated characteristics: *Intelligent, Precise, Brisk, Powerful, Authority, Director, Successful, Good Taste, Sensual.* (947 applications)

This is the phase of Saturn's 4th which is associated with the high places of worldly power and responsibility. As a result of the preceding phases Saturn is here invested with the full measure of authority due to him. He has borne responsibilities, exercised self-control, and probably acquired wealth and now, for good or ill, in phase four he must exercise the power he has won. If his intentions have been ordinate he will probably sustain his authority with dignity, carry his responsibilities faithfully and with intelligence and wield his power justly and with restraint. He will tend to experience the loneliness of the long-distance runner or the isolation of the man at the top and, because worldly power is given an added dimension by the element of, or the semblance of, spiritual power, it is a phase which (if the nativities of popes and cardinals we have are reliable) is often associated with high ecclesiastical office. Indeed, there is evidence to be found in Gauquelin's results which suggests that this phase of Saturn's 4th tends to be a feature of the priestly vocation generally; at least this is evidently the conclusion to be drawn from Figure 48 which shows (after Gauquelin) the distribution of Saturn in the nativities of 884 priests collected in France. The phase four emphasis in this distribution is clear. These priests would be born in the nineteenth century in a Catholic country at a time when a greater measure of influence and power (and perhaps a more rigid self-control) were associated with the life of the priest. (Michel Gauquelin mentioned to me that this distribution was not very clearly confirmed by nativities of priests collected in other European countries, the emphasis shifting in the direction of phase one. I have not seen the figures but this is what one might expect with the shift to more protestant countries.)

Where wealth or power has been achieved as a result of greed or inordinate ambition or self-aggrandizement, a phase four Saturn verges towards miserliness or tyranny (Hitler and Mussolini had this position), and this of course produces the situation where the native is shunned or isolated again at the start of phase one.

One may notice in passing that even where wealth or power has been well-earned there is often the inclination as well as the means to indulge a taste for the refinements of good living (*sensual, good taste*) and this may apply to ecclesiastics no less than others.

And so we see again, with this harmonic as with others, that each harmonic is based upon a specific circle of psychological experience. Each such cycle tends to manifest in practice as a spiral of upward progress. In the case of Saturn, at the end of phase four a situation has been reached when either the soul, through selfishness, has failed to learn the lessons of this Saturn cycle and ends, shunned and isolated, to start again at phase one in a condition of deprivation, or, if the lessons of true service and self-giving have been learned,

responsibilities faithfully borne and duties discharged, then at the end
of the cycle there is a more or less inevitable enlargement of the
sphere of service. Promotion. ("Thou has been faithful over a few
things; I will make thee ruler over many things."). But when this
happens and a new and larger sphere is entered upon, whatever it
may be, one is back at phase one in the position of the "new boy"
with the consequent feelings of uncertainty and isolation at the
beginning of a new cycle.

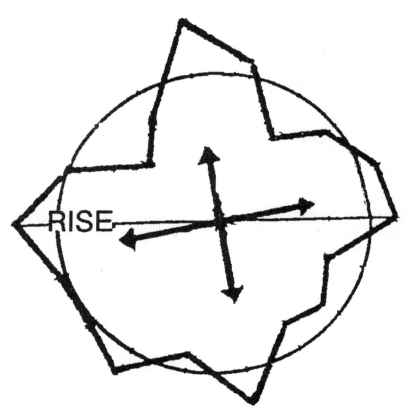

Fig. 48 The distribution of Saturn in the nativities of 884 French
priests, showing the strong fourth phase orientation. After
Gauquelin.

The Moon[†]

There is a tendency, so far as the testimony of the poets is concerned, to equate the Moon with womankind and to discover in both an element of paradox, inconsistency or variability. No doubt there is in fact the same consistency here as elsewhere but it is evidently one in which the emotional nature (itself a fluctuating force) plays an important part.

But whatever the explanation it is true that we do find contradictions and paradoxes in the lunar spectrum and with this in mind it is worth adopting a slightly different procedure with the moon, giving a fuller list of traits for each phase so as to communicate as much of the flavour of each phase as possible.

In a general way there appear to be two principal poles in our spectrum, one at roughly phase 75°, the other at about 255° and this of course means that we cannot begin phase one exactly at the angle. On the strength of the empirical evidence, we need to begin phase one about 5° or 10° past the angle. (We have constructed our lists of traits starting 10° past the angle - phase 40 - but it may be that 7.5° would be better - see Figure 49.)

Fig. 49 The phases of the Moon's fourth harmonic.

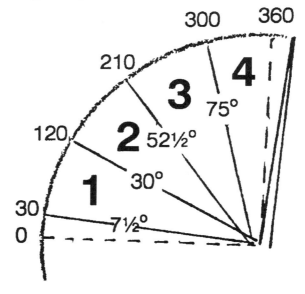

Phase One (Phase 40-130)

Indicated characteristics: *Amiable, Lively, Youthful, Spirited, Bold, Imaginative, Fancy(ful), Moving, Lyrical, Pure, Light, Tranquil, Wise, Solemn, Philosopher, Eccentric, Member of a Group.*

In order to understand this somewhat assorted list of characteristics, one might consider the word *youthful* which scores very highly indeed. The word seems innocuous enough and at first sight not very revealing, yet there is something in this phase of the Eternal Student. One may think, perhaps, of the characters in Puccini's *La Boheme*: at one time *lively, amiable, spirited,* and *bold,* at another the *wise* and *solemn philosopher,* at another the *lyricist, pure* and *tranquil, imaginative* and *fanciful,* and all this with a touch of *eccentricity* and (since these are characteristics which thrive on an audience or at least call for a few boon companions) *'in a group'.*

One cannot, it might be supposed, go through life playing such a role (although, indeed, this *is* the typical lunar phase of the actor) yet for those with the Moon in phase one, the inner life, inner values, the world of the imagination, of vision, of truth in art, all remain important and far more 'real' than the world of everyday experience. It is a phase of the Moon's 4th which is common to writers and artists of all kinds and indeed of all who seek the emotional truth.

But one has only to reflect that this phase (notably the very beginning of it, see Figure 50) is the lunar phase of the politician to realise that those who seek the emotional truth have only got *their own* emotions to go on, and in fact politicians of all parties show the same tendency to this lunar position. Considering what emotions are roused by politics (especially in the breast of the Eternal Student) we should have no difficulty in understanding that politicians like poets really are motivated by emotions aroused by their visions of a better world and more abundant life for the people, and that it is only their subsequent contact with the harsh realities of office that gives rise, in a quite secondary way, to that appearance of cynical expediency which is widely believed to be characteristic of politicians. (Anyone who thinks that politicians have nothing in common with poets and the writers of imaginative fiction has probably never read a party manifesto; it is only policies that are dictated by Saturn.)

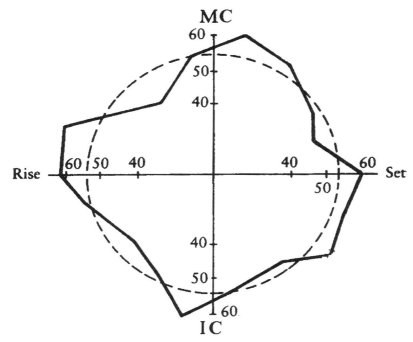

Fig. 50 The distribution of the Moon in the nativities of 993 politicians. From *Les Hommes et les Astres*, Gauquelin.

There may be a few degrees difference along our spectrum of qualities between the politician and the poet, but the essential visionary characteristic is the same in both, and this should bring it home to us that however eloquent or moving either may be, it is only in the degree that the emotions have been universalised or otherwise brought into conformity with reason that great art or truthful rhetoric will be produced; in the degree that they have not, only some kind of special pleading can result. As with our earlier planetary examples all four groups of 'professional' data show the same result for this and the other lunar phases, but for the sake of variety we will show the distribution of the moon for these (phase one) characteristics in contrast with those for phase three given later and this is shown in Figure 51.

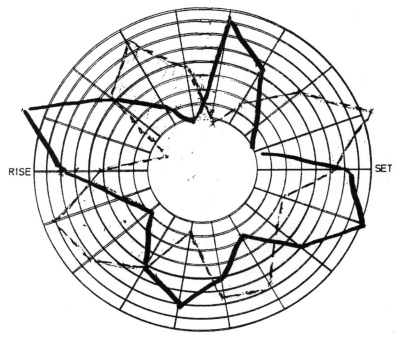

Fig. 51 The first and third phases of the Moon's fourth harmonic; the first phase characteristics are plotted by the bold line, the third phase by the lighter line.

Phase Two (Phase 130-220)

Indicated characteristics: *Courteous, Temperate, Elegant, Worthy, Cultured, Good Taste, Careful, Benevolent, Likes Family Life, Methodical, Organiser, Shy, Simple, Reflective, Skilful, Chaste.*

There is a rather telling gap in our spectrum between about phase 110 and 150 (not a total blank but only a few traits) and this is hardly surprising, for a striking change takes place in this interval, from the idealistic preoccupations and relaxed gregariousness of phase one to the restrained orderliness of phase two.

This is a somewhat 'low-keyed' phase; the love of beauty of phase one now verges towards *elegance, good taste, culture* and *courtesy, shy, simple* and *temperate*; this phase is said to *like family life*, yet one suspects that it is the home more than the family which is enjoyed, for the native of this phase is evidently better at dealing with inanimate things (such as furnishings) than animate ones (such as children). These people are *skilful, careful, methodical and good organisers*; very capable, one suspects, in the office and in business routine generally where the quiet, practical good sense is valued. Typically the native of this phase is orderly in conduct and appearance, well-groomed and with the emotions under firm control (*temperate, chaste, careful*). (A good example of the Moon in this phase might be Coco Chanel: "For forty years the Chanel suit has been a world-wide symbol of classic fashion . . .. Timeless simplicity was the trademark of her enduring style . . ..").[6]

Phase Three (Phase 220-310)

Indicated characteristics: *Courageous, Passionate, Hardworking, Director, Animates others, Influences others, Steadfast, Tenacious, Independent, Industrious, Combative, Self-willed, Cold, Powerful, Silent, Secretive, Solitary.*

This highly formidable list of characteristics can leave no doubt as to the forcefulness of the Moon in this position. It is one which has a very vivid realisation of the requirements of practical affairs and much drive and determination in implementing them. There is usually a grasp of financial matters and an interest therein.

Needless to say for most people this phase does not manifest in any extreme form but if we want to look for the 'type' we might feel it was represented by the tycoon or captain of industry - powerful, hardworking, tenacious and often something of a loner (*secretive, solitary*), or - a more extreme manifestation - the gangster, powerful, cold and ruthless (for example, John Dillinger, Clyde Barrow).[7] But these are extremes: the essential point is the realistic grasp of affairs, the thoroughgoing approach to the conduct of mundane life and the tendency to assess situations with the head rather than with the feelings. (The position tends to be characteristic of thinkers generally.) But the talent is for handling things, events and processes rather than ideas or people (as people). It is the polar opposite of phase one, which is liable to be kind-hearted, idealistic, sociable and impractical. The distribution of the Moon for the two types of characteristic is shown in Figure 51.

Phase Four (Phase 310-40)

Indicated characteristics: *Frank, Personality, Sensitive, Verve, Clear, Quiet Hobbies, Ironic, Violent, Popular, Stubborn, Abundant.*

This phase, which occurs for about 15° before the Moon reaches the angle and for 5° or so afterwards, presents us with another curious mixture of qualities. It retains some of the strength and directness of phase three but has become more sensitive and the inner life stronger. The emotional nature is intensified during this phase and so is liable at times to go out of control and even erupt violently. It is the phase, I believe, which exhibits the strong lunar sense of the needs of living things and is very, one might say, life-orientated.

One way in which one can assess the nature of a particular phase when, as in this case, one has fewer traits than usual on which to form a judgement, is to contrast it with the opposite phase. Phase two, as we have seen, is well-ordered, even demure, the emotions well-contained, elegant, temperate, chaste. Well, then, we may be sure that phase four will incline in the opposite direction. Often the natives of this phase seem to be "bursting out all over"; they can be exuberant (Lee Trevino), roistering (Henry Miller), outrageous (Salvador Dali), overflowing (Proust), vital (Marilyn Monroe) or, in a different way, they may exhibit a sort of rough-diamond quality which is more concerned with helping living things to flourish than with observing the conventional niceties (Albert Schweitzer). It is also evidently the phase of the champion of feminism (Betty Friedan, Germaine Greer, Emily Pankhurst et al).[7]

There is a well-recognised lunar type, the Scots nanny, firm but kindly, whom one might associate with this phase, the firmness being more marked the nearer the Moon to phase three, the kindliness more in evidence as it nears the angle. After the angle it sometimes seems to slide into eccentricity. (Even as one writes, visions arise of Margaret Rutherford[8] in stage or screen roles as a slightly dotty nanny or governess or even headmistress of St Trinians.)

Again the characteristic *abundant* is signalled very strongly on the border of this phase and phase one, and seems to express that element of fertility and abundance of life which can be so characteristic of the Moon in this position. It can be a very maternal phase and also one which is deeply interested in human nature and its needs, and not in an academic way but wanting to "get involved" and to help in some way - which beings us back to the politician who means so well by mankind and so often finds that good intentions are not enough.

Before leaving the Moon it is interesting to observe how often we find, in the lunar spectra, words which are used of the Moon itself (*pure, chaste, clear, silent, secret, lucid, brilliant, cold, light, abundant or fertile*) or which are used in relation to watery surfaces (*tranquil, reflective*) or which refer to the image-forming capacity so often attributed to the moon, to water and to silver[9] (*imaginative, fancy*).

This brings us to the end of our survey of the 4th harmonic. It should not be necessary to emphasise that when one is dealing with such broad categories the scope for variations within the type is very great and there will often be cases where the distinctive character of a planet in a particular phase of the 4th is largely lost because of countervailing factors; nevertheless, when the life is seen as a whole the effect will usually be discernible.

CHAPTER VIII - NOTES

1   *The Geometry of Meaning* by Arthur Young, Delacorte Press/Seymour Lawrence, USA, has some useful reflections on the four phases as principles.

2   Sometimes there are more than ten or twelve characteristics indicated for a given phase and this is particularly true of the 4th harmonic, but the work of compiling the distributions is tedious, hence - since the choice of one word rather than another at a specific phase in the spectrum usually makes no significant difference to the result (since all words at that point in the spectrum will, by definition, yield the same wort of distribution) - the decision to keep the list of typical characteristics to ten or twelve.   When it is necessary to omit words from the spectrum in compiling the graph, I normally omit (1) words of weaker amplitude, (2) characteristics which are already well represented by other words, (3) words which are least revealing, eg 'middle class', 'lecturer' etc. Occasionally there are fewer than ten words available (although not in the 4th) and sometimes there are too few words to form a reasonable empirical judgement of the nature of a particular phase.

3 The nativities of Churchill, Adenauer and De Gaspari are given in *The American Book of Charts* by Lois Rodden, Pub: Astrocomputing Services, San Diego, Ca USA, that of De Gaulle in *Fowler's Compendium of Nativities* by Jadwiga Harrison, Pub: L N Fowler & Co, UK.

4 The introduction of sports champions, as such, into this debate is a red herring much beloved of those who wish to belittle or obscure Gauquelin's work. The true category identified by Gauquelin is *not* sports champions but those who possess certain forceful characteristics. So little has the "Mars effect" to do with sports champions as such that it is only by going to the most extreme lengths of taking the cream of the cream among sporting high achievers that Gauquelin can be sure of getting a significant showing of the appropriate forceful characteristics in a collection of nativities which are not specifically collected on the basis of the true category.

When Gauquelin can leave sports champions behind and collect nativities on the basis of the *true* category (ie those displaying a high degree of assertiveness) then it will not matter whether his subjects are sports champions, pastry cooks or undertakers - the "Mars effect" will be equally present.

5 Carter CEO, *The Astrological Aspects*, L N Fowler & Co, UK.

6 The quotation is from Lois Rodden in her comment on Coco Chanel in *Profiles of Women*, Pub: American Federation of Astrologers.

7 The charts of Dillinger, Trevino, H Miller, Proust and Schweitzer are given in *The American Book of Charts*, Lois Rodden. Those for Munroe, Friedan, Greer and Pankhurst in *Profiles of Women* by the same author, and Barrow and Dali are to be found in *The Circle Book of Charts* by Stephen Erlewine, all published USA.

8 I know of no chart for Margaret Rutherford; the reference is intended only to illustrate a type.

9 In *The Seven Metals* (Astrological Journal, Autumn 1980) Nick Kollerstrom brings out well the 'lunar' characteristics of silver.

CHAPTER IX

Some Metaphysical Implications

"The Certainties of Science are a delusion. They are hedged around with unexplored limitations. Our handling of scientific doctrines is controlled by the diffused metaphysical concepts of our epoch. Even so, we are continually led into errors of expectation. Also whenever some new mode of observational experience is obtained the old doctrines crumble into a fog of inaccuracies."

A N Whitehead: Adventures of Ideas

"If we look ahead it is already possible to say that Astrology seems destined to lead all other branches of knowledge out of the blind alley of unspiritual rationalism and materialism . . . and effect the reconciliation that Science so ardently desires with Belief. Such a development is essential if we are to survive the present spiritual crisis which threatens western culture with eventual disaster."

Prof Dr L Cunibert Mohlberg of the Vatican Institute of Christian Archaeology in "Candi's Letters to Tschu"

Although it may seem at first sight that the results set out in the foregoing Section and the discoveries implicit in them have a limited applicability in the scientific field, yet it will be found upon deeper acquaintance that they have a radical bearing upon the whole background of scientific thought.

The reason why astrology is rejected so uncompromisingly by orthodox science is not because it has been subjected to an impartial scientific examination and judged in the light of the results. It is rejected *prima facie* because it is seen to be fundamentally at variance with certain widely accepted scientific concepts. If astrology is true then some of the *basic assumptions* of empirical science are false.

"What mustn't be true, can't be true": this is the logic which inspires the vehement rejection of astrology in scientific circles.

The enormous confidence which Science places in the validity of its results and in the scientific world-view which it has built up, springs from the special and admirable methods of scientific enquiry which it has evolved and with which we are all now so familiar: theorising is dangerous, ideas about the nature of things must be rigorously compared with the observed facts, and techniques of extracting the truth from these facts must be refined and perfected.

So far, so good; but it will be observed that the repudiation of astrology by modern science is consequent upon an *abandonment* of these very methods which it has found so reliable and developed to such good purpose, and an *embracing* of that very tendency to make theoretical assumptions which it professes to hold in abhorrence. Had it turned its powers and resources to an imaginative *investigation* of astrology, science would have had literally no difficulty at all in discovering the truth about it!

It is an outstanding illustration of how all scientific enquiry is conditioned by the framework of subconscious metaphysical assumptions in the mind of the scientist.

One thing must be made absolutely clear at the outset of this section: there is no disparagement here of the positive content of modern science: what it has established upon a secure foundation, what it has truly accomplished along its own lines and in its own proper fields of enquiry - these things are not called into question, and the use already made of statistical techniques testifies to our respect for these.

It is the things which science has ignored to which attention is being drawn and which form the subject of this section.

As we saw in chapter II, philosophy recognises in a general sense four species of cause: final, formal, efficient and material. The final cause is the end or purpose for which a thing exists; the formal cause is the idea or formative principle of which it is the embodiment; the efficient cause is that which actually produces or gives rise to its existence (the means by which the formal cause is implemented); and the material cause is that out of which it is made.[1]

Although in the strict sense each of these species of cause may be said to have an inner and outer aspect, yet it is also true in a general sense that final and formal causes are more interior, and efficient and material causes more exterior.

At the time of the Renaissance the forerunners of the present empirical tradition in Science carefully cut truth in half. They decided to keep efficient and material causes because the criteria of proof in these fields were deemed by them to be more accessible and real, being based upon sense perceptions and facts, and they decided (because they were in reaction against the excesses of rationalism of the later Middle Ages) to throw away formal and final causes, deeming the criteria of reason by which these causes are known and demonstrated to be less certain than those of the senses.

The story is taken up by A N Whitehead in a chapter entitled 'The Origins of Modern Science' in his *"Science and the Modern World"* -

> "Science has never shaken off the impress of its origin in the historical revolt of the later Renaissance. It has remained predominantly an anti-rationalistic movement, based upon a naive faith . . ..
>
> "Of course, the historical revolt was fully justified. It was wanted. It was more than wanted: it was an absolute necessity for healthy progress . . . but it was not a protest on behalf of reason.[2]
>
> "There is however a Nemesis which waits upon those who deliberately avoid avenues of knowledge. Oliver Cromwell's cry echoes down the ages: 'My brethren, by the bowels of Christ I beseech you, bethink you that you may be mistaken.'"

To begin by cutting truth in half and throwing away the dominant and regulative half is not a good basis for arriving at a knowledge of the causes of things. Yet this is what empirical science did. But when it threw away formal and final causes generally, it threw away the Great Formal Cause; the concept of a Divine Order and Harmony and Justice as overshadowing and formative forces in the world. It was left to other institutions and to the ingrained instincts and intuitions of ordinary men and women (including, for the most part, scientists themselves when they had closed the doors of their laboratories) to keep alive these concepts.

But, scientists may protest, it was not our function to deal with ideas of this sort; such matters belong to the field of religion. But this is not true. It is the office of science to preserve, cultivate and expound *truth*, and every aspect of truth has its appropriate science, interior and spiritual aspects of truth no less than exterior and natural ones; and if science neglects some of these avenues of knowledge then erroneous action follows upon partial knowledge and a disordered society results.

If the neglected avenues of knowledge are such that in effect a half of the whole sphere of truth is denied, so that all sciences are cut off from their sources in the subjective and super-sensible orders, and if this denial is reiterated and perpetuated through a number of generations, only such education being provided for the young as upholds, tacitly or explicitly, this schism in the sphere of thought, then the inevitable result is a society in which the young grow up to find themselves in a world divided into two camps. As with individuals so with societies: if there is incoherence within, there will be incoherence without.

With what difficulty are men brought to a perception of the origins of their disorders!

How is this rift to be healed?

Of course, the healing process has already started; everywhere the hard shells of scientific materialism are breaking open as they fail to contain any longer the new ideas now germinating in men's minds. Nevertheless the old concepts still dominate everyday life and the established institutions of the day.

In the last resort, it is the office of ideal philosophy to remake the world; it alone can restore order and set all things in their proper places.

But at present the world is deaf to this voice. What is needed is some kind of knowledge which will at least open men's minds to the kind of solution which is required and the direction in which it is to be sought - and which can speak to both sides of the present impasse in terms which each can understand and acknowledge to be valid: to Science in terms of the quantitative analysis of scientific data; to Religion in the language of spiritual philosophy - the language of those timeless truths which the mystical philosopher has expounded from age to age.

It is the writer's conviction that astrology occupies, in this context, a unique position and is the science par excellence which is adapted to fulfil this reconciling role. It would not be the first time that the stone rejected by the builder had become the head of the corner.

From time immemorial, astrology has stood between heaven and earth - between the spiritual and temporal orders. The true astrologer inclines neither to the exclusive contemplation of the inner world of first causes, nor to the excessive pre-occupation with the outward world of effects, but turns from the one to the other, allotting to each its place, interpreting the former to the latter, and striving to ordinate the latter in the light of his vision of the former.

When true astrology is distinguished from its accretions and distortions and when the history of this science is known and viewed without prejudice, it is to be seen that the high-watermarks of astrology are the high-watermarks of civilisation itself, when the inner and outer aspects of truth attained for a time a condition of balance in men's minds and rendered human life and thought fruitful.

It is a curious and perhaps seldom noticed fact that the great changes in the currents of human thought are often marked at their outset by a change in man's beliefs about the stars. It is as if his concentration upon things proximate and mundane rendered him forgetful of the larger realities of his station, but that a sudden new vision of the calm plenitude of cosmic life brought him again to a recollection of the verities of his estate.

> Mysterious Night! When our first parent knew
> Thee from report divine, and heard thy name,
> Did he not tremble for this lovely frame.
> This glorious canopy of light and blue?
> Yet neath a curtain of translucent dew,
> Bathed in the rays of the great setting flame,
> Hesperus with the host of heaven came,
> And lo! Creation widened to man's view.[3]

It is at these moments, when man's vision suddenly expands to take in new perspectives - the nodal points, as it were, of the great rhythms of human thought and civilisation - that the astrologer is liable to appear briefly[4] and often it would seem symbolically (one remembers a visitation at Bethlehem) upon the terrestrial stage, a representative of the perennial philosophy and the perennial religion, to join one age to another and all things to heaven.

The need to restore heaven and earth to one another in present day life is clear and urgent. "The unleashed power of the atom", wrote Einstein, "has changed everything except the way men think." *This is precisely what one would expect. Physical discoveries bring physical changes - it is metaphysical discoveries which change the way men think.*

In this sense, the rediscovery of the true principles of astrology, with their vast potentialities, by the scientific world, will prove of infinitely greater importance and be productive of much more far-reaching consequences than the discovery of atomic energy. Those who have not contemplated the potentialities of this science can have no conception of the revolution which its re-introduction into the scientific field will have. *Today the difficulty is to persuade men of its truth; tomorrow the difficulty will be to persuade them to keep a sense of proportion about it.*

But just as the initial effect of the discoveries of the Renaissance was a liberating one but their subsequent effects enslaving because they led to an excessive emphasis upon external aspects of truth, so the initial effect of the re-discovery of astrological principles is liable to be an enslaving one, because of attempts to misapply them by the remnants of a materialistic age[5] but their subsequent result will be liberating because of the ordinating effect upon the world of thought of the underlying concepts upon which astrology must inevitably be seen to stand.

The re-assimilation by science of the truths implicit in such results as those described earlier *can have one end, and one end only*: the reunification of the entire field of science so that all possible objects of knowledge, from the heights to the depths, from the innermost recesses of deity to the last and most transient of phenomena, are seen to coalesce in one perfect scheme of truth entire and seamless from first to last: all sciences rooted in the First Science; all causes in the First Cause; all lives in the First Life; all substances in the First Substance.

If it should be objected that too great an emphasis is being attached to the part which astrology can play in effecting this reunification of thought, it must be emphasised again that astrology is not here envisaged as usurping the role of other disciplines but that it is accorded this importance because it is so precisely fitted to the needs of the present situation as demonstrating the indivisibility of two different orders of truth which have become wrongly sundered, and as providing the means whereby the sharp and admirable instruments contrived by modern science can themselves be turned to the destruction of the false elements in that same science.

The changes in scientific thought of which we have been speaking will, as we have tried to indicate, be consequent upon the restoration of formal and final causes (but especially formal) to their proper places in the world of thought. Let us examine more closely the bearing of astrology upon this issue.

Aristotle taught that there are ten ways in which existences express themselves; ten ways, that is, in which the characteristics of things are communicated to us. These are according to their substance, quality, quantity, relation, place, time, condition, situation, activity and passivity. One is aware that these ten categories have been roughly handled by some commentators but they remain, for the mystical philosopher, a complete integral and sequential scheme, revealing the manifest symbolic attributes of things, from their most *intrinsic* characteristic in substance to their most *extrinsic* in passivity.

The astrologer starts as it were in the middle of this scheme, working *backwards* from the symbolism of time (to which the symbolism of place is intimately related) to draw inferences about qualities and substances, and again *forwards* to predict the character of the activity and passivity of things, what they will do and what will be done to them, which are their most extrinsic attributes.

In this sense astrology takes as its immediate object of study *the symbolism of time*. Thus Prof Tomaschek in the article quoted on p. 253 says that from the astrological viewpoint celestial phenomena may best be considered as "qualitative functions of time and space". It is this same idea which was extended by Jung (who fully accepted the astrological position) into the much-quoted dictum: "Whatever is born or done at this moment of time has the qualities of this moment of time."

But Time has no symbolism *in its own right* and moments of time do not have qualities *in their own right*. Qualities depend upon substance and substance depends upon a subjective union of being, life and intelligence. Thus it is Proclus' definition of Time as "the measure of the lives and motions of the cosmos" which has special relevance for us. In this sense astrology is the study of the influences of the lives of the cosmos one upon another and especially of the great primary lives (the "first-born thoughts of God") upon the lesser lives. In this sense astrology may be properly considered as the Larger Biology.

But again Plato's definition of Time as "an everlasting flowing image of Eternity" takes the issue a step further for this implies that the lives of the cosmos are vehicles of Eternal Ideas; that what is *spread out* in time and space has a *unitive subsistence* beyond time and space; that the endless chain of efficient causes and effects in time is unfolded in accordance with a body of formal causes; that the evolutionary process is, as the word implies, an unfolding of something within; that the Dancers in the Great Dance perform their steps to a certain Music which they hear and, even, that behind the Dance and the Music there is a Great Choreographer and Musician.

At this point one may refer to the problem which confronts those who find it entirely credible that, say, the Moon's position might have a *current* effect upon rainfall or even perhaps upon human glandular systems,[6] or that current planetary tensions in the solar system could produce electromagnetic and suchlike disturbances which might, in some roundabout way, trigger off earthquakes and so on, but who nevertheless find it impossible to accept the implications of such a concept as the doctrine of nativities which postulates a relationship, not between *current* terrestrial phenomena and *current* celestial phenomena, but between current and future terrestrial events and celestial phenomena at a past moment in time: in this case the moment of birth.

But such a possibility is a necessary corollary of the recognition of the dominance of formal over efficient causes, for in accordance with this relationship, actual events move in harmony with *both* these orders of causation; with the efficient proximately, with the formal at one step removed, so that sometimes the actual and palpable efficient cause seems to be the significant causal factor (as would be the case with the phenomena mooted in the first half of the previous paragraph) whereas at other times the action of efficient causes is lost to view as they slip from the strictly natural into the cryptic order,[7] so that the perceptive observer is left to infer, from a scrutiny of events, the role of formal causes set in motion by the higher order of soul which is the true order of action.

In this sense the chain of circumstances which leads up to the moment of birth, its outward and efficient causes, appear, like so much else in the mundane world, to be merely haphazard and fortuitous. But we have seen in the foregoing results that the moment of birth *has* relevance to the characteristics of the person born despite the fact that these are clearly determined before birth. Of course, we have taken as our object of study a temperamental susceptibility to a certain disease (poliomyelitis) as related to one single celestial factor (the sun's longitude) at the time of birth, and this by itself is perhaps not adapted to show the relationship we speak of in such simple, obvious and clear-cut terms as other features which might be taken.

The phenomenon of red hair, for example, has been used to illustrate the point. This is sufficiently obvious and just sufficiently unusual to provide a clear-cut test. The horoscopic indices of red hair are known in a general way and *could* theoretically be formulated with a fair degree of precision; further, they commonly depend upon quite small changes in the passage of time. But the fact that a person shall have red hair is physically determined long before birth and presumably at conception. Yet the phenomenon is clearly shown in the natus. This can only mean one thing - *that there are forces at work which attract, as it were, the birth to an appropriate symbolic moment in time* - like attracting like.

One sometimes hears the question asked: How can the hour of my birth possibly affect what I am? The answer of course is that it does not - it is what one is that affects the time of birth.

To digress, one might add that what is being said here of the Aristotelian category of Time applies equally to the other categories. One may illustrate the point by reference to the category of quality. The qualities are the manifold symbolic shapes, colours, sounds, smells etc with which substances clothe themselves. Thus each person has a characteristic bodily conformation, carriage, colouring, voice and so on, and it is a common - might one not say a universal? - assumption that these corporeal qualities tell us something about their owner - that in fact there is some sort of correspondence between the outward appearance and the inner disposition.

The standpoint of orthodox science constantly places it in the position of having to postulate that it is the corporeal which comes first and that the aforementioned correspondence arises because men are conditioned in their behaviour by the physical. But this standpoint is evidently at variance with that of ordinary men and women who take it for granted that the physical attributes *express* the nature of something which subsists prior to the corporeal and has an altogether superior reality to it.

Just as it is asked: How can my time of birth affect what I am? - so one might ask: How can my body make me what I am? The answer is the same in both cases: they do not; it is the other way about.

The things, events and conditions of time and space have their formal causes outside time and space; the processes of efficient causation which we behold taking place in the phenomenal world are mere mechanisms whereby formal causes are implemented.[8]

Thus, to return to the time of birth, the fact that all kinds of evidently chance factors, medical decisions and so on, appear to affect the moment of birth is totally irrelevant, and indeed illusory - this is the chain of efficient causes in time which is, in reality, overshadowed by a body of formal causes above Time.

This body of formal causes is, in its inner, unitive and spiritual aspect called Providence and in its outer, multiplex, natural and cryptic aspect called Fate. *Fate is simply the name given to the body of laws by which appropriate actions are connected to appropriate effects (however remote) in the world.* If it were not for them the mundane order would be a chaos and it would not be possible to feel any confidence that any course of action would lead to the kind of effects which it was sought to accomplish.

The laws of the cryptic order are, as we have indicated, based upon processes of occult attraction and repulsion whereby the downward-tending life forces tend to clothe themselves in appropriate manifest forms.[9] Thus the symbolism of the moment of birth does not depend primarily upon celestial "influences" but simply upon the attraction of like to like, the incarnating soul being drawn into time at a moment when conditions are like itself and to a mundane vehicle which accords with its own nature and purposes.

Thus Simplicius[10] says that the astrologer judges the character and purposes of the soul from an examination of the nativity just as one tells from the examination of the tools which a man uses what trade he follows and even, in some measure, his degree of skill . . . "for the most skilful workmen use the most delicate tools". He continues in a passage which is worth quoting at length:

" . . . there is accordingly some connection between the fatal revolutions of the heavens and the movements of Souls which take bodies at certain times: not, indeed, that the aspects of the heavens compel Souls to desire this or that, but they are concordant with their desires. For just as in cities there are sacred seasons and holy places for the assembling of the more serious among the people, and also places devoted to display and popular pleasures where gather the lower kind of people, the idle and wanton; and thus from the places and seasons we can form an opinion as to the habits and character of those who frequent and celebrate them, so in a similar manner we may say that from the aspects of the heavens we can infer the characters of the Souls on account of their bodies, which are generated in correspondence with these aspects.

"For since the Justice of the Divine Goodness has decreed under Fate the effects that the stars shall produce in their respective positions, He sends down at the appropriate times those Souls who require certain disciplines for their purification. For all these things are brought into the right relation through the power of necessity and natural affinity.

"Fate, therefore, does not coerce the inclinations of the Soul, nor constrain her freedom, but the Souls themselves fit themselves for this fate or that, and each according to her true dignity has an instrument corresponding to her needs. Hence, as has been said, it is not surprising that the tendency of the Soul's inclinations can be judged from the constellations in the heavens.

"But although the particular kind of life embraced by each Soul is chosen in accordance with a former disposition and dignity, each human being has it within his own choice to use his abilities for good or evil. Thus it may happen that he who has chosen the life of a merchant may live worthily, while he who has preferred the study of philosophy may act unworthily. And because each kind of life, whether of a farmer, sailor, or musician, is chosen by the Soul herself according to her former disposition, and assigned to her by the Creator according to her merit, whilst the Soul herself decides the degree of excellence of her own life, we praise or blame men according to their behaviour in their callings and not for the callings themselves."

This passage goes some way towards making clear the relationship of astrological beliefs to the problem of free will. Some readers will have been disquieted, and some no doubt outraged, by the suggestion advanced, with evidence in chapter VIII that the vocation of the priest is indicated in the scheme of the nativity. "Surely, of all things", they will say, "the priestly vocation is a spiritual and not a natural thing: this is dragging heaven itself down to earth."

But since when has the gift of ministry been different from any other gift?[11] *This vocation, like all others, is conceived by spirit and born in matter through nature.* The most spiritual things, if they are to obtain a manifest expression on earth, must pass through nature and establish a corporeal basis for their activities. If the soul who has resolved to serve God and his fellows in this way or that could not depend upon being born with a corporeal and destinal vehicle appropriate to its own freely chosen purpose, there would, as we have said, be chaos at the very roots of mundane life. *Astrology does not only bring heaven down to earth; it lifts earth and all its activities up to heaven.*

In the closing pages of *The Republic*, Plato introduces the story of the man named Er, a Pamphylian, who, left for dead upon the battlefield, sees in a vision the regions between heaven and earth where the souls of men are ascending from, and descending to, their lives on earth and where those seeking incarnation are choosing the kind of lives they will have. *The story is an allegory*, of course, and heavily overlaid with a distracting amount of symbolism at that, but the essential features are distinguishable. Each soul, even though it chose "in accordance with a former disposition" has, essentially, a free choice as to the kind of destiny it will have: the measure of its health, its wealth, its vocation, a roving or settled, public or private life, and so on. Most choose sensibly but some are rash and seek a destiny which although superficially attractive will, in effect, involve them in situations which they cannot sustain either morally or in some other way. In this sense the wise soul is content with a restricted destiny and even, in some cases, one which places great restraint upon it if such accords with its true purpose.[12]

At this point Socrates, who is telling the story, breaks off and with great earnestness says to his listeners that of all the kinds of knowledge *this* is the one we should prize and cultivate most - the ability to distinguish what is good for us, what it is we may safely and wisely desire for ourselves and towards what objects our free volitions should be directed.

It is interesting that we have from Jesus an almost exactly parallel admonition in: "Wherefore if thy hand or thy foot offend thee, cut them off . . . and if thine eye offend thee pluck it out and cast it from thee; it is better for thee to *enter into life* with one eye, rather than having two eyes to be cast into hell fire." (*Matthew 18, 8-9*). In other words, it is better to choose a restricted lot which accords with our purpose than a fuller one which may be the occasion of errancy. There have been those who have taken the above advice literally and severed offending members, but this is plainly absurd; the time for choosing and accepting such limitations is *before* the soul confronts Lachesis and Clotho and Atropos and passes beneath the Throne of

Necessity. After that has happened, although the freedom of the will remains, the freedom of action is circumscribed - circumscribed not by a harsh fate but by a beneficent one which imparts and maintains those conditions which the soul has sought and needs for the accomplishment of its purposes, which it has freely chosen, beheld and ratified by a mystical act of the enlightened volition.[13]

Astrology does not tell us something *new* about freedom of will or of action; it merely *confronts* us in clear-cut terms with the extent to which what we already know should be carried. From the side of religion we are told that we cannot by taking thought add a cubit to our stature; what astrology shows is that this principle extends more deeply into the conditions of incarnation than we may lightly suppose if we can get away without thinking clearly about it or being brought face to face with the facts.

And from the side of science the geneticists tell us the same sort of thing about the element of heredity in human life.[14] So that even if the pronouncements of the geneticists represented the whole story, which they do not, we should still have to acknowledge that once conception had taken place a great many things are determined for good or ill.

But astrology shows that patterns of destiny run in families in a manner which goes far beyond what genetics would easily recognise or acknowledge as springing from hereditary causes in the ordinary sense. This is, astrologically speaking, because family horoscopes show family likenesses, and this in turn is because of the operation of the law: like attracts like. Thus such similarities of destiny in families arise, not through the inherited link *as such* (this is merely the efficient cause of certain types of similarity), but *primarily* through the links and similarities in the psyches (the seat of the formal causes of individual characteristics, interior and exterior) of those born within families, and *secondarily* through the similarity of stellar configurations (that is the similarity of cosmic conditions) under which they are born.

The linking factor of heredity *is included* in the stellar scheme and does not add anything to what is indicated therein. This is the kind of thing which is a matter of common everyday knowledge to the astrologer but quite unknown to other types of scientist. The one takes the knowledge for granted; the other rejects it out of hand as absurd. And so the hostility between the two kinds of knowledge is perpetuated. But in the long run there is no need for such things to remain matters of dispute or conjecture. They can be put to the test.[15]

There is one final question which may be touched upon in this section: What ought we to mean by such words as "chance", "random", and so on? These are words which play an important part in the 20th century vocabulary and a great many conclusions of one sort and another are drawn upon the assumption of their having a certain significance.

A statistician writing on the "Laws of Chance" in a widely read book on statistical methods writes:[16]

"There are certain notions which it is impossible to define adequately. Such notions are found to be based on universal experience of nature. Probability is such a notion. The dictionary tells me that 'probable' means 'likely'. Further reference gives the not very helpful information that 'likely' means 'probable'. It is not always that we are so quickly made aware of circularity in our definitions. We might have an extra step in our circle and bring in the word 'chance', but to judge from the heated arguments of philosophers, no extension of vocabulary or ingenuity of definition ever seems to clear away all the difficulties attached to this perfectly common notion of probability."

It has been said that if one wishes to understand the thought of an age, one should look, not at those things which are deemed to be in need of proof, but at the things which are taken for granted, which are assumed *not* to be in need of proof. Such concepts are usually those which are, or are said to be, "based on a universal experience of nature" or words to that effect. In other words, they are mysteries; mysteries, that is, in the sense that a really intelligible account of them - one which goes to the roots of the matter - is not forthcoming from those who take them for granted. In order to give an intelligible account of anything, the appropriate scientific concepts are needed (using the word scientific in its strict sense) but the empiricist rigorously abstains from allowing himself to form any concepts upon the subject of formal causes. This effectively prevents him from thinking clearly about what is commonly called chance.

If, as our writer says, the philosophers have been making heavy weather of this subject, we will not labour it here, but it is, or should be, obvious that the notion of "laws of chance", however convenient for practical purposes, is (like the idea of an "uncertainty principle") a contradiction in terms. Law is law, principle is principle - neither has anything to do with chance or uncertainty.

Clearly, if the main theme of this section is true and every chain of efficient causation is constantly being moulded by a body of formal causes, then events which appear to be haphazard and unpredictable from the outside are in fact orderly and predictable when viewed from within.

We say that an event happens by chance when we cannot estimate or discover the total operation of the efficient causes involved in producing it. When we spin a penny, the forces which would give heads or tails are normally too complicated and too finely balanced for us to say which it will be.

But behind the multiplex character of the external causes of an event, there is a simple inner formative factor which is accessible upon its own terms - for example through the symbolism of time. This is the basis of the idea of divination. This is not an irrational process, nor unscientific. It is rational because it depends upon a knowledge of noumena; it is scientific because the principles upon which it depends are demonstrably true.

The results given in chapter VIII belong, in reality, to this class.[17]

One searches in one's mind for some means of imparting an insight into these issues to those whose entire intellectual training fits them not so much to *misunderstand* the subject as to look straight, uncomprehendingly, through it. Perhaps the following illustration will serve.

In the case of poliomyelitis which we took for the purposes of our experiment, one is dealing, in effect, with three groups of people: Those who do not come in contact with the virus; those who do come in contact with it but do not succumb to paralysis; and a much smaller group who come in contact with it and do succumb.

If we consider the phenomenon of Premium Bonds,[18] we have again three analogous groups: Those who do not buy them; those who do buy them but do not win significantly; and a much smaller group who buy them and do win.

Now the mechanism which indicates the numbers of winning bonds is assumed to have one outstanding virtue - namely that it picks *at random* and without, as it is said, fear or favour. And this is true when viewed in ordinary terms since the mechanism is designed, presumably, to give, in terms of efficient causation, the maximum of unpredictability.

But when looked at from the inside, as it were, the situation is quite different for, in fact, the problem of differentiating the three groups is theoretically no different in this case than it is with poliomyelitis. Precisely the same methods could be employed to distinguish the three groups from one another in both cases.

Thus we see that whilst in terms of efficient causes "Ernie" is a machine devoted to picking random numbers, from the point of view of formal causes there is no such thing as randomness[19] and we find that it is simply a machine for distributing a certain kind of wealth to those to whom it is due in accordance with certain conventions of the mid-20th century.

This will strike some as outrageous but there is no point in disputing the matter. The appeal is to scientific experiment. No amount of fulminating against "fatalism" by those who do not understand *and have probably never attempted to equip themselves to understand* the profound paradoxes of that subject will alter the fact that formal causes are as certainly linked to their effects as efficient causes. Every law links a certain kind of cause to a certain kind of effect in a predictable way in given circumstances - otherwise it would not be a law. The two things which it is specially desirable to know about a law are: How does it contribute to the universal good? and: To the action of what superior laws is it subordinated?

For over 300 years scientists have asked themselves with ever-increasing penetration and success *HOW* things happen. Because of this we now have a race of scientists who are specialists in the knowledge of how efficient and material causes are related to their effects. All honour to them and to the rigour with which they have pursued their search for truth. But it does not seem to occur to them that there is another (and much older) race of scientists who from ancient times have asked themselves *WHY* things happen and so are specialists in the knowledge of how formal and final causes are related to *their* effects.[20] This has always been the distinguishing characteristic of the knowledge of the sage. By knowing things in their essences he perceives the secrets of their activity and passivity, no matter how complex and apparently unforeseeable when viewed externally.

These two types of knowledge, the inner and outer, are complementary. The coming re-affirmation of the rightful place of the knowledge of formal causes is destined to exert a transforming effect upon the whole field of human thought and will touch every science and branch of knowledge without exception.[22] In some fields its effects are not hard to see but in others they are difficult for those conditioned by our present modes of thought to envisage. There are, however, a host of tacit assumptions about the nature of things which regulate men's opinions, and indeed their very search for truth, in every sphere. Because of the over-emphasis upon efficient causes, social and political doctrines have become distorted, our history books have come to contain the most shallow and faulty judgements of men and events, and right scientific criteria in every field have become displaced. If, for example, the philologist is asked about the meaning and origin of language he will answer in historical terms, explaining how certain linguistic changes came about, but he will make no reference to the symbolism of articulate sounds which lies behind and controls all outward developments of language. It is evidently upon the unfoldment of this latter study that an effective universal language must wait.

This last sentence gives some indication of the way in which the developments we have been speaking of accord with the needs and tendencies of the present time, for their effect will be, above all, to *simplify, harmonise* and *unify*.

NOTES ON CHAPTER IX

1 Aristotle's four causes are detailed in chapter II.

2   When Whitehead speaks here of "reason" and of the "anti-rationalistic" character of modern science, he is speaking of rationalism in a quite different sense, of course, from that used in the second quotation at the head of this section which refers to "*unspiritual* rationalism and materialism".

The "reason" spoken of by Whitehead (and in the paragraph which precedes the quotation) addresses itself to spiritual and universal ideas - to a knowledge of noumena rather than of phenomena as such.

3   The octave of J B White's sonnet *To Night* which Coleridge spoke of as - "the finest and most grandly conceived sonnet in our language". Commenting on these lines, A N Whitehead writes: "The excess of light discloses facts and also conceals them. It distorts the facts for human observation. It is one task of speculation to urge observation beyond the boundaries of its delusive completeness and to urge the doctrines of science beyond their delusive air of finality." (*Adventures of Ideas, CUP p. 199*).

4 So in the past, but it would seem that the coming age must be one in which Astrology (under whatever name) will occupy a central position in human thought.

5   One reason for anticipating that the theories advanced in this book will make their way in the world more rapidly than many scientific theories have done, is their ready applicability in all sorts of commercial undertakings. What astrologers call the "earthy" mentality, which verges towards scepticism and even obtuseness when appealed to on grounds of abstract truth, is suddenly found to be endowed with extraordinary flexibility and perceptiveness when it is pointed out that a profit is to be made.

6 Disturbances among psychiatric patients and the incidence of fires and of certain types of crime are among examples of human phenomena which have been related to the lunar cycle.

7   However, the laws of the cryptic order can be regarded as the nethermost aspect of the laws of the natural order. They govern the interpenetration of the forces of nature with matter. They are regulated by laws of occult attraction and repulsion based on numerical potencies.

8   This overshadowing of the course of events is to be seen in all the affairs of life. Again and again, momentous events *seem* to hang by a thread. Ask any married couple how they met and it will be found that in nearly all cases there was at least one point at which the conditions of their meeting apparently hung upon the slenderest thread of circumstance, which could (so one would think to view the matter casually) have turned out quite differently. But does this mean that the marriage of these two people was an accident? Certainly the scientific materialist and the scientific humanist think so, for they live in a world of accidents. But most ordinary people, and all those who believe that they live in a cosmos rather than a chaos do not believe any such thing or that events transpire in so haphazard a manner.

Can one at this point hear an outcry? Fatalism! The dread word! But what is fate? It is one thing to explain this; it is quite another to see this profoundly difficult concept in its true terms and in its proper relation to other concepts.

9   This power of inner formative principles to clothe themselves in appropriate manifestations is, of course, especially recognisable in the world of artistic creation where the ideas contemplated by the artist inspire their own expression. To give a simple example: Elgar, upon being asked how he produced the terrifying sound in *The Apostles* where Judas goes out and hangs himself, said that he simply "*saw* Judas in the extremity of his remorse and *heard* it on the muted horn." This is the common process of all artistic creation, and works of art achieve integrity and greatness in proportion to the dignity of their formal cause and the degree to which the artist (as the efficient cause) has identified himself with it and allowed it to dominate the material under his hand. Another aspect of this law is that those who contemplate and identify themselves with great purposes are thereby endowed with great energies.

10   The passage quoted is from Simplicius' Commentary on the Enchiridion of Epictetus.

11   There is, for example, a charming dialogue in "The Little Flowers of St Francis", Chapter VIII, which illustrates the difference in a relative sense between what is truly ours and what is a 'gift'. It is the one in which St Francis expounds to Friar Leo wherein perfect joy is to be found. (p. 15 in the Everyman edition.)

12   As Yeats was fond of observing in this context: "There is no deformity but saves us from a dream."

13   The position of the soul assuming incarnation is essentially that of any person embarking upon an important undertaking. If, for example, a man proposes to build a house, he does not put a spade hopefully over his shoulder and set off for some likely spot to dig the foundations. He considers first the best time and place for building and having found a good site he enters into negotiations for the tenure or freehold of the land and thereby assumes certain legal responsibilities and privileges. He then draws up plans, probably in consultation with an architect, and after that contracts with a builder to provide certain skilled labour. Finally he will order the necessary materials and arrange for them to be delivered on certain approximate dates in order that the work, once begun, shall proceed without delays.

   In all this he repeatedly commits himself to future courses of action - future responsibilities: but having committed himself he does not later complain that his freedom is circumscribed by the agreement he has entered into, because those agreements were the result of his own free choice. And if he runs into unforeseen difficulties he knows that he must stand by his agreements and do the best he can in the circumstances.

   This is, figuratively speaking, the basic position of the soul assuming a physical corporeal existence - that of someone who enters into a bond in order that a purpose can be accomplished.

   To extend the metaphor, the snag, one might say, is that whereas the consequences of some contracts are of limited extent and easily calculable, others are complex and may have implicit in them more than had been foreseen. In this respect, the legal contract which comes nearest to that of incarnation is marriage, simply because it is so many-sided in its consequences. Katherine Whitehorn wrote light-heartedly but penetratingly on this subject in The Observer (22.9.63) under the title: "Missing Marriage Lines" -

"What always intrigues me as I hear them gulping out 'I do' is the thought of all the other contracts they are making without realising it. The person could hardly say 'Dost thou, Algernon, promise to laugh at this woman's jokes, push the car till it starts and bring her sherry in the bath?' and the congregation would be surprised to hear the bride whispering 'I do' to the proposition that she should keep quiet at breakfast, find the things her husband has put down only a minute ago, dash it, and refrain from telling his employer what she thinks of him. Yet these are the agreements which really give the marriage its shape."

So, too, with incarnation; it is the implicit contracts, one might say, which give a life its shape.

14 One may quote Dr D C Darlington, FRS: "All the spermatozoa which beget the living population of these islands could be contained in the space of one pin's head. Within twice that volume we could put the whole substance of the nation's heredity. That amount of matter determines what we are and what we may be. Nor is it just for a few months or a few years, but for the whole of our lives and down to the casual gesture and the susceptibility to accidental infection sixty, seventy and eighty years ahead." (From a talk: "The Coming of Heredity" given on the BBC Third Programme some years ago: I have no record of the date.)

Incidentally, the two opening sentences of this quotation should be sufficient answer to those who object to astrology on the grounds of the relative smallness and remoteness of the planets. In these days, surely, no one can believe that physical size has much relevance in matters of this kind.

15 It is very tempting to go in for detailing experiments which would or should elucidate questions of this kind and one can easily overlook the problems and uncertainties which might, in practice, tend to make clear-cut results so difficult to obtain.

In theory, however, to demonstrate the truth of what we have been saying here, one could take four groups of pairs of people. In the first group the pairs would be twins; in the second group they would be pairs of people born on the same day (and within the same average time-limit as twins) but unrelated; the third group would be pairs of (non-twin) siblings, and the fourth, pairs of people unrelated but roughly the same age to within a year or so. These last would in effect serve as a control group. It cannot be too strongly emphasised that it would be by using groups 2 and 4 only that the essential astrological position could be demonstrated. The bringing in of twins and siblings is a refinement designed to elucidate the relationship of these matters to heredity, but which brings in all sorts of complications and should ideally be left until after the central issue has been clarified by a comparison of groups 2 and 4.

The problem would be to devise a means of measuring the similarity of the pairs in each of the four groups when it is held that the closeness of similarity would be the order given above, twins being most alike, those born close together next, the siblings next and the others last.

The presumed fact of the greater similarity to one another displayed by the pairs of group 2 in contrast to those of group 3 would show that closeness in time of birth was of greater significance than a shared heredity in producing similarities, but the greater similarity of twins in contrast to the pairs of group 2 would reflect only the fact that there is a special and known common element of destiny (that of a common family) between members of group 1 which would be expressed horoscopically in ways (and notably in micro-harmonics in the time rhythms linking the births) which are unknown and possibly indistinguishable to present astrological practice.

It is possible (though for various reasons not certain) that this latter supposition could be confirmed by further subdividing the twins into identical and fraternal twins and comparing these two groups with a third group of pairs born *very* close together in time on the same day, when it might well be found that such pairs would be more alike than fraternal though less so than identical twins. But this would be a difficult experiment to arrange since the time interval between the births would need to be both accurate and very small indeed, certainly not more than ten minutes.

It may be worth saying, if anyone is thinking of carrying out such experiments as the foregoing, that there is a strong case for consulting *beforehand* those who have specialist knowledge of the issues involved. There would be plenty of pitfalls, such as for example the tendency which would exist to base the measurement of similarity upon factors in which the hereditary transmission of characteristics was already known to operate. This would be rigging the experiment in favour of the orthodox genetic viewpoint. There are many other types of similarity than those which the geneticist would be likely to favour.

In actuality, comparisons of the sort we have been suggesting are more difficult to make than one would suppose. For example, twins and siblings are virtually never given the same name, whilst those born close together in time often are; again, the death of a parent is an important psychological event and those born on the same day often experience this at the same age. But twins *must* do and siblings can *never* do. Thus straightforward comparisons are not always possible.

It is very probable that initial attempts at comparisons of the kind suggested would give obscure results and that repeated efforts would be required to discover the best basis upon which to make relevant and informative comparisons.

Again, it may be enquired if there is any factual basis to justify such experiments. So far as a general tendency towards similarity among those born on the same day is concerned, there is abundant testimony. All kinds of examples from all kinds of sources are to be found in the literature of astrology. Instances of those born *extremely* close together in time come to light only by chance and infrequently; nevertheless, anyone interested can, over the years, collect examples.

For instance, some years ago two little girls, Jean Henderson and Joyce Ritter, aged 3, became next-door neighbours in White Plains, New York State. Their physical similarity was such that they were repeatedly mistaken for one another by parents and neighbours. It was discovered that they were born within five minutes of each other in the same hospital. One weighed 8 lbs 3 oz at birth, the other 8 lbs 3.5 oz. It was said that they walked, talked and looked alike and had common tastes to a remarkable degree. Their teachers found that they thought and wrote alike and had difficulty in distinguishing them (however as their marks were usually the same, this did not seem to matter). Both children had similar backgrounds: their fathers both worked at the same air-base and the girls both occupied the same position in a family of four - boy/girl/*girl*/boy. A careful examination (even of physical features, such as the formation of teeth) showed them to be much more alike than most fraternal twins.

16 *Facts from Figures* by M J Moronay, Chap 2, p. 4 (Pelican Book).

17 But perhaps someone will be able to demonstrate, in relation to, say, the 120th harmonic, that those born every third day approximately tend to have some form of vitamin deficiency which renders them vulnerable to poliomyelitis - thus bringing the whole picture into line with ideas of efficient causation. Actually, it is *taken for granted* that there *are* always efficient causes operating between formal causes and their manifest effects in the world, but the more deeply one sees into the truth of the situation, the more clearly one sees, as Plato saw, that the ideas in the mind of the artist are of surpassing interest and relevance, whereas the tools in his hand are of relatively trivial interest. In the one case, one is looking at something which is truly intelligible - in the other, at a merely inert and variable mechanism.

18 For the sake of the uninitiated, these are British Government Bonds, the interest upon which is distributed monthly by lottery, with prizes ranging from £50 to £250,000. [Since modified.]

19 The fact that there is, in the absolute sense, no such thing as chance, does not - as it seems to the writer - invalidate most of the practical applications to which this concept is put for the purpose of determining statistical probability and so on. However, it does mean that there are certain pitfalls in that field to be guarded against (some of which are already recognised in pragmatic terms). To take an extreme example, a study has recently been made of educational problems in this country based on an analysis of the background and development of 5000 children *all born in one week*! *(The Home and the School*, by JWB Douglas.) If the theme of the present book is true, then it is not merely possible or probable, but absolutely certain that this group of children will exhibit a host of common features (in their relationships, backgrounds, aptitudes, characteristics) which are not typical of the population at large. Thus *general* conclusions based on such an analysis are liable to be misleading.

20 Most of the thinkers of antiquity dealt with causality in terms of formal causes. In doing this they inevitably used *symbolic* ways of expressing things; if these symbolic terms (for example, such concepts as 'fire', 'earth', 'air', and 'water') are taken literally as if they were intended to refer to the phenomenal world and to efficient causes, then they naturally make the old expositions seem primitive and

simple-minded. This is just what the learned professors of later times have done, expatiating upon the "superstitious" beliefs of men who were in reality, however, looking at a deeper level of truth than their detractors have their eye on.

NOTE ON THE APPENDICES

In John Addey's original conception of this volume he had planned to have various appendices covering the details of

1) The Gauquelins' methods
2) His own methods
3) Observations on the vocabulary of Character Traits
4) The harmonic analysis of the planetary distribution for each specific trait
5) Rudolf Tomaschek's essay *Observations on the Basic Problem of Astrology*

The last is reproduced as Appendix III. Tomaschek (1895-1966) was Professor of Theoretical Physics at the University of Munich and a dedicated research astrology. His thoughts on the basis of astrology represent one of the few attempts from within establishment physics to engage with astrology and its implications.

The problems of working with **character traits** are treated at various points within the main text. No details of John's additional observations on the vocabulary of Character Traits have been found as such. John, like Francoise Gauquelin, was very aware of the problems of language and especially of translation. As they say in French, *Traduire c'est trahire*, to translate is to betray. By definition John Addey was working with English translations of descriptive words and phrases gathered for the most part from French texts. Working closely with, and thinking about, character traits for so much of the time during the last years of his life, John was acutely aware that the words we use to describe people, even when well translated, are always pointing beyond outward behaviour and character to deeper ideas and qualities. No doubt this Appendix was intended to discuss these wider issues

The **Gauquelin's methods** have now been well documented in Michel Gauquelin's own *Written in the Stars* (Aquarian Press 1988, ISBN 0-85030-615-9) and most recently in Suitbert Ertel and Kenneth Irving's *The Tenacious Mars Effect* (Urania Trust 1996, ISBN 1 871989 15 9)

It is planned, later this year or early next. to make available the technical details of **John Addey's own methods** together with the publication of **the planetary distribution and the harmonic analyses for each specific trait word**. Because of the highly specialised nature of this material and its present condition, (as many hundreds of pages of computer print-out and hand-drawn tables and listings), this will be released in image form on compact disc. If you would be interested in obtaining a copy of the disc when it is released, send your name and address to: UT Publications, 17 Rossiters Hill, Frome, BA11 4AL.

We have also added here the full text of *Astrology Reborn* which as one of Addey's most clear and concise statements on the philosophy of astrology and its implications. Likewise we have included the text of *The Discrimination of Birth Types* which illustrates the harmonic principle at work in the field of medicine.

ASTROLOGY REBORN

*The text of John Addey's 'C E O Carter Memorial Lecture'
delivered at the Astrological Association's annual conference
at Fitzwilliam College, Cambridge, 4 September 1971.*

The theme of this, the second Charles Carter Memorial Lecture, is that astrology is evidently about to undergo a rebirth and a period of new growth. It will be no ordinary rebirth and no ordinary period of growth. From being an outcast from the fraternity of sciences, it seems destined to assume an almost central role in scientific thought.

What reasons are there for saying this? We may note first that in all science there is, or should be, an interplay between the inner and outer, between the idea and the fact, between the conceptual and observational orders. In the larger sense the conceptual dominates the observational, if only because we make our observations and select and interpret our facts in the light of what we believe - in the light of our conception of the kind of reality we are dealing with.

Nevertheless, the external aspect of science plays an important role too, because the changing conditions of the phenomenal world continually require science to be re-expressed and adapted to the solution of new problems.

There is another point to notice and it is this: all human progress is from thesis, through antithesis to a new and higher synthesis. The period of thesis tends to be dogmatic and authoritative, to rely heavily on tradition and to look more to the unchanging world of ideas and so to enjoy a consequently greater stability. The period of antithesis tends to be more sceptical and to try to test the inherited teachings and traditions against actual experience. From the interplay of these two should come a higher and more complete synthesis which represents, in terms of that cycle, maturity and balance.

The obvious example of this process is that of childhood (which has a stability derived from the acceptance of parental authority), adolescence (which must try to throw off the traditional rules and find out for itself by experience), and adulthood (which eventually accepts that the traditional ways had much good in them and is all the stronger for having proved this by experience and found out their weaknesses and faults).

In order to see where we now stand scientifically in relation to this process, we must review very briefly the history of western thought during the past two millennia.

Before the Renaissance there had been a long period in which a certain view of the universe (within and without, spiritual and material) had prevailed. It was a thoroughly ordered view of things. Theocentric and hierarchical in conception, it was above all rational, in the true sense, for it saw all things proceeding from a Divine First Cause, through secondary and subsidiary causes to the last and least of manifested things.

Notice that the whole essence of this system was its orderly procession from unity into multiplicity. Every part was subordinated to a larger whole which, being dynamic, expressed itself *through* the parts of which it was the parent and origin. Without the presubsistent whole the parts would not have existed, nor would they have had any reason for existing. It was a system in which matter was considered to be passive, receptive, inert and nescient, and in which spirit was considered to be active, creative, dynamic and the source of all intelligibility in the worlds of form.

Between spirit and matter, this world-view conceived of a third principle which it called Soul, which was partly like one and partly like the other and was the intermediary by which the realities of the higher and inner were communicated to and manifested in the outer and lower.

This was the great thesis which men inherited at the time of the Renaissance. It had been enunciated by Pythagoras and Plato (though it was not original to them), fortified (through the work of Plotinus and others) with other elements in the thought of antiquity and taken up, in large measure, by Christian philosophers and theologians to provide a continuous tradition of thought which retained its essential character right down to the Middle Ages.

This was the tradition of which the true astrology has always been an integral part, for in its hierarchy of productive principles the primary cosmic substances had a necessary place - in the words of the Platonists the heavenly bodies were "the first-born thoughts of God"; "born", that is, in the sense that they were the primary lives of the manifested universe.

Astrology, in this sense, was as homogeneous with the thought of Pythagoras and Plato as it was with that of St Thomas Aquinas and St Albert the Great in the thirteenth century.

But sooner or later, if man is to progress, thesis must be followed by antithesis. That which has become the settled dogma must be challenged, at whatever cost, or human thought crystallizes into rigid forms which stifle progress, and in the later Middle Ages this rigidity had, indeed, set in.

Just as the thesis, then, had been that the spiritual and unmanifested world was the primary reality, so the antithesis must needs be that the manifested and material world was the real. And so, at the beginning of the so-called Renaissance, men began to turn their observational powers with an altogether new enthusiasm upon the world about them. Increasingly they began to place their confidence in observed facts and to reach, inductively, from these observations, their own conclusions about the nature of things.[†]

In the absolute, if not the immediate, sense, this was a retrogressive step, for in abandoning that hierarchy of principles rooted in intelligible causes, they overthrew the basis of all higher philosophy and, indeed, of all rational thought. For how can reason flourish where matter, the very principle of *un*reason, is taken as the starting-point of science?

To quote A N Whitehead:

"Science has never shaken off its origin in the historical revolt of the later Renaissance. It has remained a predominantly anti-rationalistic movement, based upon a naive faith. What reasoning it has wanted it has borrowed from mathematics which is a surviving relic of Greek rationalism, following the deductive method. . . . Of course the historical revolt was fully justified. It was wanted. It was more than wanted: it was an absolute necessity for healthy progress . . . It was a sensible reaction; but it was not a protest on behalf of reason."[‡]

[†] One can see that, ideally, these two views of reality, the "inner" and the "outer" should be in a state of balance, each being accorded its proper place; and it is arguable that the great cultural achievements of the early Renaissance were the product of just such a state of balance when men's minds were still grounded in the old philosophy but when they were opening their eyes to the wonders of the manifested world.

[‡] *Science and the Modern World, Ch 1.*

Empirical scientists and their converts have constantly declared that astrology is an *irrational* subject - in contrast, of course, to their own brand of science which they deem to be rational. But this is an inversion of the truth.

In reality it is always the inner content of facts which gives them their intelligibility. One can never arrive at a larger truth by analyzing and reducing things into their component parts; this always leads down into greater materiality and into greater unintelligibility. It is only by inquiring to what higher, co-ordinating formative principle anything is a subject part that one can really make sense of it.

So, if we stand back a little from the developing course of events so as to see what has really happened and what is happening now, we can see that the scientific tradition of the past three centuries has been no more than a necessary diversion.

When we speak about the restricted ideas, the limited horizons and localized beliefs of those who are shut off from the mainstream of thought and life we use the word "provincial". But Whitehead points out that it is possible to be provincial in time as well as in space and he suggests that the tradition of modern empirical science is an example of just such provincialism in time.[†] It has been a backwater, astonishingly cut off from the great sweep of human thought, into which scientists have retreated for a while to repair the tools of their trade and to remedy some of the negligence of their immediate predecessors.

We know with what success their labours have been attended. Indeed, the very limitations they imposed upon themselves - or which were imposed upon them by their historical origins - have been the key to their remarkable success in the field of methodology. No one should belittle what is good in these achievements.

But they have clearly been gained at a huge cost in the erosion of spiritual values, and not only in spiritual values as such, for *all* values are rooted in spiritual values.

What man believes, that he will become. Modern science has believed that all things emerged from the primordial slime; but since all things return, sooner or later, to their parent substance or idea, we ought not to be surprised, as we struggle against the rising tides of pollution - mental, moral, aesthetic and physical - if this same science

---

[†] *Op Cit* Preface.

now seems to be returning us a fair way to that very primordial slime in which it believes we had our origin.

However, all is not lost; the nadir, in some ways at least, is passed and the situation may yet be saved. Furthermore, if the overthrow of the old order at the time of the Renaissance seemed in retrospect, remarkably swift, the collapse of the central concepts of modern science appears to be taking place far more swiftly; every decade now brings remarkable changes - almost, one might say, every year.

Now, before we go on, there are two things which must be emphasized; the first is the supreme importance of the concept which lay at the heart of the old philosophy, of a hierarchy of principles, so that every higher cause is the origin of a multitude of effects on a lower plane, each of which expresses one aspect or function of the whole to which it is subordinated. From this we may understand that the originating idea or substance is not only the cause of its effects but is also, and constantly remains, the organizing unity which gives coherence and intelligibility to their developments and activities, in time as well as in space.

The second thing to emphasize is that this concept has always been one of the essential truths of astrology, and astrology, conversely, has always been an integral and necessary part of the tradition of thought (the "perennial philosophy") to which this doctrine is central.

Now if it is true - and it is true - that science is about to undergo a transformation in its thinking about first principles, it is to this idea that we must expect it to revert and we may consider, first, what signs are already visible that it is doing just this, and secondly, we may inquire how far it has progressed towards recognizing - even if only in a primitive form as yet - the involvement of the heavenly bodies and their motions in this new vision of scientific relationships.

Before we do this there is an unanswered question which we cannot altogether ignore here, even though we cannot fully elucidate it either. It is the problem of why modern scientific thought has difficulty with this conception of a hierarchy of principles, subordinated and superordinated one to another, as a key to the understanding of the universal constitution of things.

What in fact is the nature of these principles? To answer this question adequately cannot possibly be attempted here. They are not abstractions; they are certainly not products of the human mind. Man can think of these principles because they are there (and because they are within man as well as external to him); they are not there because man thinks of them.

There are a number of ways in which these principles may be understood, but the difficulty in gaining a real insight into their nature is always the same. It amounts to the difficulty we have, especially after a long period of materialistic thinking, of understanding the properties and characteristics of *spirit*. This is the key, for it is the dynamic and connective characteristics of spirit which enable wholes to express themselves in and through parts, and to organize and maintain the activities of their parts; and these properties are communicated by spirit even to the vital and formative principles of existences in gross matter. It is as if spirit (call it the divine spark, if you like) retained a footing in even the least and lowest of material existences.

So, bearing in mind that we shall not expect those who have been trained in the empirical tradition to have a real conception of the realities towards which they are groping their way, what evidence is there that they are moving in the right direction?

As many of you will know, among the foci of interest in the scientific world at present are the symposia recently held each summer at the Villa Serbelloni on Lake Como, where Professor C H Waddington of Edinburgh University has gathered together groups of leading biologists, mathematicians and physicists to explore the possibilities of a "firmly founded theoretical biology."

The striking feature of the discussions at the Villa Serbelloni is that, from every branch of science there represented, come arguments along the same theme, and that theme is that the practice of taking things to pieces to unravel their secrets - the process of "reductionism" as it is now called - does not, in the end, appear to lead anywhere and that the opposite hypothesis, that the nature, purpose and interrelationships of the parts must be considered as subordinate at each stage to their governing wholes - this is the hypothesis which work in these fields now seems to require.

The results of these symposia may be found in *Towards a Theoretical Biology*, edited by C H Waddington. There is also *Beyond Reductionism* by Koestler and Smythies, which gives the papers and discussions from a similar symposium at Altbach in Austria, organized by Arthur Koestler.

John Davy, in an article in *The Observer* magazine, gave an admirable description of these developments last year[†] and since the summary form of his article, written for the lay reader, lends itself well to our purpose, it is from that that I take the following quotations.

First of all the biological viewpoint.

"Molecular biology assumes that the instructions for co-ordinating an animal's various parts, for directing it to its 'goals', are coded into the [genetic] blueprint. But copies of the blueprint sit inside each cell of an organism: how does one blueprint know what instructions all the others are issuing? How does one cell keep in step with another? How does each part 'know its place' in the organism as a whole?

"A number of scientists at Serbelloni emphasized that however this control is achieved, it must be involved with the *hierarchical* nature of living organisms; each organism consists of organs, which consist of tissues, which consist of cells, which consist of a variety of molecules, which consist of atoms, which consist of fundamental particles . . . At each level the parts serve a whole on the next higher level which somehow organizes the parts of which it consists.[‡]

"The 'reductionist' tradition of science assumes as a matter of course that a complex phenomenon must be explicable in terms of something simpler. The cells must explain the organ, the molecules must explain the cells, . . . etc. Perhaps the most surprising event at Serbelloni was that this assumption was explicitly challenged by a physicist. . ."

This challenge came from Prof David Bohm of Birkbeck College, London, who argued "that the apparently chance behaviour of particles at one level, in fact reflects an orderly pattern at a higher level. . . ." At Serbelloni Bohm suggested that there is an analogous situation in biology and that rather than the parts of living structures

---

[†] Do we or don't we understand the secret of life? *The Observer Magazine*, 15 February, 1970.

[‡] Notice that the phrase "of which it consists" is the phrase of someone accustomed to think in terms of the empirical viewpoint. The whole does not "consist" of the parts, it presubsists them. The Arsenal Football Club does not consist of its Chairman, Manager, players, etc; it was there before they were born and will probably be there when they are dead, but it has within it certain principles or potential modes of manifestation which continually tend to embody themselves in a Chairman, Manager, players, etc.

determining the whole, the whole may determine the parts. Perhaps 'hierarchies of order' are as fundamental a feature of the universe as 'particles'.

"Bohm admitted that such an idea runs contrary to all usual scientific habits and is therefore difficult to digest."

One aspect of the capacity of the dominant whole to organize its subordinate parts which has impressed the Serbelloni group most is the self-organization of living things in time:

"At the heart of this problem is one central problem: the *organization* of living things - their capacity to arrange and maintain their cells and their organs as coherent wholes or 'organisms'. And again and again, in discussing this problem, the suggestion was made that the answer would have to do with the peculiar relation of living things to *time*."

And again: "Whatever ideas and experiments emerge out of this rich and complex endeavour, they are likely to centre on rhythmic processes in time."

And so we see that, with suitable cries of astonishment, scientists are in fact groping their way back to the idea of hierarchies of order, orders in which each unitive principle is the parent of a multiplicity of effects at a lower level.

The next step must be (and it cannot be more than ten or, at the most, twenty years before this is explicitly and clearly recognized by scientists) that, with more suitable cries of astonishment, it will be realized that the cosmic bodies are the primary unities of the manifested cosmos and that their motions and interrelationships are the primary determinants of the patterns in time - those "rhythmic processes" - which characterize all natural processes of growth and unfoldment.

I said that the scientific recognition of this could not be delayed for more than ten or twenty years, but, in fact, it could be and should be already recognized, or at least strongly suspected, and the only thing which prevents it from being already seen is the unmanageable diversity and superabundance of scientific information published today, allied to the natural reluctance and incapacity of scientists (one might say of men generally) to examine thoughtfully results, however scientifically sound, which cannot be readily assimilated with their present concepts and world-view.

The fact is that the past ten or fifteen years have seen a remarkable accumulation of scientific results which point clearly to the relationship between natural phenomena and cosmic forces. Let us consider some of these.

One of the best examples of such studies outside the astrological field is the work of The Foundation for the Study of Cycles, of Pittsburgh, Pennsylvania. With a continuous programme of extensive and penetrating cycle analysis going back to their founding in 1940, this Foundation has built up a very large catalogue of well-authenticated cycles in the occurrence of human and natural phenomena in many different fields.

For much of this period the Foundation has been, to some extent, up against the same problem which we face in a more pronounced form, namely, that despite the high scientific standards they have maintained, their subject of study has stood somewhat outside the circle of accepted scientific research. The reason for this, of course, is the one with which we are now familiar, that regular cycles of events which continue to repeat decade after decade and, in many cases, century after century, in such social phenomena as economic and trade cycles and the occurrence of civil and international strife, not to mention cycles in biological, meteorological and medical phenomena, etc - these all presuppose some higher, unitive, regulating pattern or mechanism which the scientific fraternity has been loath to acknowledge.

But in the past few years all this has suddenly changed dramatically and the conferences now organized by the Foundation's European Division - The International Institute for Interdisciplinary Cycle Research at Leiden - have been attended by scientists from all over Europe. They have come as individuals or as representatives of some of the ever-growing number of societies (such as the Group d'Etude de Rythmes Biologiques, which coordinates French cycle research) which are now interesting themselves in the study of fluctuating phenomena in many branches of science.

One of the projects which they have put in hand is that of a ten-volume catalogue of cycles and for this they have some 87 scientists collecting and collating cycle references in 17 languages and in 39 branches of science.

In many of these fields scientists are content to observe cyclic phenomena without offering firm conclusions about the originating causes of their cycles, but there can be no doubt that the overwhelming, and growing, body of opinion now looks to extra-terrestrial factors as the regulating mechanisms.

But quite apart from the rapidly expanding work of the Foundation for the Study of Cycles under its remarkable president, Edward Dewey, there are countless programmes of research proceeding all over the world into circadian and similar rhythms, very many of which are explicitly related to extra-terrestrial causal factors.

One ought to mention, in passing, the increasing variety of phenomena which have been linked with sunspot cycles - (only a few weeks ago, Russian scientists announced that influenza epidemics correlated with these periods) - and alongside this, one must place the discovery that these sunspot cycles can be described very largely in terms of the harmonics of planetary periods; a discovery which caused *The Times* to comment in its Science Report that this might provide "a sound scientific basis for some astrological predictions." The report continued:

"The radiation from the sun is one of the prime hazards to manned space flight, so we find the curious anomaly that the dates of future space flights might be chosen using the textbook astrological techniques of Kepler to predict periods of low sunspot activity."[†]

Now if we survey all these many developments in the world of orthodox scientific research we shall find that the all-pervading concept is that of regular rhythms in the occurrence of natural and human phenomena.

If we turn to the world of astrological research we shall find that in all the leading examples of such work (and here I must include the work of Professor Gauquelin, whatever he may protest to the contrary) the same concept is to be found; that of regularly recurring rhythms.

Now I know that there are those who say that John Addey has a bee in his bonnet about the harmonics of cosmic periods, and I know that there are those who believe that what I have been saying on this subject for many years is just some specialized application or aspect of astrology, that it is like, say, horary astrology, something one can either take or leave alone, according to taste. In reality this is not

---

[†] *The Times*, December 5, 1970. John J O'Neill, Science editor of the *New York Herald Tribune* and the first science writer to win a Pulitzer Prize, made the same observation over ten years ago. He also wrote, "Astrology is one of the most important fields for scientific research today, and one of the most neglected . . . There is absolutely nothing unscientific about engaging in research in this field . . . scientists today cannot look down on astrology; instead they must raise their eyes to take in the wider horizons that astrologers have preserved for them."

the case. The real position is that it is only by seeing astrology in terms of the harmonics of cosmic periods that we can begin the task of re-expressing our study, in all its manifestations, in clear scientific - I mean really scientific - terms.

In this respect, exactly the same principles underlie both astrology and all those subjects of enquiry, which I have been speaking of, now attracting the attention of orthodox science. There is no longer any dividing line, in principle, between them.

What we have in place of a "dividing line" is a graduated assortment of scientific results, some of which at first sight look like the familiar products of orthodox scientific enquiry, some of which seem to belong quite clearly to the field of astrology, and some of which could belong to either. To complicate matters, some of the first group have been produced by astrologers while some of the second have been produced by opponents of astrology. But they all embody the same principles and will ultimately be seen to belong to one science, the name of which is astrology.

It is true that there are many astrologers who have misgivings about attempts to approach astrology through the methods of science. "How do we know," they say, "that if we begin by adopting their methods, we shall not end by adopting their philosophy?"

My dear friends, this is not the position; *this is not the position at all!* How could scientists, as we have been accustomed to think of them, convert us to their way of thinking when they are no longer able to sustain their old beliefs themselves? We are not even in the position, as we have sometimes liked to think of ourselves, of a David pitting our strength against the Goliath of Modern Science. Science today - and I am speaking of the heart and core of the scientific world-view which has prevailed for the past 300-odd years - is not so much like a Goliath as like a great simpleton who is even now in the process of falling over his own bootlaces into the dust from which he will not rise again.

I hope indeed that we shall become more scientific in our methods, but we certainly need not fear their philosophy (if one can call it that) when they themselves are already deserting that philosophy in order to rejoin the road which we have never left.

There is indeed a difference between us and orthodox scientists and it is quite simply this: that we have a clearer grasp than they have of the principles towards which they are now turning.

Modern science has far greater resources than we have and their methods are better, but their thinking about scientific problems is behind ours. And this is why I have taken up so much of this lecture in setting the present situation in its historical context, because, unless we understand our position - our strength and our weaknesses - *vis-a-vis* modern science and shake off our timidity about it, we shall not have the confidence to take advantage of our basically strong position or the open-mindedness to move forward to that synthesis of the best elements in those two world-views I spoke of earlier, and so make use of the valuable methods developed by science to help us, where necessary, in clarifying and, indeed, rethinking and re-expressing the principles of our science.

What then are these principles which I believe we have a fresh opportunity to clarify and re-formulate?

Obviously they are manifold but there are certain key ideas which lie at the very heart of our science, which we all tacitly recognize, which have the widest applicability for us, but which we have now come to see only in terms of rigid traditional concepts which, in the interests of easy transmission, have been drastically over-simplified.[†]

I would like to take up most of the remainder of this lecture in looking closely at one of these ideas and showing, if I can, how a fresh approach could revitalize our thinking and our grasp of practical procedures.

The idea I want to look at is the one I have been speaking about throughout this lecture. It is that astrology belongs inherently to that tradition which sees the whole manifested cosmos, and everything in it, as being brought forth by a hierarchy of principles, proceeding from unity into multiplicity by stages - stages in which each superior principle is the parent of a number of effects at a lower level, each one of which, in turn, has its own centre and unity from which still further effects proceed at a yet lower level.

Now, in this procession from unity into diversity it is the character and properties of the successive formative principles which determine

---

[†] One of the themes which might have been included in this lecture, had circumstances allowed, is the whole question of how traditions become corrupted, what kind of things happen when they do, and how they are to be restored. The (to some extent inevitable) shedding of the less central elements of a tradition by its custodians when they have their backs to the wall, is one of the most common disintegrative effects. Alan Leo did much simplifying; Margaret Hone carried the process to even greater lengths.

the number and variety of the subordinate effects and also the number of stages through which they pass in their unfoldment.

For this reason the symbolism of number is an integral part of astrology; it is embedded in all the rules of horoscopy and we use it, consciously or unconsciously, in every facet of our science.

Alongside this one may place the re-discovery of the fact, which has always been implicit in the rules of astrology but which I believe my own work has made clear, that the symbolism of number is expressed primarily (for us) through the harmonic relationships of planets in the circle.

Let me explain and illustrate this.

Pythagoras taught that there were only nine basic numbers and that all numbers beyond nine were repetitions. Our system of numeration exemplifies this for we use only nine numbers plus a nought to indicate the return to unity and the beginning of a new cycle. (That is, when we reach nine we return to one with a nought after it.)

What is the explanation of this? It lies in the truth that all things, between their innermost unity and their outermost expression, pass through nine stages.

Now I know there are those who believe that distinctions of this sort are merely arbitrary conceptions of the human mind which have no reality other than that given to them by our own thoughts. This is a heresy which has arisen as a by-product of an era of scientific materialism which cannot conceive of inner realities except in these terms.

With what order of truth *are* we dealing then, when we say that all things unfold through nine stages? It is the same order of truth, for example, which says that man is tripartite: spirit, soul and body. This is not an arbitrary distinction: it corresponds to a clearly definable reality. Furthermore, this example (of the tripartite nature of man) also has a direct bearing on the symbolism of the number nine, for, in fact, we are not dealing merely with one trinity - a "vertical" trinity one might say, thus:

SPIRIT	1
SOUL	2
BODY	3

but also with a "horizontal" trinity, by which each of the first three are triple in character:

STATIC   DYNAMIC   IDEAL   1 | 2 | 3

Here we have a problem of nomenclature. Perhaps the terms *static, dynamic* and *ideal* are the most apt. For just as spirit is static, soul is dynamic and body is ideal (in the sense that it is through body that ideals are actualised and so made manifest), so we can say that spirit has static, dynamic and ideal aspects which are the *source* of all secondary static, dynamic and ideal elements; that soul has the same three elements and is the *means* whereby they are implemented; and that body has the same three elements and so is the *vehicle* through which they are all outwardly expressed. Thus we have a combination of two trinities which gives us the nine stages through which all things unfold in passing from their innermost subsistence to their outermost expression.

$$1 \quad 2 \quad 3$$

$$4 \quad 5 \quad 6$$

$$7 \quad 8 \quad 9$$

Thus the number nine is especially connected with the process whereby the innermost root idea is ultimately connected to its outermost full unfoldment and expression.[†]

We can now ask how this fits in with our ideas about the number nine in astrology. Probably the most important manifestation of the number nine in practical astrology is to be found in the *navamsa* chart which is given such great prominence in Indian astrology. As was explained in a recent issue of *The Astrological Journal*,[‡] the navamsa chart is really a diagram of the planetary positions of a chart

---

[†] Thus Proclus says that the soul "proceeds enneadically (ie according to the number nine) . . . that it may proceed to the last of things after departing from the monad." Quoted in Thos Taylor's translation of the *Timæus* of Plato (note 17 on line 36b, p. 537 of volume II of the *Works of Plato*, Prometheus Trust, 1996).

[‡] Harmonics and Hindu Astrology: Charles Harvey, *Astrological Journal,* Spring 1970.

shown in terms of the ninth harmonic. (That is to say the chart is considered as having nine cycles of 40° each: one complete zodiac from 0° Aries to 10° Taurus, one from 10° Taurus to 20° Gemini and so on.)

One statement I have seen about the navamsa chart is that it stands in relation to the radical map as the fruit to the tree. This we can now see to be appropriate, for the number nine in our diagram represents the complete realization, or fruit, of what is implicit in the number one or root idea.

Again the navamsa chart is said to show the marriage partner and the marriage generally. Here again we can now see the reason for this, for the two ends of this ninefold process are like two poles which must be brought together. "One" represents the root identity and original potentiality; "nine" represents the ultimate ideal to be realized. The bringing together of these two is symbolized in marriage.

While casting about for an example of an outstanding marriage which might serve to illustrate this point, it was suggested to me that Robert and Elizabeth Barret Browning might be a good case to take.

Upon obtaining the natal positions of these two, I found that I needed to go no further than the first map I converted to the navamsa - that of Elizabeth Barrett Browning.[†] Here Venus is exactly on the seventh cusp in the navamsa and in trine to the navamsa Sun in 17° Scorpio. Since Robert Browning had the Sun in 17° Taurus we can see, without going any further, that the navamsa describes both the felicitous nature of the marriage and also something about the marriage partner. (The maps have other interesting features, too, of course.)

One may mention in passing that this characteristic of the number nine, of marking out the successive stages of unfoldment of an idea, is the reason why, in numerology, it is customary to add up the digits of any number in order to arrive at the *root* number from which it is derived.

This practice had always mystified me because, of course, to add up hundreds, tens and units as if they were all the same thing seemed illogical. But what one is really doing, when one adds up the digits of a number, is finding out what is the root number in which a larger number had its origin in a series of ninefold progressions.

[†] Born: March 6, 1806, 7.00 pm, Durham.

Here we have a piece of occult lore which has seldom been clearly explained but which is now confirmable and explicable in scientific terms.   This was brought home to me when we had all our collections of sun positions, in all the available collections of data held by the Astrological Association, subjected to harmonic analysis by computer.   These included some 20,000 sets of birth data.[†]

This point can be illustrated by reference, for example, to the largest single collection of birth data, that of 7302 Doctors of Medicine.[‡] (Those who find elaborate mathematical examples unnerving may omit this part, continuing on page 216.)

In this collection of data the Sun's longitude at noon was tabulated according to the total number of times it occupied each degree of the ecliptic.   This gave 360 totals showing the distribution of 7302 solar longitudes.   (The crude totals are given in *The Astrological Journal*, Autumn 1969.)

This distribution was then subjected to harmonic analysis in order to discover the rhythms present in the distribution.   The analysis was carried from the first to the 180th harmonic and the results of this analysis are given in the table shown on the following page.   Each harmonic is numbered and described according to its amplitude and phase angle.[§]

This harmonic analysis has many interesting features (for example, the harmonic which shows the highest amplitude of any of the 180 possible harmonics, is the twelfth - which may be said to correspond to the traditional twelvefold division of the Zodiac, showing that this has the most vigorous presence of all the rhythms governing this solar distribution), but the point with which we are here concerned is the *procession by nines* and the reader's attention is drawn to those harmonics which fall at intervals of nine places from the 7th, that is

---

[†] These include the birth data of 7302 Doctors of Medicine, 2875 Artists, 2492 American Clergymen, 1970 British Clergymen, 1970 Control Group ditto, 1024 Polio victims, 970 Nonagenarians and 710 Judges.

[‡] Extracted by Rupert Gleadow and Brigadier R C Firebrace from the Registrar of Medical Practitioners   1850-1900.

[§] The amplitude shows the strength of each particular harmonic as a percentage of the mean distribution; the phase angle shows where the 'peak' of each wave-form falls in relation to the point 0° Aries, the wavelength of each harmonic being taken, for this purpose, as 360° in extent.

the 16th, 25th, 34th, 43rd, 52nd, and so on, all numbers of which the digits add up to 7.

I call these the successive *subsistences* of the number 7. Thus 16 is called the second subsistence of 7, 25 is the third subsistence and so on. (I do not know if any other term exists.)

Now if we show diagrammatically the *phase-angles* of this series of harmonics, from the 7th to the 178th, by marking them on a 360° dial, we find that they are distributed in the circle in a manner which is anything but characteristic of a random distribution. As can be seen (Fig I), all except one of the 20 phase-angles in this series fall virtually in one half of the circle, and the exception (the 52nd) has a very small amplitude. This is a remarkable result but it is only one of many similar ones which could be given.[†]

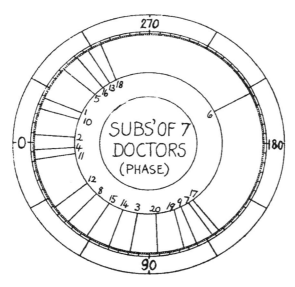

Fig. I

[†] It should be added that the total distribution of all 180 phase angles in this analysis shows no significant bias in the circle - as can be seen from the first diagram (a) below, which gives the number of phase angles falling in each 30° of the circle.

H: Harmonic   A: Amplitude   P: Phase

H	A	P	H	A	P	H	A	P
1	5.2	86	62	3.7	251	123	2.8	84
2	2.2	66	63	2.5	194	124	1.4	70
3	2.5	171	64	2.6	217	125	.6	20
4	2.5	17	65	3.5	99	126	3.4	93
5	2.8	15	66	3.0	156	127	1.3	342
6	4.0	239	67	1.2	338	128	3.3	114
7	.7	336	68	1.4	295	129	1.8	193
8	2.7	139	69	3.4	354	130	1.8	204
9	1.8	235	70	4.6	46	131	4.7	241
10	4.3	274	71	1.9	289	132	4.2	305
11	1.7	110	72	1.1	317	133	1.9	57
12	6.2	229	73	3.6	340	134	1.2	184
13	1.1	262	74	3.0	327	135	2.5	211
14	1.9	82	75	1.2	39	136	1.8	235
15	1.2	100	76	2.1	91	137	2.4	326
16	2.2	356	77	3.9	66	138	4.2	59
17	2.2	162	78	2.1	337	139	3.5	225
18	1.0	133	79	2.2	115	140	2.7	322
19	.6	158	80	1.3	287	141	2.8	343
20	2.3	277	81	1.0	235	142	2.4	309
21	2.8	349	82	1.5	249	143	1.2	330
22	1.2	340	83	4.0	64	144	3.5	28
23	1.9	1	84	2.3	7	145	2.0	353
24	2.4	240	85	3.3	211	146	2.7	95
25	4.7	82	86	3.1	175	147	3.3	216
26	3.6	284	87	2.6	34	148	5.1	26
27	2.2	201	88	4.5	342	149	2.3	138
28	.5	125	89	3.7	264	150	1.5	31
29	3.0	34	90	1.4	260	151	1.3	128
30	1.5	83	91	1.6	222	152	2.4	344
31	4.5	178	92	2.2	88	153	1.1	127
32	.9	285	93	2.0	328	154	1.2	33
33	2.1	102	94	1.3	262	155	1.2	144
34	4.2	4	95	3.4	66	156	1.2	284
35	3.1	265	96	2.4	170	157	4.5	98
36	2.0	108	97	2.3	9	158	3.4	221
37	2.3	332	98	.8	348	159	1.5	40
38	1.8	223	99	3.0	146	160	1.8	295
39	2.8	249	100	3.1	302	161	1.3	291
40	1.4	284	101	1.0	305	162	2.0	357
41	3.1	186	102	3.8	3	163	1.2	174
42	3.3	340	103	2.2	311	164	2.1	205
43	2.8	318	104	1.5	86	165	1.2	89
44	.2	235	105	2.4	333	166	3.1	225
45	.6	184	106	2.6	37	167	.7	98
46	2.2	107	107	1.9	120	168	2.1	246
47	1.1	184	108	3.3	293	169	2.4	108
48	1.2	266	109	.8	234	170	2.8	122
49	1.4	55	110	1.3	81	171	2.7	328
50	1.5	347	111	3.5	68	172	.9	164
51	1.9	317	112	3.4	35	173	3.0	1
52	1.2	207	113	1.3	311	174	1.3	43
53	.9	288	114	1.9	225	175	.8	159
54	2.1	163	115	2.6	302	176	.8	118
55	1.1	311	116	3.7	127	177	.3	227
56	1.8	190	117	5.3	128	178	1.3	94
57	5.8	112	118	2.3	255	179	2.1	140
58	2.5	88	119	2.9	332	180	3.5	270
59	1.5	273	120	1.5	324			
60	1.6	97	121	2.7	206			
61	1.8	124	122	3.0	82	Total values	7302	

By way of comparison, here too are the phase angles of those harmonics which are subsistences of 7 in (b) the solar distribution on the birth dates of 1970 British Clergy and (c) on the birthdates of 970 nonagenarians. This last example is of extraordinary and far-reaching significance. (These two illustrations comprise the first to the 10th subsistences only.)

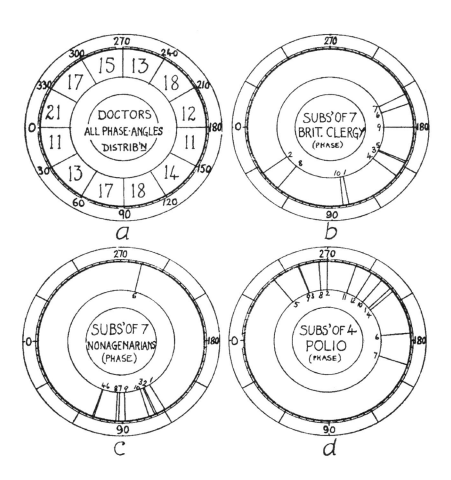

It is not only the subsistences of the number 7, of course, which are significant in results of this kind and, for comparison again, I give the distribution of the phase-angles of those harmonics which are subsistences of 4 (13, 22, 31, etc) in the nativities of 1024 polio sufferers (d).

The significance of this type of result is no doubt difficult to envisage, but the effect is to produce distribution peaks or troughs at intervals of 40°, since harmonics which are nine places apart will coincide nine times in the complete circle.

What it amounts to is this, *that each one of these sets of birth data - doctors, artists, nonagenarians, etc - are, when analyzed in this way, just like different crystalline substances, each one characterized by a different numerical structure.*

Over half a century ago, D'arcy Thompson, in his memorable book *On Growth and Form*, commented on the reluctance of morphologists (in contrast to, say, astronomers or chemists) to raise their study to a science by the proper employment of mathematics. It was as if they saw in the teeming forms of nature, in the lineaments of the growing plant or the convolutions of the snail's shell, mysteries too deep and too varied to lie within the scope of clear numerical expression. Yet Thompson and others have since shown how mathematical laws are at work in all the forms of nature.

Now science must learn that the lineaments of human character and the convolutions of destiny too, fall, no less, within the scope of number; for if it is true that God made 'every plant of the field before it was in the earth, and every herb of the field before it grew', it is no less true that He measured the ways of man before he was in the womb, and made him an embodiment of ideal and divine numbers.

Here is another example of the numerical basis of the larger astrological symbolism, and one from which I want to go on to show (what I believe is a new discovery) how, in principle, the genetic code is expressed in terms of astrological symbolism.

In the *Astrological Journal* of Spring 1970 I contributed an article on the symbolism of the number five as applied to human affairs, and I showed that one basic pattern applied to all the different manifestations of this five-fold symbolism. I illustrated it, you may recall, in terms of the various faculties, the five senses, the five-fold structure of the hand, the Indian Caste system, the five types of government described by Plato in his *Republic* and in other ways too.

I showed that this five-fold order was always constructed in the same way with a unity above, a unity below and a triad in the middle, although this sometimes appears as a unity with four subordinate principles.

For example, man has three *groups* of faculties: the affectional, the volitional and the mental; or heart, will and mind. The unity above these is soul (which is their source, centre and principle of coordination). The unity below is body through which they all manifest outwardly.

Soul

Heart   Will   Mind

Body

Each of these can be further sub-divided into subordinate five-fold groups of a *corresponding* nature. If we take one of the original five, say 'mind', we can divide the gnostic powers (starting with the highest) into intuition, reason, estimation or judgment, instincts and senses thus:

The point to insist upon, perhaps, is that divisions of this sort are not merely arbitrary; they correspond to real truths about the constitution of man (and other things too, of course). This five-fold division in things human is of great antiquity and is expressed by man in countless different ways and embodied in a great variety of human institutions. It is of so universal a character that it has passed into the language with such words as *quintessence*, for you will see from the examples that the fifth and highest order of the group always contains the essence of the four lower orders.

To go a step further we can now see that if we take a section right across this five-fold type of hierarchy in human nature (and of course there are other numerical divisions besides the five-fold one) we might arrive at an example of this sort:

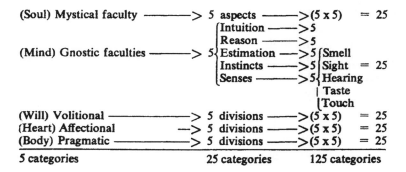

On the left is our original five-fold division of man; in the middle we have each of the original five subdividing into five branches each, giving 25 categories of things in that column; and in the third column a further splitting into fives gives 125 categories in that column of which we have given the five separate senses as an example.

Now if I am right in insisting that the sub-harmonics of the whole circle are numerically correlated with the appropriate subdivision in the hierarchical organisation of the whole, then it follows that, for example, special qualities or defects of the five senses will be shown in the 125th harmonic in the horoscope, and that special characteristics of the faculties at the 'higher' level will be shown in the 25th harmonic, and so on.

Let us take Helen Keller[†] as an example. Here, you will remember, there were severe impediments at the level of the individual senses, but no impairment of the intelligence at a 'higher' level. So we shall be looking for manifestations of the 125th harmonic, the wave length of this harmonic (125th part of 360°) being 2° 52.8'.

The positions of Sun, Mercury and Saturn in her chart are shown in the diagram (Fig II) and we see straight away that Mercury is close to the square of Saturn. But if we look closer we see that the square

[†] Born 27 June 1880 at 'about 4.00 pm', Tuscumbia, N Alabama (*Astrology*, Dec 1952).

has an orb of 2° 52' - exactly the wave-length of the 125th harmonic (to within 1') which therefore means that these two bodies will again be in exact square in the 125th harmonic.

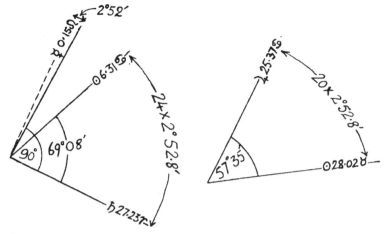

Fig. II   Fig. III

If we look at the angle between Sun and Saturn we find it to be 69° 08' and here again we find this to be an exact multiple of 2° 52.8' (24 x 2° 52.8' to be precise, again to within 1'). Thus in the 125th harmonic Sun is exactly conjunct Saturn showing the severe blockage of the powers of self-communication *at that level.*

But Saturn does not impose any restriction at the higher level, that is in the 25th harmonic.

On the other hand, let us take the positions of the philosopher Bertrand Russell[†] who, you will recall, was not only an outstanding thinker but who also retained his physical faculties in good order up to the age of 98. (Fig III.)

Here we find the angle between Sun and Jupiter to be 57° 35', and in the ordinary course of events we should call that a sextile and have done with it. However, in the light of our present enquiry we now notice that this Sun-Jupiter angle is exactly 20 x 2° 52.8' (again to the nearest minute) and thus, since 20 is a multiple of 5, he has Sun

---

[†] Born 18 May 1872 at 5.45 pm, Trellek, Monmouthshire *(Astrological Journal,* Spring 1970 where a misprint gives the time as 5.45 am).

conjunction Jupiter not only in the 125th but also in the 25th harmonic.

I hope these illustrations will serve to demonstrate the principle I am trying to get across. *It is that the hierarchical arrangement of the principles in the human constitution gives the key to the descriptive harmonic relationship between the appropriate points in the horoscope.*

This is quite simply the 'quantum' principle expressed in terms of natural man. It may be said that intelligence is above nature, and so it is, but soul works on matter through *nature.*

But once that is established we can immediately go much further.

All the characteristics of the physical body are determined by the genetic make-up, and are transmitted genetically from parent to child. But the body is what it is *because man is what he is*; all the parts of the body are an expression of the inner constitution of man. If the body is to be a true vehicle for the whole man then there must be an appropriate part or attribute of body corresponding to every one of his inner and higher attributes. The body is like a physical microcosm; its every detail is an expression of something in human nature as a whole.

For this reason, the harmonic relationships in the horoscope, immensely complex as they are, provide the basis of a complete genetic code and a total description of the genetic characteristics communicated from one generation to the next.

I have chosen to give this particular application of the doctrine of harmonics in this lecture because the science of genetics has been for some time a focus of interest in the scientific world.

The position is that geneticists now know or can deduce a great deal about the genetic transmission, its nature and processes. For this reason, and with the prospect dangling before us of being able to improve genetic strains and eliminate inherited disorders, there has been much talk about what is called genetic engineering - that is, the direct mechanical interference with the genetic process to accomplish these apparently desirable objects.

But I believe that the wisest, most thoughtful and knowledgeable masters of this subject have come to the conclusion that the real prospects of genetic engineering are, for one reason and another - and not least on the moral score - no more than a tantalising mirage, which may appear feasible upon first sight but which, in fact, are entirely impracticable.

Is it possible that, as one avenue closes to science, another is opening up, and that we have the key to it? Is it possible that as the possibility of the mechanical control of genetic processes is seen to be a false aim, the prospect of controlling them through a true understanding of the right times and seasons for conception is opening up? This may seem a remote possibility at present, and it is certainly not an immediate prospect, but once the principle is established, the rest will follow. Plato himself points to this possibility in the eighth book of *The Republic*.

The simplest example and the simplest potential application of this principle relates to the actual prevention of contraception. We know that this can be accomplished by mechanical means - by contraceptives, that is - but there are those who hold that this is a wrong method and most others would presumably admit that it looks like a second-best method. Catholics urge that a method based upon natural rhythms should be used and pray for an improvement in the scientific understanding of this problem. There is no doubt whatsoever in my mind what the nature of that improved understanding will prove to be. In the meantime we must await the removal of the barrier of scientific prejudice which prevents certain lines of enquiry being followed up by those who have the means to follow them.

To revert to the genetic theme, one of the papers presented at the Serbelloni Symposium mentioned earlier, was given by R C Lewontin of Chicago University and had the title 'On the Irrelevance of Genes'.

In the accepted view of genetics, inherited traits are individually determined by genes of which there are conceived to be many thousands within each chromosome - 46 chromosomes in the case of man. But Lewontin, indicating that inherited traits do not normally appear singly but in associated groups determined by their chromosomal origin, declares that the new picture which is emerging is one in which genes entirely disappear, leaving only the chromosomes as wholes.

This is another example of the assumption of parts within wholes and it is, of course, fully in accord with the astrological picture (where groups of associated traits are regarded as springing from one astrological factor) and especially with the concept of harmonics where the same principle is brought into much sharper focus.

In this connection, one may ask if the time is not rapidly coming when geneticists, turning away from the laboratory approach, will gain far more enlightenment as to the nature and structure of the genetic inheritance from considering, for example, the statement of the neoplatonic philosopher Proclus (known, by virtue of his deep identity of thought with Plato, as the Platonic Successor), that there are in the soul 105,947 monads,[†] a monad, in this context, being one centre or unit in the hierarchy of principles, from each of which flows a range of subordinate effects at a lower level.[‡]

I have especially discussed one application of the law concerning the harmonics of cosmic periods: that in relation to genetics. But its implications are vast and it can be applied throughout the whole field of science. The knowledge that the number of every substance is a sub-multiple of its originating substance (and I use the word substance in its philosophical sense as applying to spiritual as well as natural substances) will be one of the central pillars of the science of the future. It has already been acknowledged in one field in the form of the Quantum Theory of physics and as we see, is becoming a source of interest in other respects. But this principle is of universal applicability and is the key as much, for example, to new forms of curative medicine as to the discovery of new forms of power based on the principle of resonance. It is, in fact, the key to all vibratory phenomena.

One result of these developments in the sphere of astrology will be a very great increase in the predictive potential of our science, and I am speaking now of the new and enlarged astrology which is also the true astrology.

Are we prepared for such an increase of predictive power? It has been said[§] that mankind has already passed, in recent centuries, through three demoralising experiences. The first was the realisation, through the Copernican revolution in astronomy, that the earth was not at the centre of the universe and to many men this had the effect of seeming to dwarf the significance of man himself. The second was

---

[†] The Commentaries of Proclus on the *Timæus* of Plato. Trans: Thomas Taylor (1820), Vol II, p 109. (Also quoted as footnote on p. 210).

[‡] In *Beyond Reductionism* (page 197) Koestler calls these 'holons'.

[§] The following remarks are based upon some editorial comments of Edward Dewey in *Cycles* of August 1970.

the Darwinian contribution to science which, again, seemed to many to humble man even still further. The third was the advent of modern psychology which showed man just how far he was the puppet of unrecognized drives and pressures from the irrational side of his nature.

Insofar as the construction placed upon these three discoveries by some was demeaning to man it was a mistaken interpretation. His true nature and dignity was really undiminished by any of them.

But a fourth and I believe still more shattering experience lies just around the corner and its impact will be felt in the next twenty years. It is the revelation of just how far the ebb and flow of human events and activities take place in response to the all-various pressures of cosmic forces.

The reaction to this discovery - which will be fortified by many different kinds of scientific evidence - may be severe and a wave of fatalism may sweep over men. Nevertheless, in the long run the experience will be a salutary and beneficial one, for Renaissance man and his successors have come to accept a totally false view of the nature of free will and to believe that it consists in subjugating his environment to his own self-interest (usually a very narrow self-interest) in defiance not only of the natural order but, often, of the moral order too.

This is a totally false kind of freedom.

True religion, indeed, has always pointed man the way, and astrology has always been on the side of true religion, for it is a God-centred science. But when the established church weakly turned its back upon astrology at the behest of a debased science, it lost its strongest ally. If it had upheld the right position of astrology as carefully as did, for example, Albertus Magnus and Aquinas, the story might have been different. As it is it lost its grip on certain first principles and, with it, by degrees, the allegiance of the people. An example, perhaps, of the salt losing its savour.

Taking the long view we can see that it is not until man has been forced to the realisation of just how far, and in what respect, he is *not* free, that he will be able to see clearly wherein his true dignity and liberty do consist, and that these, indeed, when they are realised, stand above nature and above all the fatal revolutions of the heavens.

Then indeed, if he is not in the meantime overtaken by Nemesis, he can begin, with safety and humility, to build a new golden age. But I suspect, as the Duke of Wellington might have said, that it will be a damned close-run thing!

THE DISCRIMINATION OF BIRTH-TYPES IN RELATION TO DISEASE

Reprinted from a pamphlet first published by the Astrological Association in 1974.

There are many problems in the field of medical research which may be said to devolve upon the question of genetic types and the relative inherent susceptibilities of different kinds of people to certain classes of pathological disorder.

That such inherent predispositions exist is so obvious and well-recognised that no special justification of their importance is called for. The concept of inherited diseases and inherited susceptibility to particular disorders is a familiar one and has always had a place in medical study and practice. So likewise the closely related, if not identical, question of constitutional physiological types.

All prophylactic medicine must concern itself with this issue. If steps are to be taken to anticipate and prevent certain ailments then the prophylactic measures are best administered where a real susceptibility exists or where it is greatest. A campaign of universal inoculation, for example, might be wasteful if it could be shown that only some people had a significant predisposition to the disease against which the inoculation was directed and it might even be altogether mistaken if it were known that, for other people, the inoculation itself carried a risk. Similarly it is well known that some drugs, whilst they operate beneficially in most cases, produce very serious side-effects in a few, due evidently to some special constitutional tendency in the patient.

But the problem goes further than this. Unless there is some objective yardstick for distinguishing physiological types and their characteristic ailments, there may easily arise a tendency to attribute to accidental, precipitating causes of disease what should really be ascribed to some inherent constitutional cause which is the dominant and determining factor.

Some classic medical controversies have centred upon this problem. For example, it is widely held that cigarette smoking is a cause of lung cancer and there can be no doubt that some connection between the two things does exist. Yet there have always been a tenacious, and often well-informed, few who have maintained that the relationship between them is not a simple matter of cause and effect but that both smoking and lung cancer are common features of a certain psycho-physiological type; and in support of this they educe arguments tending to show that the acknowledged facts of the case point at least as well to this sort of relationship as to a straightforward causal one.[1]

To be fair to the proponents of this view it must be said that their case has never been fully answered, and so the possibility remains. But, whatever the truth, it must be admitted that this is one instance where a sound, objective and comprehensive method of discriminating between different constitutional birth-types would contribute substantially to the elucidation of the problem of disease incidence and the principles of prophylactic medicine.

In the past decade or so there has grown up a very vigorous movement in the field of biological studies which has set out to re-assess the foundations of biology and in the process has put forward postulates which have inverted many of the traditional modes of approach to the understanding of living things. In particular there has been a tendency to revert to the conception of the hierarchical organisation of living things; to the principle that behind *parts* of organisms is a co-ordinating *unity*, or a hierarchy of unities subordinated and super-ordinated one to another, and this not only in terms of their structure in space but also of their development in time so that the life movements of all living things are seen as expressions in time of a co-ordinated life-process which is organised and maintained throughout a lifetime by some regulating whole.

This is leading biologists to turn to the study of the relationship of living things to time, their continuity in time, their order in time, their time-responses, their growth and development in time and, above all, as I believe, *to their origins in time*.

I have tried to show elsewhere[2] that this conception of hierarchies in nature and their expression in temporal life-processes, if it is to be fully understood, must be seen in terms of the life of nature as a whole.

If there are hierarchies in nature, where is the *summit*, in nature, of those hierarchies? There can only be one answer to this question. All living things are generated, live and evolve in a cosmic environment and, if the principle of a hierarchical organisation in nature holds good, then it is to the rhythms and sub-rhythms of the cosmic environment that the life-rhythms of living things must be subordinated.

In this context, I believe that all the rhythms of nature are based upon harmonics of cosmic periods. This is the basis, among other things, of the existence in nature of so-called circadian, and other similar rhythms.

Man, on his corporal side, is part of nature. Thus the key to the discrimination of physiological types in man is to be found in the correlation of men with their distinctive times and seasons, and especially with their origins in time.

This statement must inevitably appear, on the surface, to be a singularly obscure one and a further discussion of its theoretical basis might not, for most readers, contribute very much to its clarification. It seems wisest, therefore, to tackle the subject in terms of actual examples.

We shall therefore try to show:

(1) that there is strong evidence (evidence which is all too easily rejected on metaphysical grounds) to support a relationship between the time when a person is born[†] and the diseases to which he is prone and, by implication, to his psycho-physiological type, and

(2) that the key to this relationship is to be found in the harmonics, that is the rhythms and sub-rhythms, of cosmic periods.[‡]

In order to show that medical research has already, from time to time, pointed to the truth of our first thesis, we shall draw, in respect of (1) upon two studies (or groups of studies) by medical statisticians which have already been published. But in respect of (2) we shall depend upon an original study of our own which is, however, part

---

[†] Time, in this context is taken in its widest connotation: the epoch, the century, the year, the month, the day, the hour . . .

[‡] By 'cosmic periods' we mean any natural period of time derived from cyclic events in space, such as the rotation or revolution of the earth or the orbital, synodic or diurnal periods of heavenly bodies.

of, and consistent with, a series of researches carried out by the author (and others[3]) in this and kindred fields.

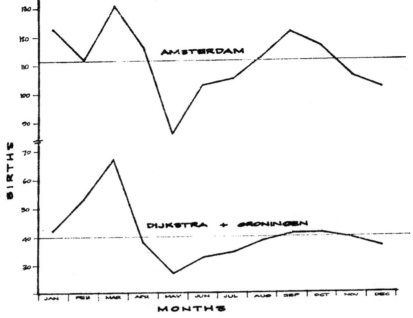

Fig. A

Let us then take as our starting-point the article by BKS Dijkstra in the Journal of the National Cancer Institute (Vol 31, No 3, Sept 1963) in which he described an examination of the dates of birth of 330 lung cancer sufferers in Holland and concluded that they showed a significantly abnormal distribution both by *year* of birth and also by *date* of birth. In the latter case, the births showed a peak incidence in March and a low incidence in the summer months and Dijkstra suggested an explanation linking these two factors with certain physiological effects which could be brought about by a deficiency, in the one case, and an abundance in the other, of Vitamin A in the diet of the newly born child. (Milk has a low Vitamin A content at the end of the winter, a high one in the summer.)

In the correspondence in the British medical journal, *The Lancet*, which followed the publication of Dijkstra's paper, two other Dutch sources sent in their sets of monthly totals of lung cancer birth-dates.[4] They were the University Cancer Registration Centre, Amsterdam, and University College Hospital, Groningen.

Since Dijkstra's cases totalled only 330 and University College, Groningen, only 150, we may reasonably and conveniently put these two sets together for comparison with the much larger total of 1320 cases from Amsterdam so as to provide ourselves with the best available comparison of large totals.

Here are the two sets of Dutch lung cancer birth-dates as distributed by monthly totals from January to December (Fig A).

It will be seen that these two distribution patterns present a thoroughly consistent picture.

Before the additional data had been sent by the two above-named Dutch sources, the significance of Dijkstra's figures had been challenged by the Royal Marsden Hospital's Institute of Cancer Research, Chelsea,[5] where an analysis had been made of the birth-dates of 2042 men dying of lung cancer in Southern England during 1959 and 1960. In this study the high incidence of March births was no longer in evidence and, instead, the peak came in the Autumn. Yet, leaving aside the question of how far Dutch and English cancer cases can be treated as strictly comparable, the distribution of the English lung cancer births was not so grossly dissimilar from the Dutch ones that the case for *some* sort of seasonal rhythm was destroyed, and if the distributions are considered by three-monthly totals, then their underlying similarity becomes apparent (Fig B).

Some time later, in *The Lancet* of 5 September 1964, WJJ Sauvage Nolting wrote from Holland to say that in a much larger survey of 15,091 cancer cases, of which one-third were cancer of the lung, 'a distinct seasonal variation' was shown in the distribution of birth-dates, a variation 'which, moreover, proved to be identical for the different categories of cancer'.

Altogether, the case for some sort of seasonal rhythm in cancer births seems to be very strong indeed, though it must be regarded as an unexplained phenomenon for the Vitamin A deficiency theory was evidently soon discarded.

We must now consider the work of a Scottish surgeon pathologist, T W Lees (at one time of Law Hospital, Carluke, in Scotland, more recently of the Provincial Laboratories, Prince Albert Island, Canada). Comparatively little has been heard of this work, considering its penetration and scope, and perhaps there is a definite reason for this which will be mentioned shortly.

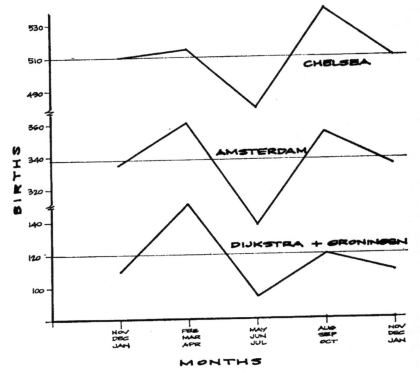

Fig. B

It is impossible to do justice to Dr Lees' researches and conclusions[6] in the space of a brief summary but an outline, at least, of one particular aspect of his work must be attempted.

This has consisted primarily of a study of the incidence of various types of cancer among different age-groups during the past century or more. It is well known that different types of cancer show changes in their incidence over the years, some (such as Leukaemia at the present time) showing an increase, whilst others (such as cancer of the gullet at present) are declining; some reaching a peak (such as lung cancer today) whilst others (such as lip and tongue) almost disappear.

The 15 commonest types of cancer in males and four in females (19 in all) were analyzed by the incidence of mortality at specific ages *and in every case it could be seen that the rise and fall had followed, or was following, a similar pattern.*

It was invariably found, with each and every type of cancer, that when the incidence was considered by age-groups it was the youngest age-group which reached its peak incidence first, (indeed it is in the youngest age-group that a significant increase is first to be observed) and as higher and higher age-groups are considered the peak incidence occurs later and later in time.

It is vital that the significance of this important finding should be clearly recognised. Each type of cancer does not begin to appear first among the older members of the community *as one would expect it to do if it were being caused by some factor in the environment.* Rather it is as if it were suddenly found that new generations were being born with an increasing tendency to a new type of cancer but no longer showing so great a susceptibility to those types which were widespread when they were born or in the preceding decades.

Thus it can be shown that the peak incidence of any one type of cancer is reached, not among all age groups simultaneously, but that it is *one particular generation which shows the highest incidence at every age.* The highest incidence of that type of cancer among people in their thirties is reached when *that* generation is in its thirties; the highest incidence among forty-year-olds is reached when *that* generation is in its forties and so on up the scale to the higher ages. And of course, by the time that generation is old and showing a very high death rate from that type of cancer, the death rate at the lower ages will long since have declined, since by that time new generations are being born whose tendency is to a different type of cancer.

For example, Fig C1 shows deaths from cancer of the larynx by ages during each 5-year period between 1906 and 1960.

It will be seen that the highest death rate among those aged 40-50 occurs in 1916-20; this gets steadily later until among those aged 70-74 it occurs in 1941-45. We can now re-draw this graph (Fig C2) using the same data but arranging the age-group lines so that the horizontal scale is no longer the *year of death* but the *year of birth.* We now see that the highest death rate for laryngeal cancer at every age occurred, approximately at least, among those born in the 1860s.

Fig D shows deaths from lung cancer on the same basis as Fig C2, that is among generations of men *born* in five-year periods between 1846 and 1931. This graph was given by Lees in the early 1960s.

The difference now is that this graph is drawn on a logarithmic scale so that the *proportionate* increase or decrease at each age is shown by a *proportionate* rise or fall on the graph (ie a 10% change occupies the same space on the vertical scale whether it be a change from 9,000 to 10,000 at the higher ages, when the disease is relatively common, or 90 to 100 at the lower ages, when it is rare).

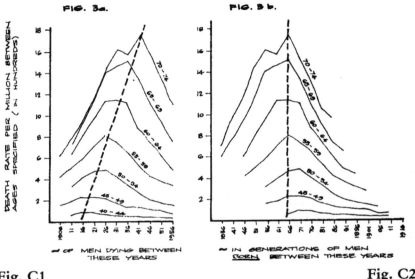

Fig. C1   Fig. C2

In this graph the continuous lines represent the observed death rate up to 1960, the dotted lines represent the predicted death rate, the latter being given on either of the two assumptions: (1) that the curves will continue their shape or (2) that lung cancer will behave as all other types of cancer have been shown to behave.

Dr Lees shows that the increase and decrease of each type of cancer can be represented by a roughly symmetrical curve, the base of which extends over a period in the order of 150 years (although he pointed out, in relation to the graph given - Fig D - that the decline is usually more rapid than the one given and that the predicted death rate for all ages over 50 was probably too high). In the case of lung cancer it will be seen that it is those who were born in approximately the first decade of this century who show, at every age, the greatest tendency to the disease.

Of the relationship between smoking and lung cancer Dr Lees says: 'The sternest critic of the theory that smoking causes lung cancer is the behaviour of the disease itself . . . Forty years ago when tongue cancer was in its heyday it was "caused" by smoking, but now it has almost disappeared. Today smoking "causes" lung cancer because that has gone up fifteen times but not cancer of the larynx because that has gone down to one-third; all smoke passes over the larynx and the association of smoking with laryngeal cancer thirty years ago was as good as that with lung cancer today.'[7]

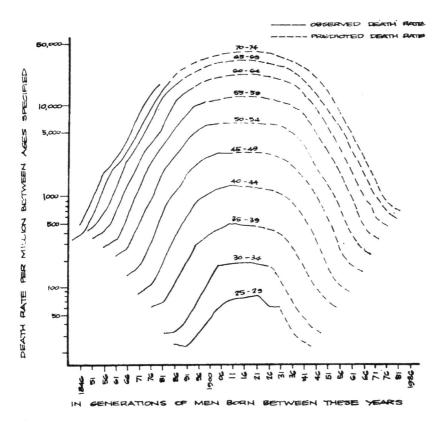

Fig. D

The sole reason that the death rate from lung cancer has continued to rise in recent years is that the 'lung cancer generation' is now reaching the age of 70 and more, and so the very high incidence of deaths from lung cancer among those over 70 has offset the falling death rate at all lower ages. But now, as Lees predicted fifteen years ago, the two forces are balancing and by the early 1980s it will be falling at all ages.

'From time to time the intensity of some specific factor in the environment rises in parallel with the increase of some cancers. It is then claimed to be the dominant "cause". Sooner or later, however, the intensity of the "cause" and the level of the alleged "effects" part company.'[8] This stage has already been passed in relation to smoking and lung cancer. The facts speak for themselves: the lung cancer mortality rate for those under 35 has been *falling* for nearly 25 years; it has been falling at all ages below 45 since 1955 and at all ages below 60 since about 1965 - and this at a time when there was certainly no decline in cigarette smoking and among the very age-groups who smoke most cigarettes.

The crude association of smoking with lung cancer is not questioned, but proof of association, no matter how overwhelming, is not proof of causation.

In actuality it can be seen that each type of cancer is related primarily to some factor *which operates from birth.*

One is reminded again of the conclusion drawn by Dijkstra who, having examined his evidence from various points of view and having placed these different aspects of the evidence side by side wrote: *'Mathematically this means only ONE factor is responsible for its (cancer's) origin . . . the question is where to look for that one factor. All three curves suggest the moment of birth.'*

The striking feature of the two pieces of research which have been described - and the one to which attention is particularly drawn - is that in both cases the researcher was driven to the conclusion that, for whatever reason, there was, in the problem of cancer causation, some crucial factor to be considered which *operated from birth.*

Confronted with such a discovery the natural reaction of the present-day scientist, accustomed to think primarily in terms of proximate material and efficient causes, is to search the infant or pre-natal environment for some extrinsic factor which would induce a permanent constitutional predisposition to the ailment in question (Dijkstra's suggestion was the Vitamin A deficiency).

However, it is possible that this is not the only way, or even the best way, of looking at the problem and it is interesting to note that Dr Lees (insofar as he considers the point) appears to find that the observed facts do not favour explanations in terms of efficient causes - for example cigarette smoking; rather, he sees (in his 'wave theory' of disease incidence) only the sweep of some larger 'biological law' moulding the course of events; he has even used the term 'inexorable'.[9] Such thoughts, one suspects, do not readily accord with our modern viewpoint on such matters. We like to be able to correlate neatly, the rise of cancer of the lip with the use of the clay pipe, lung cancer with cigarettes and so on. But if such correlations do not fit the facts then Dr Lees must be a better scientist and not a worse one for saying so candidly.

We may reflect that in another age men would have seen the outward chain of efficient causation as being subject to and moulded by a higher order of formal causes and they would have reflected that the seat of the formal causes of disease in man is the soul. Thus perhaps even so down-to-earth a psychologist as Professor Eysenck is nearer the truth when he sees both smoking and lung cancer as common characteristics of a certain type.

We do not always realise what an overshadowing role metaphysical concepts play in determining what is to be accepted and what rejected in the field of scientific enquiry and discovery. Certainly Dr Lees' researches are worthy of a far greater degree of attention than has been accorded to them.[10]

We have seen that Dijkstra pointed to significant fluctuations in the *year* of birth of lung cancer sufferers and he and others to *seasonal* fluctuations in their births. We have also seen that Lees points to much larger fluctuations which affect whole generations.

It is the writer's contention that all these fluctuations are based on the harmonics of cosmic periods.

In order to illustrate the principles and to show, furthermore, that such fluctuations in birth times relate not only to generations, to years and to seasons, but also to days and to hours, it will be necessary to change diseases.

The author has not had access to any large collections of cancer birth-dates but having worked for some years with children suffering from paralytic poliomyelitis, a large number of birth dates of sufferers from this complaint were available to him.

There is no anomaly in this change from one disease to another; the principles involved are the same in both cases and in this connection it is of interest to note that Lees has also studied the long-term fluctuations of poliomyelitis and has predicted that it will return in the mid-1980s, affecting, in middle life, the same generation which it originally attacked in infancy and, later, in adolescence.

Our poliomyelitis data, then, consist of two groups of children who contracted poliomyelitis before the age of 16: 443 cases from Queen Mary's Children's Hospital School, Carshalton, Surrey, and 580 from the National Orthopaedic Children's Hospital School, Stanmore, Middlesex - 1023 cases in all.

There are a number of temporal rhythms which can be shown to relate to poliomyelitis-prone births, but it is essential in this instance to keep the outline of our case clear and its basis as simple and uncontroversial as possible. Therefore the period we shall examine is the year of 365.25 days approximately, the period of our planet's revolution around the sun. (This of course is the basis of those seasonal variations already observed in connection with cancer-prone birth-dates.)

In order to study the rhythms, within the year, of our births it will be both simpler and more accurate if we convert our birth dates into solar longitudes. The sun's longitude on a given day scarcely differs from one year to another but it is easier to deal with 360 (degrees in a circle) than 365/366 (days in a year).

Our basic data consists, therefore, of 1023 solar longitudes, being the sun's position (eastward from the vernal point), to the nearest whole degree, at noon, on the day and year of birth of children with poliomyelitis. Distributed round the 360° circle of the ecliptic these give us 360 totals each representing, to all intents and purposes, the number of such births on a given day of the year.

Fig. E

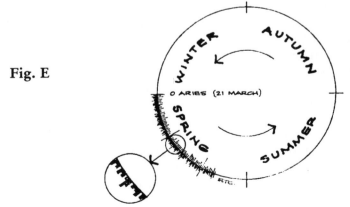

In order to visualise clearly what is involved we can picture the circle of the year with the total number of cases for each degree blocked in as in Figure E.

With only 1023 cases spread through 360 degrees the total for each degree is not going to be high: an average of less than three per degree; but, as we shall show, this thin spread is not an impediment to our purpose.

Now when Dijkstra and others studied the seasonal distribution of cancer birth dates, they divided the circle of the year into twelve months and gave a total for *each month*.

We are now no longer interested in such monthly totals[11] since our purpose is to show the presence of much shorter rhythms than can be revealed in this way. Where Dijkstra considered the yearly distribution of births month by month we shall examine the birth rhythms *within* each twelfth part of the circle.

This may seem an unlikely exercise but other researches by the writer have given abundant justification for such a study.

Fig. F

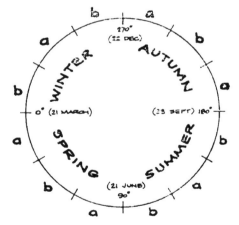

In dividing the circle of the ecliptic (around which the sun appears to travel) into twelve 30° sectors, we are in effect dividing the year into twelve *approximately* 30-day periods and we are to investigate whether there are significant and consistent rhythms at work within these periods which throw up certain times when polio-prone births tend to occur and others when they do not.

For this stage of the investigation we shall, in the first place, take all our 1023 birth dates, converted into solar longitudes and distributed round the 360° of the circle, and show them as thirty degree-by-degree totals for two groups of alternate 30° sectors round the ecliptic. In other words we are diving the 360° into twelve 30° sectors, calling these alternately 'a' sectors and 'b' sectors (Fig F) and showing the sun's degree-by-degree distribution in *all the 'a' sectors put together* compared with its distribution in *all the 'b' sectors put together*. Fig G shows the result.

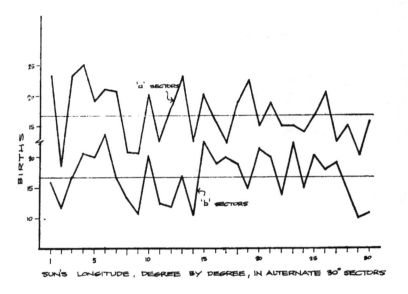

Fig. G

Now although the fact may not be instantly apparent (especially to the eye unaccustomed to such comparisons), the two distribution patterns shown in Fig G are exceedingly similar. A close scrutiny will reveal this to be so. In fact the similarity is such that it would occur by chance less than once in 100 times.[†]

If this similarity is not a chance one then, what exactly does it imply? If implies that within each 30° sector (roughly within each

[†] The coefficient of correlation is 0.512 (t=3.14) but for the control (see below) - 0.053.

30-day period) there are birth rhythms at work which have a special relationship to poliomyelitis-prone births, and because those rhythms are operating to produce a definite distribution pattern of such births within the 30° period then (to take a leap forward) those rhythms must all be sub-harmonics or sub-rhythms of that period.

And as they are harmonics of that period then we shall be able to see their presence even more clearly by subdividing the 30° period by the whole numbers - that is by 2, 3 and so on - and examining the distribution of births within those shorter periods.

Fig. H

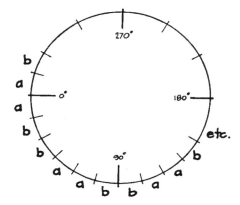

If, for example, we divide the ecliptic into 24 sectors of 15° each and again compare 'a' and 'b' sectors as shown in Fig H then the degree-by-degree distribution for the two groups is as follows (Fig I).

The similarity of distribution of births within these (approximately) 15-day periods is now quite clear. The fundamental rhythm is of course the 24th harmonic of the circle, a wave of 15°. But superimposed upon this there are two other vigorous harmonics present: the 48th (showing as two waves of 7.5°) and the 120th (showing as five waves of 3°). We may illustrate how these three rhythms combine to give the distinctive distribution shown in Fig I as in Fig J.

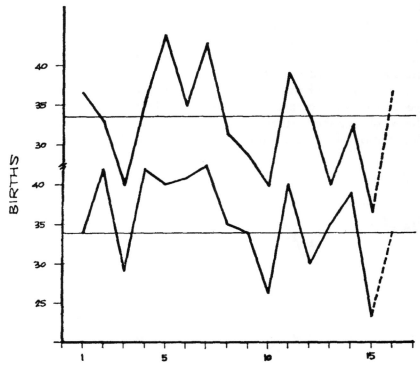

Fig. I

Comparing the bottom line in this, Fig J, with the distribution shown in Fig I, we can see that the forces at work shaping the distribution of polio-prone nativities within each 24th part of the year consist primarily of three harmonics of the annual cycle of which the 120th (3°) is a particularly strong presence.

The shape of the wave complex in the bottom line of Fig J is analogous to the sound wave of a note sounded on a musical instrument. When such a note is sounded the pitch of the note is represented by a fundamental wave form (top line), but to this are added sub-harmonics of that same note and these vary from one instrument to another to give the characteristic 'timbre' of the instrument upon which the note is sounded. Here we have just such a wave complex which is repeated over and over again, twenty-four times in each complete circle.

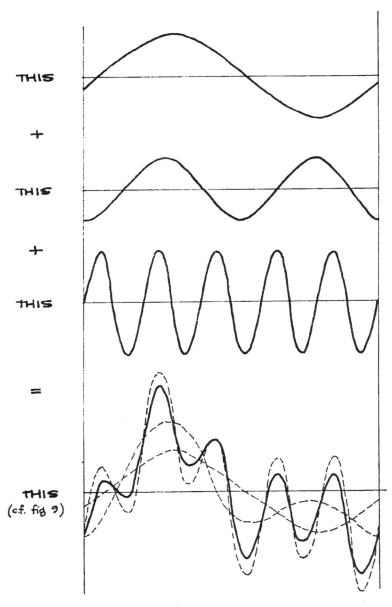

THIS

+

THIS

+

THIS

=

THIS
(c.f. fig 9)

Fig. J

The thin spread of cases (less than three per degree on average) is such that our characteristic wave 'signal' would seldom show up in any one 15° sector but, by dividing our distribution pattern into 24 sectors and collecting these sectors together in two groups of twelve, the random elements in each separate sector are cancelled out and the 'signal' is left showing.[12]

If we think again about Fig G, we shall realise that of the possible sub-harmonics of that 30° sector of the circle, we have extracted so far (ie in Fig I) only those which will fit into half the period - that is those which result from dividing the 30° sector by two and its multiples.

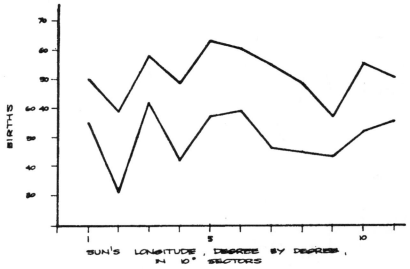

Fig. K

We can test the distribution pattern for the presence of the third sub-harmonic of that 30° period (ie a wave of 10° in length) by dividing our original distribution round the circle into 36 sectors of 10° each and comparing the distribution in alternate such sectors. Fig K shows the result of this exercise. The dominant 'note' here is the basic wave of 10° - the 36th harmonic - but some of the sub-harmonics are clearly to be seen.[†]

[†] Notably the 144th (4 x 36) and the 180th (5 x 36).

In order to test the validity of these findings two things are needed: a control group and a new set of polio birth-dates.

Strictly speaking the control is not needed. The sun's apparent daily motion varies but little during the year and such variation as exists is *entirely* eliminated when the ecliptic is divided, as has been done, into twelve sectors which are then added together. The same is true of variations in the birth rate at different times of the year. However, in order to eliminate doubt, a control collection of birth-dates was made. Our original total of cases was 1023, and these were derived from two main sources; therefore the control group was made up of 512 (= 1023 divided by 2) random birth-dates of school children from three different localities, the yearly total of birth-dates in the control being, for each year, just half of the yearly total in the larger group. (In other words the distribution by years was the same for the control as for the polio births.)

An examination of the control group of birth-dates confirmed that the rhythms observed in the polio birth-dates were not, as will be seen later, common to births generally.

In order to obtain a further batch of birth-dates of polio sufferers recourse was had to an article which was published, with an appeal for birth-dates, in the 'Infantile Paralysis Fellowship Bulletin'. This was not a very satisfactory method of acquiring data (since it introduced a slight element of selectivity) and one would have preferred to extract the information direct from medical records; however, no access to such records was available at the time. Some 257 replies were received, not a large number but enough to test against the earlier results, and these had the added element of accuracy provided by an approximate birth-*time*.

The special feature of the results we have described was that the distribution of the birth-dates (represented by the solar longitudes) was dominated by the sub-multiples of the 12th harmonic of the annual period. Not all this series of harmonics were equally important; the 12th itself (a wave of 30°) was insignificant in all three sets of results but apart from that one and the 120th harmonic, which was outstanding, it was the lower sub-multiples of the 12th, that is the 24th, 36th and 48th, which were most strongly marked both as to the amplitude of the waves and the consistency of their phasing.

A complete harmonic analysis of all four sets of data (3 groups of polio and the control) was done by computer from the 1st to the 180th harmonic (the number of harmonics required to describe fully the distribution for 360 separate degree-totals) and it was found that the Infantile Paralysis Fellowship data agreed with each of the two original sets of data even better than they agreed with each other. The harmonics which were sub-multiples of the 12th were again very prominent in terms of amplitude and were in close agreement as to phase.

To round this off on a more technical note: As an appendix we give the harmonic analysis for the three sets of polio data and the control from the first to the 50th harmonic[13] plus the 120th harmonic.

What one is looking for in these results are rhythms which appear both *strongly* and *consistently* in the data. *All* harmonics are present to some extent in any complex wave form such as we are dealing with here; the really important and significant harmonics are indicated by high amplitude together with consistency of phase from one set of data to another.

Fig L shows, on the top, the geometric mean amplitude of each of the first fifty harmonics for all three sets of polio data (the amplitude being expressed, for each harmonic, as a percentage of the mean distribution). Beneath that is shown the phase angle required to cover the difference of phase between the three sets of polio data for the same 50 harmonics. (A single pair of harmonics can differ in phase angle by up to 180°; three harmonics may require up to 240° to cover their phase difference.)

It will be seen that among these harmonics only three, the 24th, 36th and 48th are outstanding both as to amplitude *and* phase agreement for all three sets of data. To these should evidently be added the 120th harmonic (a wave of 3°) which shows a mean amplitude for three sets of 17% whilst a phase angle of 79° covers their phasing.[14]

The details may be summarised as follows:

| | Stanmore | | Carshalton | | IPF | | Overall | Control | |
Harmonic	Ampl	Phase	Ampl	Phase	Ampl	Phase	Phase Diff	Ampl	Phase
24	12.5	118	10.2	107	8.5	50	68	6.5	139
36	8.4	147	15.9	185	18.1	186	39	6.5	331
48	7.7	176	12.0	239	11.1	226	63	6.7	236
120	11.5	133	22.2	54	20.4	112	79	4.3	9

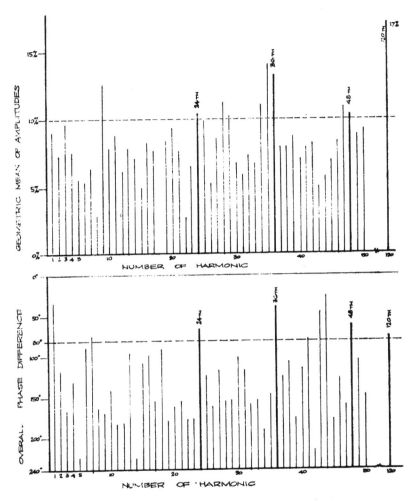

Fig. L

In Figure L the overall phase difference has been shown for each harmonic up to the 50th. Eg if the phase difference between the nth harmonic in data sets 1 & 2 is 30° and in data sets 2 & 3 is 60° in the same direction, the overall phase difference for the nth harmonic is 90° as shown right. If the corresponding amplitudes in the 3 data sets are 2%, 4% & 8% the geometric mean is 4% (cube root of the product of 2, 4 & 8). Of the first 50 harmonics only the 24th, 36th & 48th have overall phase differences less than 80° *and* mean amplitudes greater than 10%.

Finally it may be stated that if the distribution of all 1280 cases is plotted in terms of the 12th harmonic - that is the distribution in all 30° sectors put together, the series in which all sub-harmonics of the 12th are precipitated - then the resulting degree-by-degree totals show a deviation from the mean which would occur by chance only once in 1000 times (see Table).

─────── TABLE : ───────

Degree	Polio Cases	Control Cases	
0	33	11	
1	47	20	
2	25	9	
3	45	14	X^2 TEST ON DISTRIBUTIONS
4	58	16	
5	47	12	
6	53	20	
7	48	17	
8	30	21	*Polio cases:*
9	26	20	$X^2 = 57.7$
10	46	17	0.1% level (such a distribution occurs,
11	34	22	by chance, once in 1000).
12	37	24	
13	56	19	
14	36	18	
15	54	21	*Control cases:*
16	46	16	$X^2 = 21.1$
17	39	14	This value is exceeded by more than
18	53	20	half of such sets ,randomly distributed.
19	55	19	
20	41	21	
21	49	19	
22	38	13	
23	46	15	
24	38	13	
25	50	17	
26	49	17	
27	36	16	
28	35	14	
29	30	17	
	1280	512	

To sum up, it is upon evidence of this order that the writer suggests that there appears to be a basis for the differentiation of geno-types and the measurement of their susceptibility to different types of disease *to be found in the relationship of human births to the harmonics of cosmic periods*, and although the foregoing example has been worked out entirely in terms of the harmonics of the annual solar period - or rather, of the terrestrial revolutionary period - there is (on the basis of this research) at least a *prima facie* case for supposing that the same principles may apply in terms of other cosmic periods and this has in fact been shown to be so.[15]

CONCLUSION

The ancient science of astrology treats of the symbolism of time and of the symbolic relation of things brought forth in time to the ideas which substand all generation.

Upon the great ocean of generation are rollers which span the centuries and ripples which are but minutes and seconds. All are based upon the harmonics of cosmic periods which measure out the motions of the primary lives of the cosmos.

'Time is the measure of the lives and motions of the cosmos'. (Proclus)

'Time is an everlasting flowing image of eternity'. (Plato)

Modern research has shown that all the traditional lore of astrology which has been handed down from remote times is based upon the symbolism of cosmic existences and their periodic revolutions but that it has in the process of transmission, become ossified into rigid formulas and doctrines from which the illuminating principles have largely been lost.

The key to the interpretation of the numerical relationships within the birth chart is to be found in the hierarchical structure of man and nature by which all things are rooted in and proceed, in due order, from the unity which is their cause and origin.

To recover the pure Pythagorean principles of number symbolism as they relate to the microcosm and the dynamic interrelationships of its parts and principles, is perhaps the foremost task of astrology today.

NOTES

1 See, for example, Prof H T Eysenck writing in the magazine *Encounter:* Aug 1964.

2 *Astrology Reborn:* J M Addey, See appendix I

3 See, for example, the work of Prof Michel Gauquelin of the Laboratoire d'Etude des Relations entre Rhythmes Cosmiques et Psychophysiologiques, 8 Rue Amyot, 75 Paris 5, France: Now published in 16 volumes. French and English Parallel texts.

4 *The Lancet:* 4 Jan and 11 Jan 1964.

5 *The Lancet:* 14 Dec 1963.

6 See *Smoking and Lung Cancer* and *The Wave Theory of Cancer Mortality* by T W Lees, MD, both published by the author.

7 *Smoking and Lung Cancer.* (See Note number 6 above.)

8 *The Wave Theory of Cancer Mortality*, pp 27. (See Note number 6 above.)

9 In a letter to the *Sunday Telegraph* of 22 March 1964.

10 Leading medical journals have been very resistant to the publication of Lees' work, as he himself avers. One of the few occasions on which he was given a hearing was in the *Sunday Telegraph* of 21 Feb 1965. In publishing his views, the *Sunday Telegraph* commented editorially:

CHALLENGE ON CANCER

"So enormous is now the professional and financial interest in cancer research which follows certain lines and so weighty is the official influence behind the campaign against smoking that it is virtually impossible for a critical view to appear in the medical press.

"With due sense of our responsibility to sufferers and their doctors, we publish this week on the opposite page the views of a pathologist who challenges current assumptions from the basis of his own experience with a large number of individual cases. He poses questions arising from the statistics which no one has answered.

"*The Sunday Telegraph* will be pleased to give publicity to authoritative answers. In particular we seek some explanation of why, if smoking causes cancer, this disease as it affects the tongue and larynx should have declined at a time of rapidly increasing smoking. That the Minister of Health may have been wrongly advised seems incredible, but it is not impossible."

(One phrase in this statement should be corrected: Mr Lees was not challenging current assumptions merely from 'his own experience of a large number of individual cases' - although he certainly had such experience - but from the total mortality figures of the Registrar General.)

When the *Sunday Telegraph* received no response to its plea for an 'authoritative answer' to Mr Lees' case, it tried again:

CIGARETTE CASE

"Last week we published the views of Mr T W Lees, a surgeon pathologist, questioning the current statistical assumptions about smoking and lung cancer. We invited authoritative answers to this minority opinion in the confident expectation of receiving them. We have received none.

"This is astonishing and even alarming. Millions of pounds are contributed to cancer research. Surely there should be at least one man in this vast medical industry to justify a belief, which has been widely publicised and to which even the government has been committed."

The following week an 'answer' was printed from C M Fletcher, MD, FRCP, of the Royal College of Physicians Committee on Smoking and Health. He did not attempt to deal with Mr Lees' evidence but wrote that:

"Eight independent committees of medical men and scientists in five different countries and one WHO committee have in the past eight years reviewed all the evidence on cigarette smoking and lung cancer and have concluded that the explanation of the association of smoking and lung cancer is due to cigarette smoking being an important cause of lung cancer . . . why, Sir, by your ill-informed attention to Dr Lees . . . do you seek to weaken doctors' efforts to save lives?"

Since then there have, no doubt, been dozens, if not hundreds more committees, all with large sums of money to spend. Each year Dr Lees' views and predictions have been ever more clearly vindicated whilst no substantial progress has been made in justifying the orthodox opinions as to the cause of cancer. Otherwise the positions remain unchanged.

11 However the comparison of monthly totals - or rather their equivalent in terms of twelve equal 30° sectors of our circle - do show a good measure of agreement. In 10 cases out of 12 the total births in each 'month' is not above average in one hospital group where it is below in the other, or vice versa.

12 An analogy may be drawn here with what sometimes happens in radio astronomy. When radio astronomers, for example, bounced radio signals off the planet Venus in order to pick them up on their return and so measure the distance to that planet more accurately, the signal which came back was so faint as to be lost amid the general random background 'crackle' from outer space picked up by the radio telescope. But because the signal was of known frequency, the astronomers could in effect filter out the random sounds and so leave the signal clearly detectable.

In just the same way, because of the thin spread of cases (only three per degree) our characteristic signal would not be visible in any *one* 15° sector of the distribution pattern but, by collecting up two sets of twelve sectors, the random elements in each sector tend to cancel each other out and the signal is left showing.

13 The provision in the appendix of the harmonic analysis from the first to the fiftieth harmonic is sufficient to illustrate the process involved and to give the facts necessary for understanding the basis of the calculations described in the text but the full analysis to the 180th harmonic is available from the author.

14 The *phase angle* is expressed by treating each harmonic wave as being 360° in length (no matter what fraction of the circle it represents) and by giving the distance along the wave (from 0° Aries) at which the peak of the wave comes.

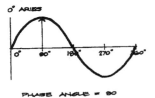

PHASE ANGLE = 90

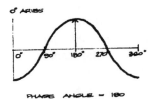

PHASE ANGLE = 180

15 See, for example, 'The Scientific Starting Point in Astrology' (*Astrological Journal*, Vol III, No 2, March 1961), reprinted in the year-book (1970) of ISAR, USA.

*Opposite we give the harmonic analysis of the solar distribution in the three collections of polio nativities together with the control set. The significance of this analysis is explained in pages 243 and 244, see also diagram L on page 245.

HARMONIC ANALYSIS OF THREE SETS OF POLIO DATA AND CONTROL

H=Harmonic A=Amplitude P=Phase

H	Stanmore		Carshalton		I.P.F.		Control	
	A	P	A	P	A	P	A	P
1	7.1	29	6.8	38	14.8	3	21.2	5
2	11.1	285	3.1	225	12.3	167	7.3	318
3	8.7	211	10.6	286	8.6	117	8.1	225
4	8.4	203	4.5	337	13.5	223	12.3	23
5	10.9	13	8.4	318	1.5	183	5.3	349
6	4.9	32	8.4	301	3.7	15	5.9	129
7	13.4	281	10.4	204	1.8	258	0.8	158
8	0.9	156	10.4	250	21.9	320	7.5	78
9	17.5	187	13.8	358	8.0	345	5.9	80
10	6.2	24	8.3	42	9.7	259	8.0	37
11	7.5	169	10.8	308	7.9	352	18.4	199
12	8.5	180	1.9	2	22.5	226	16.3	161
13	3.7	357	12.4	254	9.9	259	10.1	195
14	10.6	332	4.4	91	9.1	198	2.9	106
15	4.9	356	2.3	84	12.3	106	5.7	296
16	6.7	20	10.0	113	7.6	121	6.7	260
17	11.5	262	5.1	105	8.1	164	10.6	164
18	0.4	297	4.4	204	10.8	295	7.8	10
19	4.8	96	12.0	275	10.1	8	11.7	100
20	3.6	184	9.9	310	20.0	146	11.2	189
21	10.4	133	1.9	205	22.4	49	3.1	48
22	10.0	287	1.8	108	1.5	134	9.5	82
23	2.3	153	16.6	282	7.8	104	1.1	335
24	12.5	118	10.2	107	8.5	50	6.5	246
25	5.0	284	14.6	162	13.3	159	6.8	188
26	2.3	163	5.8	236	12.2	313	7.9	274
27	11.8	356	5.9	65	8.5	113	3.4	61
28	11.3	17	18.9	279	6.5	221	10.1	31
29	9.5	10	10.0	256	11.1	51	7.8	353
30	2.8	132	4.9	28	21.4	41	5.5	167
31	8.1	212	3.5	93	8.3	143	6.4	1
32	4.9	75	7.1	274	11.5	54	8.9	347
33	9.6	278	4.1	124	8.5	145	3.1	57
34	15.2	209	8.5	331	10.0	139	9.5	43
35	9.5	218	14.9	70	21.5	214	10.4	49
36	8.4	147	15.9	185	18.1	186	6.5	331
37	7.5	59	4.9	14	13.0	293	6.8	64
38	6.1	178	7.1	86	12.4	194	10.1	30
39	11.0	230	4.7	234	11.8	53	17.9	71
40	3.1	24	7.1	268	16.8	281	11.0	119
41	13.4	303	5.0	23	8.5	315	9.4	136
42	12.7	120	5.9	263	6.8	356	7.7	52
43	7.7	194	2.9	232	4.6	240	5.6	170
44	9.7	226	2.4	208	9.5	197	9.4	249
45	2.7	322	10.8	144	10.2	179	4.6	23
46	3.1	316	14.3	236	14.0	188	6.5	295
47	9.3	312	11.9	150	12.4	211	13.1	151
48	7.7	176	12.0	239	11..1	226	6.7	236
49	5.8	227	8.9	120	13.5	151	10.3	245
50	5.8	28	12.2	141	11.3	177	8.1	57
120	11.5	133	22.2	54	20.4	112	4.3	9

Appendix III

OBSERVATIONS ON THE BASIC PROBLEM

OF ASTROLOGY

Rudolf Tomaschek,
Professor of Theoretical Physics, University of Munich

(From an article which first appeared in *Tradition und Fortschritt der Klassischen Astrologie*)

The correlation of astronomical facts with terrestrial events is the domain of astrology, be they of a physical, chemical, physiological or psychological nature. The truth of such correlations can be demonstrated by statistical methods: that is, the correlations between the positions and aspects of the planets and angles with terrestrial events. Their factual character is beyond doubt.

Even if it were possible to treat astrology as a purely empirical investigation, however, it would still be desirable to have some conceptual framework within which to consider the correlations we observe.

There are four theories which attempt to explain the possibility of such correlations. They are:

1. That the celestial bodies actually *operate* upon terrestrial events.
2. That the celestial bodies *precipitate* events which are ripe for manifestation.
3. That the celestial bodies *synchronize* with terrestrial events.
4. That the celestial bodies *symbolise* organic cosmic forces which are qualitative functions of time and space.

1. To affect something implies a transmission of energy (e.g. by radiation or through a field of force) on to the terrestrial medium, much as the seasons are caused by the sun's rays. According to this theory, one would expect the effects observed to bear a direct relationship to the causative factors -- such as, perhaps, distance, mass, surface, temperature and so on.

This is the simplest and most obvious, yet in reality the least satisfactory explanation. It is the one which, because of our present materialistic outlook, has been accepted by many who think only superficially about the problem.

2. To precipitate something is really a variation, though a significant one, of the theory given above. It too postulates a physical energy from the planets, but in this case the quality or magnitude of the effect bears no proportionate relationship to the amount of primary or acting energy. Rather it assumes a minimum value for the initiating energy. For instance, the lighting of a fire with a match. With the match one may set fire either to a piece of paper or a house or even to a powder magazine. (This fact presented an interesting problem to the discoverer of the principle of the conservation of energy, Julius Robert Mayer, to which he devoted much thought in his latter years).

A qualitative factor can, however, easily be introduced by assuming the existence of vibrations of some sort as the basic phenomenon. This involves the principle of resonance. According to this view, the vibrations which correspond to certain effects are called into play in appropriate circumstances.

This is a phenomenon which is familiar to us nowadays through the study of electric waves. In a living room, for instance, all the radio waves of the transmitting stations of the world exist simultaneously without interfering with each other and without our noticing them. But if we have a wireless set, we can tell that they are there by (a) the sound which comes from the loudspeaker, (b) tuning in to a particular station through the principle of resonance so that we can receive whatever is being transmitted from that station, and (c) certain aids such as amplification and narrowing down the frequency (to give greater selectivity) so that one can make even the faintest signals audible. Today radio-telescopes are so sensitive that thunder storms on Jupiter or Saturn can be detected.

The difficulty about this second assumption of precipitation (which also postulates a physical relationship between terrestrial and celestial phenomena) is to be found in the fact that there exists at present no conception of the way in which the qualitative differences of vibration, which lead up to resonance, are connected with the qualitative differences of effect. That such differences exist accounts, in the psychological sphere, for the sensation of colour. The vibrational frequency of six hundred billion per second brings about the sensation red, while the frequency of four hundred and thirty billion causes the sensation green. Perhaps the colours which are traditionally associated with the planets are due to such differences of vibration.

3. The third possibility is that of synchronicity. According to this view, the totality of events is regarded as an interwoven unity which

operates and is operated upon as a whole, so that no single event can be regarded as the cause and another as the effect, but each is correlated with the other. In other words, simultaneous events correspond to one another. Accordingly the celestial bodies would have to be regarded as the hands of a single clock which indicate the total cosmic situation in which our Earth, with everything in it, is involved.

The course of events is revealed in the cosmic picture as a whole and can be read in the movements of the heavenly bodies. This total situation must be of cosmic dimensions and must comprise the whole solar system.

The position of the heavenly bodies is never at any time accidental but is like a tune in a continuous melody which can be characterised by Bode's Law and its structure. Again, through Kepler's Law not only the distance but also the velocities of the planets are determined. Thus the position of the heavenly bodies, determined by the laws of time and motion is at the same time an expression of a harmony of a higher order.

It is possible that the key to the future development of the doctrine of stellar influences lies in the recognition of the cosmic structure which is at the base of Bode's Law, as was the case in regard to the atom and the quantum theory. For this rule points to a principle which is valid for the whole solar system. Here, in my opinion, in the synchronistic approach, can be found one of the most promising avenues of research.

Briefly, however, one ought to point out that the synchronistic interpretation presupposes a *quality* of time. No moment of time can be repeated, so that no experiment can be exactly reconstructed. Seen scientifically, every moment is unique and disappears irrevocably with its potentialities and hopes into the abyss of what has been.

4. The fourth possible interpretation is that of symbolism. It presupposes an animated universe, a spiritual coherence of the whole cosmos. Goethe said: 'He who speaks of Nature must also proclaim Spirit or give tacit recognition to it.' This is an attitude which comes very close to the views of modern natural science.

Heisenberg's Uncertainty Principle is the quantitative expression of the fact that it is not possible to determine the behaviour of an elementary particle in a strictly causal fashion. It is not possible to make an unambiguous forecast about it. Even the simplest particle is seen to possess a certain 'freedom'. Only as regards a great number of particles is it possible to make a *statistically* quantitative statement. Thus, in a certain sense, one can speak of 'consciousness' or 'animation' even of the smallest particles in our world.

The English biologist, H S Haldane, says 'If the world picture of modern science is correct we must be prepared to find consciousness or life, at least in its simplest form, everywhere in the Universe.'

To use the terminology of the famous exponent of Evolution, Father Teilherd de Chardin, what is strictly determinable is only the outside of things to which there corresponds an inner principle. The richer and better organised the outward form, the higher the inner spiritual potency. Spiritual perfection and physical complexity are only two different aspects of one phenomenon. This complexity ascends from the electron to the atom, thence to the molecule, the crystal, rocks and higher, to the heavenly bodies themselves. We do not yet know what state of consciousness corresponds to a planet or a star - for instance, our Sun but to judge by the criteria given above, it must be rather highly evolved. (Interesting if fantastic speculation in this direction can be found in a book by the astronomer Fred Hoyle, *The Black Cloud*).

Those states of consciousness which are within our comprehension belong to a different branch, namely to the microcosmic complexity which has developed via the protein molecules to organic life and eventually, by way of the organisation of the brain, to the thinking faculty and egoconsciousness.

Although Man, in respect of magnitude, stands between the atom and a heavenly body, he is not in the same line of evolution. Rather is the heavenly body the pre-condition of his existence.

These reflections may suffice to indicate how we may one day obtain a scientific understanding of the symbolism in Astrology.

INDEX